ANALYZING SALES PROMOTION

TEXT & CASES: HOW TO PROFIT FROM THE *NEW POWER* OF PROMOTION MARKETING

2ND EDITION

JOHN C. TOTTEN

MARTIN P. BLOCK

DARTNELL is a publisher serving the world of business with books, manuals, newsletters and bulletins, and training materials for executives, managers, supervisors, salespeople, financial officials, personnel executives, and office employees. Dartnell also produces management and sales training videos and audiocassettes, publishes many useful business forms, and many of its materials and films are available in languages other than English. Dartnell, established in 1917, serves the world's business community. For details, catalogs, and product information, write to:

THE DARTNELL CORPORATION,
4660 N RAVENSWOOD AVE,
CHICAGO, IL 60640-4595, U.S.A.
OR PHONE (800) 621-5463, IN U.S. AND CANADA.

DARTNELL TRAINING LIMITED
125 HIGH HOLBORN
LONDON, ENGLAND
WC1V 6QA
OR PHONE 011-44-071-404-1585

CONTENTS

John C. Totten, Ph.D., is vice president, analytical and technical products, with Nielsen Market Research. In this role, he acts as a liaison between Nielsen and the academic community and frequently addresses important marketing conferences, including those sponsored by the Operations Research Society of America and the Institute of Management Sciences. Totten is currently researching ways to integrate Dun and Bradstreet's information for consumer goods manufacturers into a comprehensive set of marketing mix analysis and planning tools.

Overall, Totten's speciality is managing brand budgets relating to trade promotion, consumer promotion, and advertising media. His expertise stems from 30 years of experience with major consumer package goods manufacturers. At Procter and Gamble, he was a consultant in the areas of research and development, new product development, and market research. Totten also served in three separate senior management positions with Information Resources, Inc., as Vice President, research and development; Vice President, market response analysis; and Vice President, product standards and technical support. While at IRI, Totten developed analytical systems for measuring the impact of trade promotion on brand sales—an effort that formed the basis of a multimillion-dollar consulting business for IRI.

Totten is also active as a writer and college lecturer. He has published articles on topics such as Markov analysis, critical path planning, project management, and analysis of designed experiments using scanner data. Totten, who holds a Ph. D. in operations research from the University of California, Berkeley, is a frequent guest lecturer at graduate management programs.

Dr. Martin P. Block, Ph.D., is a full professor in the Integrated Marketing Communications Division of the Medill School of Journalism at Northwestern University, where he teaches marketing research, sales promotion, advertising, and direct marketing. In addition, Block is president of Block Telecommunications, Inc., a marketing and research consulting firm that numbers among its clients such prestigious companies as Ameritech, Amoco, Kraft, and IBM.

Block, who holds a Ph.D. in mass media from Michigan State University, specializes in sales promotion scanner analysis and telecommunications, as well as new technology research. He has served as director of Medill's Graduate Advertising Division, professor and chairman of the Department of Advertising at Michigan State University, and senior market analyst in corporate planning with the Goodyear Tire and Rubber Company.

Block has been published extensively in academic research journals, trade publications, and various books. He has been the principal investigator on several federally funded research projects, and has served as a consultant to the Federal Trade Commission.

ACKNOWLEDGMENTS

The authors thank Nielsen Marketing Research for providing data from their Nielsen Household Services consumer panel, their ScanTrack store movement database, and their Scan*Pro Monitor promotion evaluation service. Examples (sometimes with disguised brand names) include actual data and analyses from the following categories; carbonated beverages (Coke and Pepsi), a major dairy products category, frozen orange juice, pancake syrup, hot cereal, mouthwash, and ready-to-eat cereal.

Several individuals have made helpful contributions to the book including Jan Gollins, Greg Ellis, Mitch Kriss, Doss Struse, and Ken Wisniewski of Nielsen, Dennis Bender of Milward Brown, Mike Duffy of Kraft General Foods, and Tamara Brezen of Northwestern University. A special thanks also goes to Lee Cooper of UCLA and Leigh McAlister of the University of Texas, who have used the first edition in the classroom and have provided particularly useful comments.

A number of manufacturers and retailers granted permission for reproduction of their promotional material. Thanks are due to Binney & Smith; Campbell Soup Company; The Dial Corp; Dominick's Finer Foods, Inc.; General Mills, Inc.; Geo. A. Hormel & Company; Jewel Food Stores; Ore-Ida Foods, Inc., a subsidiary of H.J. Heinz Company; Pillsbury Co.; Sargento Cheese Co., Inc.; and S.C. Johnson & Son, Inc.

A Note on the Case Studies. Solutions to the cases may be ordered from the publisher. Please call The Dartnell Corporation at (800) 621-5463 for ordering information.

CHAPTER 1

INTRODUCTION TO
SALES PROMOTION

T his book focuses on the analysis of sales promotion rather than on the creation of a sales promotion strategy. Its purpose is to be able to guide readers in developing general principles and guidelines to help plan future sales promotion programs and, ultimately, strategies. Through analyzing the cases provided in this book, readers will gain experience in the planning and evaluation of sales promotion activity. While this book specifically does not deal with the creative aspects of developing sales promotion programs, it clearly points to the need for substantially more creativity in the future.

One of the first things a beginning student of communication learns is that the purpose for all communication is to influence behavior. More specifically, marketers through advertising, public relations, product packaging, in-store displays, and sales promotion attempt to influence behavior. The particular behaviors they seek to influence may vary widely with the specific marketing situation, and certainly, various tools and techniques may be applied with different levels of effectiveness.

The challenge for the marketing manager is to assess correctly the particular marketing situation, select the appropriate tools and techniques, and develop the most effective executions of those techniques. The manager must understand how the techniques work alone and together in what is usually a very competitive environment to develop the most effective promotional strategy.

The best way a manager can develop an understanding of how techniques work is by systematically analyzing past experience to gain understanding of prior beliefs and biases. Such analysis should generate some general principles and guidelines.

DEFINITION OF SALES PROMOTION. Sales promotion is difficult to define because it includes such a wide variety of activities and techniques. The term *sales promotion* refers to many kinds of selling incentives and techniques intended to produce immediate or short-term sales effects. Typical sales promotion include coupons, samples, in-pack premiums, self-liquidating premiums, value-packs, refunds and rebates, price-off packs, contests, sweepstakes, trade shows, continuity plans, and others. Sales promotion techniques can be applied across a broad range of products, from chewing gum to houses and cars. Perhaps the only unifying theme among these various methods is that they all must be *communicated to the appropriate audience* to be effective.

The other defining characteristic of sales promotion is that the goal is short term or *immediate*. Sales promotion is not used to generate long-term results or sales in the future, but rather to generate sales results now. The distinction between short-term and long-term results may certainly vary with the product category and the particular industry, making a specific time definition somewhat arbitrary. But the important idea is that the goal for sales promotion is results in the current promotional period—not in later time periods.

Promotion is, then, a collection of techniques communicated to target audiences to generate short-term sales results. Sales promotion has been traditionally viewed as a nonrecurrent selling activity, and it is often defined as such. However, this view does not reflect the current condition of frequent and repeated sales promotion programs necessary to maintain business in many product categories. Sales promotion has become an all-too-recurrent activity, so the idea of a nonrecurrent activity is eliminated from the definition here.

INTEGRATED MARKETING COMMUNICATION.   Sales promotion and all other marketing communication activities are intimately related. Marketing communication includes the traditional activities such as advertising, public relations, direct marketing, and personal selling. It is difficult to imagine any sales promotion without the support of advertising and the field sales force, and it is becoming increasingly difficult to imagine advertising or field sales-force activities without the support of sales promotion.

The term *advertising* has been defined many ways, from "salesmanship in print" to "any paid form of nonpersonal presentation and promotion of ideas, goods, or services by an identified sponsor." The first definition is certainly too broad, since it also includes most public relations activities. The latter definition is better because it reflects the important fact that advertising consists of paid messages placed in the measured media. The measured media include any medium in one of the four main categories—broadcast, print, traffic, and direct mail—in which some attempt to estimate the size of the audience for the particular medium. Broadcast media obviously include radio, television, and cable; print media include magazines and newspapers; traffic media include outdoor and transit; and direct mail includes catalogs and all the other material from broadsides to bill stuffers.

Omitted from the definition of measured media would be specialty advertising, including calendars, key chains, shirts and hats, and similar material, and a few miscellaneous categories like cinema advertising and directories. Still, these are all important marketing communication devices and can be critical components of a sales promotion program.

Advertising can be designed to achieve short-term goals, just like sales promotion, but it can also be designed to achieve long-term ones. A major argument for advertising is its ability to create an enduring brand image in the mind of the consumer. The value of a well-known brand name can be attributed to a consistent advertising effort over a period of many years. Advertising can also be used to generate immediate retail sales with newspaper advertisement headlines like "Sale Ends Tomorrow!" Advertising and sales promotion must work together, since advertising is one of the primary communication vehicles of sales promotion. The only other communication vehicle for sales promotion are the product package itself and retail-level in-store displays. Sales promotion would be very limited without advertising, though sales promotion activity can certainly be successful without the use of advertising.

A fundamental decision for any marketing manager is how to allocate the budget between advertising and sales promotion. Should more be spent in sales promotion than advertising, or vice versa? What is the best combination of advertising and sales promotion? Unfortunately neither of these questions has simple answers. The only generalization that almost always proves true is that advertising and sales promotion perform best when they are properly coordinated.

In recent years, resources have been shifting in favor of sales promotion. Annual growth rate of promotion efforts has typically been in the low teens and higher than the growth for measured media efforts. Most recently, growth in both promotion and advertising has slowed somewhat. Despite this recent slowdown in annual growth, however, promotion still dominates advertising in terms of spending.

SALES PROMOTION AUDIENCES. Sales promotion efforts can be targeted to three major groups: consumers, the trade, and employees. Regardless of the audience, the primary objective for any sales promotion effort is still the same—stimulating short-term sales.

Characteristics of Consumers. The consumer is the final purchaser and user of the product, and sales promotion efforts aimed directly toward this group are normally termed "consumer promotions." Defining the term "consumers" can itself be a complex problem, with several classification schemes commonly used. Perhaps the most basic way of classifying audiences for consumer sales promotion is to distinguish between "businesses" and "consumers." The common terminology here may be slightly confusing because there are business consumers and nonbusiness consumers, even though both are consumers in the sense of purchasing and using products and services. A consumer is a private individual purchasing goods and services usually for consumption by self or for consumption by the immediate family. A business, normally represented by a purchasing agent, is purchasing goods and services for the operation of the business. The term *consumer promotion* is used to refer to both business and consumer when the sales promotion is aimed at the final user of the product.

Characteristics of the Trade. The term "trade" refers to middlemen and retailers who intend to resell the product or service being promoted to them.

Middlemen include a wide variety of organizations, including wholesalers, brokers, jobbers, and representatives. Retailers are organizations selling directly to consumers as defined above. The purpose of "trade promotion" is primarily to stimulate the various members of the distribution chain to move the products through the distribution system, but it may have an additional purpose of shifting inventory holding. A trade promotion, then, has the objective of generating resale of the product or service with the ultimate goal of pushing these items through the various market channels. A particular wholesaler, for example, might receive both consumer and trade promotions. Trade promotions would be intended to stimulate the wholesaler to buy and sell more products. Consumer promotions would be intended to stimulate the wholesaler to buy more products that are consumed in the operation of the business, such as office equipment.

Characteristics of the Sales Force. The last group, sales-force promotions or employee promotions, refers to motivational programs usually designed for field sales personnel. Sales contests, both group and individual, are classic examples of the use of sales promotion techniques to motivate employees. An employee suggestion program is another example. Because employee promotions tend to be considered separate from other kinds of sales promotions, often as part of field sales management, they will not be considered here. Instead, the focus here will be consumer and trade promotions.

Segmenting Audiences. Like any marketing strategy, sales promotion needs to be carefully targeted to the appropriate consumer subgroup or market segment. Several ways are used to define the consumer groups that are to be targeted for sales promotion programs.

Segmenting markets is discussed in any introductory marketing textbook, and readers will know that there are three ways of segmenting consumer markets: demographics and geographics, psychographics, and product usage. Demographic segmentation involves defining subgroups according to demographic variables, such as age, income, and gender. This category also includes geographic segmentation, such as market area or zip code area. This method is particularly useful for selecting advertising media, since most media have audience delivery documenting research available in demographic terms. It has also been the most popular and traditional way of describing target markets.

The problem with demographics as a way of segmenting markets for sales promotion is that they generally do not provide sufficiently sensitive discriminations to be able to detect differences between groups. For example, it would be typical to find that the average age and income of women who redeem coupons from a specific promotion are virtually identical to those of women who do not redeem them. More often than not, demographic differences do not explain any differential effectiveness of any promotional effort. Rather, the demographic variables seem to define the limiting parameters of the market itself. For this reason, demographics tend not to be used as a way of describing market segments for sales promotion, even though they are readily provided by the advertising media.

Reasoning might suggest that the more subtle differences within a demographic market segment that account for the impact of sales promotion can be explained by psychological differences. Certainly two married women, thirty-four years old, with no children, and incomes of 35 thousand dollars per year could be substantially different in their reactions to a coupon or a contest. The problem with psychological segmentation is the lack of any standardized, or even moderately well-accepted, method of determining the psychological differences necessary to derive important segments. For this reason, psychological segmentation must also be rejected as a method, though it might become feasible in the future.

Perhaps the closest relevant variable is *deal proneness.* Rather than attempting to understand the underlying psychological process, deal proneness simply is a measure of past behavior. It measures the proportion of the time that a purchase in a particular product category has been made using some form of sales promotion. The average consumer makes about one-third of the purchases of food-store package goods using some form of sales promotion. Those consumers who make a greater than average proportion of their purchases using some form of sales promotion would be placed in a more deal-prone classification. Those who make a less than average proportion of purchases using sales promotion would be placed in a less deal-prone or a not deal-prone classification. The deal-prone classification is generally applied to a specific product category rather than a classification of overall consumer behavior.

Product usage is an increasingly popular method of segmenting markets. The fundamental idea here is that some people never purchase the product. These people are termed nonusers of the product. Those who do purchase the product, usually within some time span appropriate to the product, are divided into subcategories according to the volume or frequency of purchase. These subcategories are normally termed light user, medium user, and heavy user, depending on the amount of the product purchased. As will be discussed later, the concept of product usage is quite useful in evaluating sales promotion programs.

Product usage depends upon the *purchase cycle* of a product. The purchase cycle is the average amount of time between purchases. A more frequently purchased product would require a shorter time interval to determine the level of product usage than a less frequently purchased product.

Not only is the purchase of a product important, so is the choice of brand within the product category. Generally many brand choices are available, including, in some cases, products with no brands at all, such as generics. What seems to be important to sales promotion programs is the relative position in the marketplace of a particular brand. A dominant brand—one with more than 40 percent share of the market—may respond differently to sales promotion than a competitive brand—one with approximately 20 percent share of the market. A minor brand—one with less than 5 percent share of the market—may respond differently yet. The difference in the response should be in part attributable to the consumer's perception of the position of the brand. Premium-priced products may respond quite differently to sales promotion than a lower priced product.

A related concept is *brand loyalty.* A user of a product category can be considered brand loyal if he or she nearly always purchases the same brand, and a brand switcher can be considered such if past purchasing history shows no dominant brand. A brand-loyal individual would probably respond differently to sales promotion from competing brands than would a brand switcher. The problem with the concept of brand switching is that it is quite difficult to find individuals who exclusively purchase only one brand over an extended period of time. Normally a brand-loyal individual is defined as one who *usually* purchases a single brand allowing for occasional purchases of other brands. A typical definition might be one who makes 80 percent of the purchases of one brand within the product category over a specified time interval. Those who purchase a brand less than 80 percent of the time would be defined as brand switchers. Individuals with limited purchase history, such as those with three or fewer purchases in the period under study, might be separated out as light buyers, whose loyalty, or lack thereof, cannot be determined.

Deal proneness, product usage, purchase cycle, brand position, and brand loyalty are all important consumer characteristics in evaluating sales promotion programs. Also, while consumers are normally thought of in these terms, the same concepts could apply equally well to business. The differences would most likely be found in the characteristics of the product category.

TYPES OF SALES PROMOTION. There are two ways of categorizing types of sales promotion: source of promotion and fundamental appeal. Generally, there are two sources of sales promotion programs—manufacturers and retailers. Sales promotions that emanate from manufacturers are termed *manufacturer promotions.* Promotions that proceed from a retailer are termed *retailer* or *store promotions.* Retailer promotions may or may not directly result from a manufacturer's trade promotion. In other words, a retailer may offer consumers a promotion because they received a special promotion from a manufacturer. It is, however, the option of the retailer whether or not to offer a promotion to the consumer in response to the manufacturer's trade promotion. A retailer may also offer promotions to consumers without the benefit of a trade promotion.

There are two general types of appeals in sales promotion—interest and price. Interest appeal focuses on things other than price. While it can be argued that price is interesting, price is so pervasive as a sales promotion technique that it deserves separate consideration. Examples of price promotions are price-offs, coupons, bonus packs, refund offers, continuity plans, and special pack promotions. Examples of interest promotions include free premiums, mail-in premiums, samples, contests, and sweepstakes. Trade promotions might be considered a third category, even though they almost always involve price in the form of a trade allowance. This type of promotion, however, does not preclude the use of interest promotions to the trade.

BELIEFS ABOUT CONSUMER SALES PROMOTION. Over the years, many traditions and beliefs about how sales promotion works with consumers have evolved. Perhaps the most pervasive belief about sales promotion of all types is that it can reinforce advertising and other promotional programs. Sales promotion is normally described as a tool to get more out of advertising campaigns, and it would, of course, reinforce the same objectives as the advertising.

Apart from advertising, consumer sales promotion as a separate entity is generally thought capable of accomplishing four possible objectives. These objectives seem to be widely accepted and are often used to justify the use of sales promotion. They are discussed in the following sections.

Obtaining Product Trial. Getting consumers to try a product is fundamental to many marketing strategies. It might involve the introduction of a new product or the attempt to reach new customers with no previous experience with the product. In addition, sometimes a long-existing product that has been experiencing sales decline can be revived by reintroducing it to consumers who may have forgotten about it.

Encouraging Repeat Usage. Once a consumer has tried a product, it is necessary to get the consumer to purchase the product again. However, the consumer is generally in a very competitive environment. For that reason, an additional incentive is often necessary to keep the competitors from winning the consumers back after a successful initial trial. One of many sales promotion techniques discussed here can be used for this purpose.

Encouraging More Frequent Usage. An important source of business may be in encouraging light and medium users of a product category to become heavy users. Encouraging existing users either to purchase with greater frequency or to purchase in greater quantities can have considerable impact on the size of the market. A related objective is to cause the consumer to trade up to a more expensive line.

Neutralizing Competition. One of the most common responses a marketing manager might give to justify a sales promotion program is to defuse competitive advertising and sales promotion programs. Sales promotion can be used to hold current customers against competitive promotions by offering similar incentives. Sales promotion may also be able to take consumers out of the market by encouraging them to "load the pantry." Encouraging consumers to buy a large volume of a product presumably makes them immune to competitive advertising and sales promotion pressure.

BELIEFS ABOUT TRADE SALES PROMOTION. As with consumer sales promotion, beliefs persist about how sales promotion works with the trade. The most widespread belief is that promoting to the trade is indirectly promoting to the consumer. As a result of the incentive provided from the manufacturer, the trade will provide incentives and programs themselves to the consumer. Trade promotions are commonly thought to be able to accomplish the following three specific objectives.

Obtaining In-Store Support. Retailers are often in an adversarial position with manufacturers—negotiating over price and supply. Retailers do not automatically cooperate with manufacturer promotional programs and in-store displays, as retailers are swamped with material from most competing products. It is, therefore, necessary to provide incentives to the trade to obtain even minimal levels of cooperation in executing any in-store promotional strategies.

Manipulating Trade Inventories. The term *manipulating trade inventories* means getting retailers and wholesalers to either increase or decrease the inventories they carry in their warehouses and stores. Getting wholesalers and retailers to increase their inventories normally requires special incentives. This is because the trade, recognizing that maintaining inventory is a major expense, needs an incentive to offset the cost. If a manufacturer needs to shift inventory to the trade, sales promotion is a powerful tool. The manufacturer may even wish to reduce the trade inventory, especially if a product is obsolete, dated, or being replaced by a new line.

Expanding Product Distribution. Perhaps one of the most competitive struggles in marketing is the fight for shelf space. Getting distribution and shelf space are prerequisites to selling any product, and sales promotion is a means of obtaining them. Hence, introducing a new product requires a substantial promotional effort.

PRICE PROMOTIONAL TECHNIQUES. Price can be used in several ways as a promotional device, from price-offs to refund offers. The techniques are categorized by the way the special price is offered and communicated to the consumer. Price promotional techniques fall into the following categories:

Price-offs. A manufacturer's price-off is printed directly on the product packaging and becomes an integral part of the product's appearance to the consumers. Special labels might also be used. A retailer can simply mark down the price on the price label and shelf label. The advantage of price-offs is that they are easy for the consumer to use, and they place the product in direct competition on the shelf with other brands. Another advantage is that distribution of the promotion, or the price-off, is on the product itself. One disadvantage is that everyone who purchases the product takes advantage of the price reduction, including those who would have purchased the product at the regular price. Another disadvantage is that the shopper may not even notice the special price.

Coupons. Overwhelmingly, the most common form of sales promotion is couponing, accounting for well over two-thirds of all sales promotional efforts. Couponing has been growing dramatically in recent years, and it is now common to read about coupon clutter as a major problem, just as television commercial clutter has been discussed in advertising.

There are two basic types of coupons: manufacturer coupons, which have everything paid for by the manufacturer, and store or retailer coupons, which are paid for at least partially by the retailer. Sometimes a cooperative agreement may be in force between the manufacturer and retailer. Normally the distribution of manufacturer coupons is paid for by the manufacturer, and the distribution of store coupons is financed by the retailer.

There are many varieties of coupons, as described below:

1. Cents-Off. The product to be purchased is offered at a certain dollar amount off the regular price.
2. Free. A free product is given.
3. Buy One, Get One Free. With the purchase of a product at the regular price, a second is given free.
4. Time Release. Several cents-off coupons are positioned together with different expiration dates.
5. Multiple Purchase. The coupon offer applies only when more than one unit of the product is purchased.
6. Self-Destruct. Two or more coupons are printed over each other in an overlap manner so that both cannot be used, and the consumer must choose which one to redeem.
7. Personalized. The coupon is localized by geographic location or store and is redeemable accordingly.
8. Cross-Ruff. A coupon for one product is obtained with the purchase of another, unrelated product.
9. Related Sale. A coupon received from the purchase of one product applies to another product, which is related in some way to the purchased product.
10. Sweepstakes Entry. The redeemed coupon becomes an entry into a sweepstakes.

Coupons can become complex combinations of offers, and they are sometimes difficult to classify. A major problem with coupons, as will be discussed later, is getting them distributed to the appropriate consumers. Coupons offer many advantages: They create strong pull among consumers, provide quick response, may cost less than other methods such as price-offs (not everyone redeems coupons) or sampling, and may provide support to the sales force in obtaining good trade support that translates into distribution and shelf space.

The disadvantages of coupons are the clutter and the problem of misredemption and mishandling by the trade, which is a major problem for both manufacturers and retailers. With a new brand, coupons may stimulate additional triers to purchase the brand. With a more established brand, however, coupons are primarily redeemed by loyal users and switchers and may generate little incremental business to the brand. Moreover, coupon redemptions occur over time and may cause budgetary problems if levels of redemption have not been accurately forecasted.

Bonus Packs. Another way the consumer can be offered a special price is to increase the amount of the product offered for the same price. The advantages of bonus packs are an increase in shelf space and distribution and an encouragement to the consumer to buy more of the product. The disadvantages are that they do not enhance the long-term image of the product or produce loyal users, and they can often be easily pilfered by the trade. As with price-off offers, they may go unnoticed by those consumers not already predisposed to purchase the brand.

Continuity Plans. Another technique requires the saving of some device related to the purchase, such as stamps, that may be used for prizes or reduced prices. Some classic examples are savings stamps and airline frequent-flyer plans. The advantages of continuity plans are the requirement for high purchase frequency, the relative ease of implementation, and the extension of the purchase habit. The disadvantages are limited appeal, little trade support, and little or no in-store display. Grocery retailers frequently use continuity plans to stimulate repeated visits to the store. A typical plan might offer one volume of an encyclopedia or one item in a cookware set each week.

Refund Offers. When the purchaser sends in a proof of purchase, a refund or rebate is provided. The major advantage is that not everyone who purchases the product requests the refund. Other advantages are that refund offers are relatively inexpensive, sales forces like them, and the trade approves of them because refund offers are generally easy to display. The disadvantages are that the results are difficult to measure, refund offers do not generate trial, and they may be used primarily by already brand-loyal consumers. Also, the trade may worry about fulfillment problems from the manufacturer that the consumer may blame on the store and not the manufacturer.

Trade Promotions. Trade promotions generally take one of two forms—the trade allowance or the trade coupon. Both are forms of price promotion, but the special price is offered to the trade rather than directly to the consumer. A trade allowance is a price discount that can take a variety of forms depending upon the product category. A trade allowance might be based upon case lots, a dollar sales volume, or other measures of sales. A trade coupon, like coupons to consumers, offers the trade a special price offer when redeemed with purchase from the manufacturer.

INTEREST PROMOTION TECHNIQUES. Some promotion techniques attempt to stimulate interest other than price, in order to generate short-term sales. Often the particular interest might be in products, activities, or special events. A common promotional technique is to create special events, such as contests or sweepstakes. Several techniques fit within this general category, and they are described below.

Sampling. Providing the consumer with a free sample is a very effective means of introducing a new product or demonstrating an improvement in an existing product. Typically, a small trial size is provided, but as with coupons, the major problem is distribution of the product samples. Sometimes they can be delivered through the mass media, such as newspapers. Sometimes they must be delivered door-to-door, distributed by salesmen, or perhaps, even mailed. The advantages of sampling are that it initiates trial and may indirectly force distribution and in-store display because it may create store traffic. The disadvantages of sampling are that it is generally very expensive, may be difficult to distribute to the precise target audience, and is wasteful if the sample is discarded without trial.

Contests and Sweepstakes. The difference between contests and sweepstakes centers primarily on eligibility rules: Contests require that consumers purchase the product to enter, while sweepstakes do not. If a purchase is required, the sweepstakes may be interpreted as a lottery and may be illegal in some states. Some contests require skill to win, whereas sweepstakes require only a simple ballot entry that is drawn at random to win. Contests and sweepstakes are used to create interest in advertising, to gain shelf space, to increase trial or product image, or to increase store traffic. The advantages of contests and sweepstakes are that they build store traffic, have more easily controllable associated costs relative to advertising programs, and generate media publicity. The contest entry form may also be a source of names and addresses for the purpose of building a customer database. The disadvantages are the proliferation and clutter associated with contests and the "professional" participators (people who collect and enter all the available contests and sweepstakes but are not potential customers for the product).

Free Premiums. There are several types of free premiums, including in- or on-pack premiums, such as a toy, a gift, or a reusable container, and eligibility to purchase other products at a lower cost. Free premiums presumably extend the image of the product and increase the product's perceived value. The advantages of free premiums are that they gain display, differentiate the product, and facilitate the use of self-liquidating premiums. The disadvantages are the reduction of sales if the premium is not desirable, trade resistance if the premium is being sold elsewhere in the store, and possible pilfering and abuse in channels of distribution.

Mail-In Premiums. Several types of mail-in premiums exist, including self-liquidating premiums, free-in-the-mail premiums, and speed plans. Self-liquidating premiums are sold with proofs of purchase at just over wholesale cost. The premium does not cost the promoter anything because it is resold at the purchase cost. Free-in-the-mail premiums are gifts that are sent with proof of purchase. The promoter bears the cost entirely. Speed plans offer consumers different prices or prizes depending upon the number of proofs of purchase they accumulate. Mail-in premiums can be used to reinforce a product image or the product's advertising, increase advertising attention, generate trial, reward multiple purchases, and gain trade support. The advantages of mail-in premiums are that they often require multiple purchases and that they attract attention. The disadvantages are that they may not necessarily generate trial, it is difficult to measure their impact on sales, and usually, few tend to take advantage of these offers.

LEGAL CONSIDERATIONS.   Sales promotion is controlled by four general areas of regulation: federal antitrust law, Federal Trade Commission (FTC) regulations, Food and Drug Administration (FDA) regulations, and state law. Federal antitrust law begins with the Sherman Act and includes the later Robinson-Patman Act and Clayton Act.

Antitrust law forbids practices that hinder competition and favor one competitor over others. For example, it addresses the fact that small retailers may often have difficulty competing with the large retail chains. Antitrust law relates to sales promotion and competition by regulating trade allowances and related practices. A trade allowance must be nondiscriminatory so that large retailers are not favored over small ones. A small retailer must be able to participate as well as the large retailer.

The FTC regulations are clearly an extension of antitrust law and require that the manufacturer notify all retailers about a promotional program. The FTC also requires that the manufacturer not pay the retailer unless the retailer performs as required—that is by using the in-store display material or whatever.

The FTC and FDA both have guidelines regarding the use of cents-off labels. A cents-off label can only be used if the product has been sold at the normal price in the trading area during the preceding 30 days, and the savings to the consumer and the retailer are at least as much as the savings represented. Also the cents-off sales volume may represent not more than 50 percent of the total sales volume of the product in a 12-month period. The retailer is obligated to display the regular price along with the cents-off price. In addition, the FDA requires labeling, such as expiration dates and offer conditions to be on the label.

State laws generally apply to lotteries and govern contests and sweepstakes. If a prize is to be awarded then, both consideration and chance become legal elements. The term *consideration* refers to the expenditure of money or substantial effort required in order to enter. Chance is not considered to be present if through the exercise of sufficient intelligence and diligence the entrant can win the prize. If lots are drawn, for example, then chance is present. If chance is not present, the situation is a contest, and legal in most states; if chance is present, the situation is either a lottery or a sweepstakes, depending upon the consideration involved. Lotteries are generally not legal is most states, while sweepstakes, with little or no consideration, generally are legal.

Legal concerns in sales promotion are complex and involve several levels of government. Legal counsel should be consulted when planning a promotional program.

SALES PROMOTION SUPPORT.
The success of a sales promotion program often depends on the relationship between the program and other in-store conditions. If the program is supplemented with in-store displays or is coordinated with a special event, the program will be more successful. For the retailer this means that sales promotion programs should be coordinated with other marketing elements. For the manufacturer this means that retailer support is critically important.

Pricing. Price is one of the most important marketing variables, yet marketers do not understand it well. They generally assume that lower prices will generate more sales, but they fail to grasp the specific relationship. Consumer perceptual factors, such as odd-even pricing and price framing, are extremely important.

The only price a consumer sees is the in-store price the retailer sets. The fact that the retailer sets the purchase price is an additional complication for the manufacturer. It means that the manufacturer can only indirectly influence the final selling price.

Retailer Events. Special events ranging from holidays to special sales can be important to the success of any sales promotion program. Events can be manufactured, as well as based on traditional or seasonal events. Special sales, such as double-coupon events, can also enhance a promotion program. Many events, like shelf-price promotions, are under the control of retailer. Manufacturers can only indirectly influence the retailer. The role of events on the consumer is another area that is little understood.

Point-of-Purchase Displays. Displaying the product inside the store is a major component of any selling strategy. Any additional material in the store beyond the product itself is generally referred to as *point-of-purchase advertising.* All signs, displays, devices, and structures used as sales aids can be included in the definition. The material can be as simple as a printed card or as complicated as elaborate illuminated and animated structures that draw attention to special displays of the product. Included in point-of-purchase advertising are window signs and displays, banners, counter and check-out displays, interior and exterior wall signs, merchandise racks, trays and cases for both counters and aisles, shelf edgers, and can toppers.

Point-of-purchase displays include a wide variety of material that can be provided by either the manufacturer or the retailer. Most manufacturer-provided point-of-purchase material is more expensively produced and, perhaps, more elaborate. Retailer-provided material tends to appear to be more "homemade" and probably less elaborate. In general, the retailer is interested in short-term results, whereas the manufacturer is interested in longer term results. Whether the manufacturer or retailer provided the material, the point-of-purchase material can take advantage of virtually any of the sales promotion techniques described before. Retailer-provided material is more likely to use one of the price promotion techniques than is manufacturer-provided material.

Advertising Support. Any sales promotion program must be supported with some paid media advertising. While sales promotion programs are supported in all media, the print media are probably the most important because they lend themselves to the delivery of coupons.

Advertising media are the major means of distributing coupons, with less than 20 percent delivered by other means, including both in-pack and on-pack coupons and instant coupons. Instant coupons are provided at the check-out counter or at the product location in the store. Newspapers have the overwhelming share of the coupon-distribution volume, though delivery of these coupons is accomplished in several ways.

The largest proportion is delivered through free-standing inserts (FSIs), which account for well over half the coupons distributed through newspapers. FSIs offer the advantage of high-quality color reproduction, and they have been growing very rapidly in recent years. The next largest newspaper category is ROP, or run-of-paper, display advertising. Also included for newspapers would be Sunday supplements and comics, but these represent a very small proportion. Magazines and direct mail deliver approximately 10 percent of all coupons. In many marketing areas, newspapers have a special section once a week devoted to food and food-related items. These "best-food day" issues have a disproportionate number of ROP manufacturer coupons and are the primary choice for grocery retailers who are placing ad features and store coupons. Drug store and mass merchandiser print advertisements tends to be more concentrated in weekend editions. Beyond delivery of coupons, advertising is the most common source of the sales promotion message. Contests and sweepstakes, premium offers, and other price promotions are commonly included in advertising. Both the manufacturer and the retailer make heavy use of promotion in their advertising. The manufacturer would be somewhat more likely to use interest promotion techniques, and the retailer somewhat more likely to use price promotion techniques in the advertising. However, coupons are still the most common form of consumer sales promotion and widely used by both manufacturers and retailers.

Cooperative advertising also plays an important role in supporting sales promotion programs. Cooperative advertising is a form of advertising in which both the manufacturer and the retailer share the cost. Generally, the manufacturer provides the copy in ready-to-run form. The retailer needs only to add the local address to the copy, which can easily be done by the local newspaper, radio, or television station. The retailer buys the space or time, taking advantage of local advertising rates. The manufacturer pays some proportion of the cost of the time or space. Cooperative advertising, or co-op, agreements are tremendously varied between the manufacturer and retailer. Variation in the particular requirements of a manufacturer and in the proportion of payment make co-op a sufficiently complex subject to fill a book by itself. Cooperative advertising becomes a form of trade promotion itself, just like a trade allowance.

Even when a local retailer runs price-offs and coupons in weekly newspaper advertising, the advertising is being used to support the promotion. The importance of the advertising support can be seen by comparing the results of the in-store "unadvertised" price specials that many retailers use with advertised specials.

In this book, any time that a promotion is included in the advertising, we refer to the promotion as featured. Any time a promotion is included in a point-of-purchase display in a store, we refer to the promotion as *displayed*.

Database Programs. Many retailers, including supermarkets, are implementing database marketing programs with their regular customers. These programs are usually termed Frequent Shopper programs. They are based upon the retailer's ability to collect sales histories about their customers and implement marketing strategies designed to maintain them as loyal customers.

These programs apply the fundamental principles of direct marketing—the use of purchase frequency, recency, and amount—to a retail store. Some of these programs are using data captured through checkout scanners and shopper identification cards.

SALES PROMOTION IN ACTION.

Pledge offers a self-destruct coupon.

This coupon is good at one specific outlet of the chain.

This ad includes manufacturers' coupons plus a mail-in premium offer.

This "best food day" ad is built around a "buy one, get one free" theme.

This ad combines a mail-in sweepstakes offer with product coupons requiring multiple purchases.

This full-page ROP ad has medium sized pictures of most featured items. It also has a tie-in with in-store Point of Purchase activity for a manufacturer's promotion on crayons.

The special coupon values in this ad have a $10.00 minimum purchase requirement. Relatively few items are shown per page.

Slice into the Apple Taste!

An example of a coupon with no expiration date.

This "Dairy Month" promotion provides an umbrella theme covering several product categories and manufacturers.

This typical retailer continuity ad is designed to promote week-to-week repeat shopping, with a different selection of the glassware set offered at a special price each week.

This ad shows a joint manufacturer-retailer effort, with several coupon types, including "cents-off," and "buy one, get one free."

Suggested Readings

Blattberg, Robert C., and Scott A. Neslin.
Sales Promotion: Concepts, Methods and Strategies
New York: Prentice-Hall, 1990.

Nagle, Thomas T.
The Strategy and Tactics of Pricing
New York: Prentice-Hall, 1987.

Quelch, John A.
Sales Promotion Management
New York: Prentice-Hall, 1989.

Schultz, Don E., and William A. Robinson.
Sales Promotion Management
Lincolnwood, Ill.: National Textbook, 1982.

CHAPTER 2

SALES PROMOTION STRATEGY

D eveloping a sales promotion strategy is the primary reason for analyzing sales promotion. Sales promotion strategy consists of a simple, straightforward statement of which sales promotion tactics are being applied to what market segments in order to accomplish specific market objectives. A sales promotion strategy should be part of a larger marketing and marketing communication strategy and should not be developed without the benefit of the larger plan.

It is important to distinguish between strategy and tactics. Sales promotion tactics generally include all the vehicles for sales promotion, including coupons, bonus packs, sampling, premiums, contests and sweepstakes, continuity programs, and trade allowances. A danger in planning sales promotion programs is concentrating on the tactics and the specific executions of those tactics without regard to any strategy. Strategic thinking requires consideration of the target market and the objectives, along with the sales promotion tactics. Too many sales promotion programs lack a solid underlying strategy and, as a result, have done little else than reduce profit for the marketer.

MARKETING COMMUNICATION STRATEGY. Adopting the integrated marketing communication philosophy means that a sales promotion strategy should not be developed apart from advertising or public relations strategies. Sales promotion should be considered and applied in the context of all marketing communication and planned along with the other marketing communication activities.

Today, it is common industry practice to treat sales promotion as a separate and distinct area. It is also true that books like this one tend to compartmentalize their subject matter. Despite the philosophical view of integrated marketing communication, most of our discussion will appear to consider sales promotion by itself.

Critical to the development of any strategy is the specification of a measurable objective. Normally, in marketing, the objective is expressed in sales volume or share of market. In the past it has been difficult to use sales measures to evaluate marketing communication programs because of the potential influence of other factors, such as the quality and nature of the product itself, the selling price, and the availability of the product in stores. The tendency has been to use survey research techniques and develop pseudo-measures of performance, such as the familiar communication measures of awareness, preference, and recall.

Technology now makes it possible to measure sales with sufficient precision to evaluate marketing communication strategies. The advent of in-store checkout scanners makes possible the measurement of product sales at a level that was previously never practical.

IMPROVING PROMOTION EFFECTIVENESS.
The key to improving sales promotion effectiveness is in the evaluation of the sales promotion strategy. Evaluation must be systematic in its procedure to avoid any undue influences of past traditions, beliefs, and suppositions on the outcome. Evaluation must also be empirical and involve real measurements.

Quantifying Promotion Effects.
Evaluation must involve some numerical representation of a criterion variable. Sales volume is an excellent example of a quantified variable. The traditional communication measures, such as recall, also make use of numerical representations. Accounting practice obviously relies heavily upon this principle of numerical representation.

In order to evaluate a sales promotion strategy, a quantitative outcome variable must be used. Sales volume is clearly the best measure, if it can be applied.

Tracking Results.
Evaluation should not be a one-time effort. As promotion activity is ongoing, so should evaluation be, and any promotion plan should include evaluation.

Once evaluation is incorporated as an ongoing process then that evaluation becomes the cornerstone of the planning process. Continuous evaluation or tracking allows the promotion manager to systematically apply the history of the product category and brand to the development of any new promotion strategy. Knowledge of how the category, the brand, and various promotional techniques respond and interact can only come from continuous tracking.

If there is any fundamental principle to be applied to the analysis of sales promotion, it is that it should be continuously tracked and evaluated. The tracking methods must depend upon sufficiently sensitive quantitative measures in order to detect the critical differences.

PROBLEMS WITH TRADITIONAL METHODS.
In the past it has been very difficult to track sales promotion programs. Traditional survey research techniques do not work well for several reasons. Identifying product-category users requires contact with many respondents, since category usage is not known in advance. This process can be very expensive in a product category that has a low level of usage. If, for example, 10 percent of the population uses the product, 10 interviews would have to be conducted to find one user.

Questionnaire methods are generally based upon human memory, which can be less than perfect. Often people simply can't remember, or they confuse past events. This is especially true with frequently purchased, low-priced items. Diaries might help with the memory problem, but cooperation often deteriorates. Because questionnaires rely on human reports, there is error. The reporting error combined with incomplete reports make this kind of data extremely difficult to use.

Timing can be another problem with the traditional methods of data collection. Promotional events almost always occur after short periods of time. For example, the time for a typical supermarket promotion is one week. This means that the data must be collected over a very short period of time, which is possible but difficult for most survey research suppliers.

Adding the problem of competing stores within a market—that is, some stores running a promotion while others don't or while other run a different promotion—makes isolating a particular promotion very difficult. For these reasons, survey research methods have been used very little to evaluate sales promotion.

The only traditional method of evaluating sales promotion that has endured is comparing coupon-redemption rates. In fact, coupon redemption has often been suggested as a means of evaluating advertising. All that needs to be done is place a coupon in the ad and count the returned coupons. It is easy for a manufacturer or retailer to keep counts of the number of coupons distributed and the number of coupons redeemed and compute a redemption rate. Comparing redemption rates then would suggest that the better programs would have higher redemption rates.

For many years this is what generally passed for sales promotion evaluation. However it has many obvious problems. If a promotional program is something other than a coupon, it couldn't be evaluated. Perhaps more important, though, is that the program could not be understood in terms of product sales before, during, and after the promotional event. Also, nothing could be determined about how the coupon program relates to other marketing efforts, including advertising, displays, or other price promotions. The impact on competitive products would also be completely unknown.

Comparing coupon redemption rates falls far short of analysis of sales promotion activity. Still, it has been the only option for many years and is generally described as the traditional method. Technology and the concept of single-source data now allow considerably more sophistication in the analysis of sales promotion.

USING SINGLE-SOURCE DATA. The idea of single-source data came from the analytical frustrations of the 1970s, when marketers were attempting to answer the effective frequency question in advertising. The question of effective frequency asks how many exposures to an advertising message are necessary to achieve any result. Data were available from one supplier that measured product sales using the shelf audit and from another supplier that was providing advertising media expenditure estimates also using an audit. The difficulty was in combining the two sources so that some conclusions could be reached about the relationship between the advertising and product sales. This difficulty led to the call for single-source data, or data from one supplier using a single sample that would automatically show the relationship between the critical advertising and sales variables.

Until supermarket checkout scanner technology became available, single-source data was not a practical possibility. Single-source data was first developed in 1979 that offered both supermarket sales data and television viewing data at the household level. While more will be covered in later chapters about scanner-based and single-source data, it is absolutely clear that this data has revolutionized the analysis and understanding of sales promotion.

Weekly Scanner Sales. One of the most important characteristics of scanner-based data is the ability to easily manipulate the time frame. Because data is captured on an item-by-item basis, it is possible to aggregate data over virtually any unit of time. It is possible, for example, to compute sales for a particular product on an hourly basis if necessary.

Since the typical supermarket changes its prices, in-store displays, and newspaper advertising each week, the most logical unit of time over which to aggregate data is the week. Consumers also tend to visit the supermarket on either a one- or two-week average cycle. Time frames more frequent than one week would overcomplicate any analysis, and time frames longer than one week would tend to average away the effect of the promotion.

To explain this averaging-away effect, assume a one-week promotion in a single store. Normal weekly sales volume of the promoted product in the store is 100 units. During the week of the promotion, however, volume increased to 200 units. If the data is aggregated over a four-week period, the analysis would show a 25 percent sales increase attributable to the promotion. Normal sales volume would be 400 units (4 times 100 units), and sales volume with the promotion would be 500 units (3 times 100 units, plus 200 units). The difference would be 100 units, presumably attributable to the promotion, or a 25 percent increase (100 units divided by 400 units).

If the data were aggregated over one week, the sales increase would appear to be 100 percent (difference of 100 units, divided by 100 units). If the data are aggregated across one week, the impact of the promotion is judged to be much higher (100 percent more than normal sales volume) than if aggregated across one month (only 25 percent more than normal sales volume). Aggregating across longer time periods tends to diminish the impact of sales promotion programs.

Weekly Store Audits. The same principle of diminishing effects applies to individual stores as well. Most promotion programs are specific to individual stores or chains within a market. Many stores in a market would participate in the same promotion programs as competing stores. Analyzing the results of promotion aggregated by market then would tend to make the promotion appear less effective.

Promotion analysis, then, needs to be done with data that are aggregated to the individual-store level. This means that individual store conditions need to be recorded on a weekly basis. This will require weekly audits of display activity and newspaper featuring for each store. This weekly store audit then must become part of a single-source data system.

Purchase Dynamics. Examining purchase behavior dynamically over time is also critically important. To accomplish this, it is necessary to keep track of purchases by household. This requires identification of the household at the time of product purchase.

The scanner panel allows for this further application of scanner-based data. The scanner panel consists of a sample of previously recruited households that possess an identification card that is read along with all their purchases at the supermarket checkout. This technique allows marketers to compare purchases within a product category for a household over time and allows the consideration of such factors as purchase frequency within the category, brand loyalty, and responsiveness to prices and other promotional offers.

While there are a number of difficulties with scanner panels that will be discussed in detail later, such as problems with purchases made by a household in stores that are not participating in the data-acquisition effort, the scanner panel represents a significant step forward in the potential analysis of sales promotion programs. The scanner panel makes possible the dynamic analysis of individual household-purchasing patterns. The dynamic analysis of individual household data aggregated by week and by store makes possible the sophisticated analysis of promotion programs described here. This sophisticated analysis leads to much more profound understanding of how promotion works and leads directly to the development of much more effective sales promotion strategy.

FACT-BASED MARKETING STRATEGY. The application of scanner-based data leads directly to a new strategic marketing concept known as fact-based marketing. Fact-based marketing is entirely dependent upon understanding the relationship between actual product sales and key marketing tactics such as advertising, sales promotion, and price.

In the past, decisions about advertising and sales promotion have been made on the basis of long-held prescriptions and norms. For example, the product or brand life-cycle concept is a long-held marketing prescription that may or may not actually be true. This product concept argues that the marketing decision maker should increase advertising spending through the earlier stages of introduction and growth, and increase sales promotion spending through the later stages of maturity and decline. Scanner-based data will in the future undoubtedly provide the needed evidence to prove or disprove the concept, but for now it is in virtually every marketing textbook.

Also commonly found in marketing are such prescriptions as emphasis on advertising when the brand is dominant in the marketplace, is of high quality, is differentiable from competitors, or is in a product category that is frequently purchased. If a brand has been built as a price or promotional brand or is dependent on the retailer for its sales support, then sales promotion needs to be emphasized.

The difficulty with these prescriptions is that they are based on vague beliefs regarding the way the marketplace operates rather than on the specific sales characteristics of the brand. While prescriptions can be very useful, they can also be dangerous if universally applied. The fact-based marketing idea depends only on the sales response of the brand. If properly applied, it should always lead to the most efficient marketing strategies for a brand and should be self-correcting if any mistakes might be made. Fact-based marketing should dramatically out-perform traditional marketing in both sales and profitability.

Dynamic Analysis. Fact-based marketing begins with a through-time or dynamic analysis of brand sales. Figure 2.1 shows 13 weeks of sales data from a single store in bar chart form. Each bar represents the week's total sales, with the vertical axis

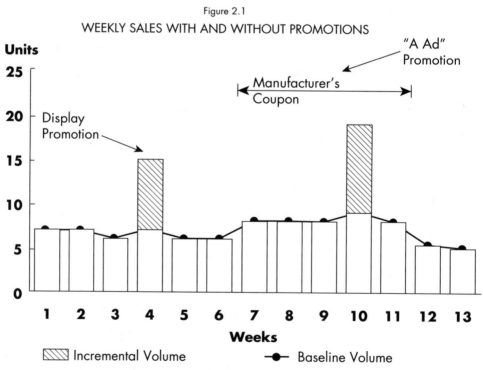

Figure 2.1
WEEKLY SALES WITH AND WITHOUT PROMOTIONS

Source: SCANPRO MONITOR

being unit volume. Most weeks show about the same level of brand sales, except for weeks 4 and 10. These two weeks each had special advertising or promotional conditions as indicated in the figure. Week 4 had a "B" ad. Week 10 had an "A" ad and a special front aisle display. The "A" and "B" ads are different versions of the product advertising. The other weeks had no advertising or sales promotion support.

The two weeks with special advertising or promotion support have considerably higher unit volume than do the other eleven weeks. The manufacturer's coupon program shown would appear to have little impact on unit volume within the store.

This suggests that the unit sales volume could be divided into two components, base volume and incremental volume. The term base volume refers to the business that would be achieved without any promotion. This base volume would be approximately equivalent to the unit sales represented in the clear portions of the bars shown in Figure 2.1.

The term incremental volume refers to the extra business added by special merchandising, feature advertising, displays, or special price reductions. The incremental volume would be approximately equivalent to the unit sales represented in the shaded portions of the bars shown in Figure 2.1 for the two special advertising and promotion weeks.

Total unit volume should equal the base volume plus the incremental volume. The same concept should work equally well for share as it does for unit volume. The analytical problem becomes the appropriate identification of base and incremental volume. The statistical tools necessary to do this are discussed in later chapters.

Base and Incremental Volume. Once incremental sales have been calculated, it is necessary to link them to advertising features, in-store displays, and special price reductions. This relationship becomes the basis for the development of strategy and evaluation.

Base volume for a brand depends upon the size of the product category and the development of the brand within the category. Base volume for a brand is also heavily dependent upon its physical distribution or its presence in retail stores. Normally, the expected time horizon for base volume changing programs is medium- or long-term—that is probably a season (13 weeks) or longer. Change factors in base volume for a brand include list pricing, distribution strategies, and advertising. Other factors include competitive product entries and the presence of heavy competitive promotions.

Incremental volume for a brand depends upon the brand's level of promotional support and the mix of promotional tactics employed. Beyond the available promotion support and tactics is the fundamental characteristic promotion response of the brand. Different product categories clearly have different responsiveness to promotion, but so do different brands within product categories. A brand's unique promotion responsiveness is crucial to its potential incremental volume.

Normally, the expected time horizon for changing incremental volume is short term. Change factors for incremental volume emphasize sales promotion and related tactics. Newspaper features, in-store displays, and special price reductions all can contribute to changes in incremental volume. Head-to-head promotions—promotions by competing brands within a category at the same time—can also impact incremental volume in some interesting ways.

STRATEGIC RESPONSE. Marketing and promotion strategy follow the logical comparison of the historical changes in base and incremental volume for a brand. Figure 2.2 shows how this comparison can be translated into a marketing strategy. This approach recognizes that total volume for a brand consists of both base volume and incremental volume.

Sustain. Perhaps the easiest situation in which to develop a strategy is the one where both base and incremental volume have been increasing. Then, the obvious strategy is to continue the marketing and promotion programs that have led to this desired circumstance. The most dangerous course of action would be to change strategy. Marketers enjoying this situation, however, need to be especially vigilant of competitive activity. Sustaining the marketing and promotion strategy does not mean being complacent.

Build Franchise. When the base volume is down and the incremental volume is up, it may mean that too much emphasis has been placed on sales promotion. In this case, it might be appropriate to shift spending in the direction of advertising or other franchise-building activity.

Figure 2.2
THE USE OF BASE VOLUME AND INCREMENTAL VOLUME
CHANGES TO CONSTRUCT A MARKETING STRATEGY

	Base Volume Up	**Base Volume Down**
Incremental Volume Up	Sustain	Franchise-Building Program
Incremental Volume Down	Trade Promotion-Building Program	Major Overhaul

A franchise-building strategy is likely to be expensive and require patience. Tactics that would build the brand franchise tend to require long periods of time to work. A variety of marketing elements should be examined, including advertising, pricing strategy, and distribution policies.

Build Trade Promotion. When the base volume is up but incremental volume is down, the suggested strategy is a trade promotion-building program. This means that the longer-term franchise-building strategies are working well, but some volume is being sacrificed, probably because of a lack of retailer support. The remedy is to offer trade promotions and allowances to encourage retailer support. Special in-store displays and related materials could be part of the trade promotion program.

Major Overhaul. When both base and incremental volume are down, a major overhaul appears to be in order. This means that neither the franchise-building activity or the short-term promotions are working as well as they should. It might mean that there are problems with the product itself or that there is significant new competition. This situation is the most serious for the brand and potentially the most difficult to fix. It is likely that this circumstance would lead to a reconsideration of the product itself as well as the entire marketing strategy.

DISTRIBUTION-CHANNEL CONFLICTS AND TRADE RELATIONS.

Developing marketing and promotion strategy depends upon the position in the distribution channel. The best promotional strategy for a manufacturer is probably not the best for a retailer and vice versa.

Manufacturers. A manufacturer is generally interested in selling the brand or brands that it manufactures and, for the most part, is unconcerned about the price retailers ask for those brands just as long as they sell them. A manufacturer is normally concerned about achieving sufficient sales volume to justify the investment in the plant and resources necessary to make the product.

The typical manufacturer has no financial interest in the retailer and views the retailer as a necessary route to the consumer. Manufacturers tend to view their competition as other manufacturers and tend to discount the importance of other brands they may manufacture as competitors. Private brands—brands owned by retailers and wholesalers—or generic or unbranded products that are manufactured by the same company are generally much better tolerated than any brand manufactured by a competing manufacturer.

The manufacturer is typically motivated by sales volume of the product at the national level. The manufacturer has made the investment in the brand franchise typically through national advertising and consumer promotion. Yet the manufacturer may need to compromise to maintain the necessary sales volume and engage in promotion activity designed to increase volume, perhaps even at the expense of the brand franchise.

Retailers. Retailers are primarily motivated by store traffic. The typical retailer would place more importance on attracting potential customers to the retail location than it would on sales volume of any particular brand. This is especially true of retailers who sell more than one brand, which is clearly the case of the typical grocery store or supermarket. It is also the case for drug stores, hardware stores, and mass-merchandise stores.

The retailer believes that the competitors are other retailers, not manufacturers. This creates a potential conflict between the retailer and manufacturer. The retailer is not concerned about the manufacturer's brand, but rather, traffic in the store. The manufacturer is not concerned about a retailer's store traffic, but rather, the sales volume of the brand through all retailers.

A promotion strategy that might be best for a retailer, then, might not be the best one for the manufacturer. Thus, it will be important to keep the strategic perspective in mind—that of the manufacturer or the retailer. Much more discussion of this conflict and its dimensions will follow.

PRODUCT-CATEGORY DIFFERENCES.
Because of the availability of data, most of the discussion here will be about consumer package goods, more specifically food products and other items sold in supermarkets. Thus, promotion strategy as it is considered here comes primarily from this perspective. Even among these food-oriented package goods, however, there are important product-category differences. So it is reasonable to expect that there would also be differences in other major types of products. Health and beauty aids, for example, generally exhibit somewhat less promotion responsiveness than grocery food products. No doubt differences exist also among general merchandise categories, soft goods, durable goods, and services.

Many of the general principles outlined here may apply to these categories, though there are no doubt some important differences. The role of fashion in soft goods must be important in promotion response. The long repurchase cycles in hard goods probably make some of the package-goods concepts, such as product usage and brand loyalty, difficult to apply. The problem of not being able to inventory most services may also be a critical factor. These differences, however, will have to wait for future editions to be more than speculation.

CHAPTER 3

ANALYSIS
FUNDAMENTALS

T o really understand how sales promotion works, it is necessary to go beyond description of the techniques and observe it in operation. Sales promotion programs need to be applied to real marketing problems with the results carefully analyzed. This needs to be done over an extended period of time to be able to generalize and begin to develop some principles of sales promotion that will be usable by the marketing manager.

Until recently, sales promotion has been managed primarily on the basis of traditional and anecdotal understanding of how it works. Neither the necessary data nor the computing power has been available to do any systematic analysis. This has now completely changed, forcing complete analysis along with careful management of any sales promotion effort in order to remain competitive in the future.

ASSESSING THE IMPACT OF SALES PROMOTION. The computer revolution that has swept the business world is just now beginning to alter the traditional methods of establishing product prices, assessing the impact of price changes, and assessing the impact of promotional activity. Computer technology has made possible the collection of purchase and sales data in ways that were previously not possible, and it has greatly enhanced the ability to manipulate and analyze that data. Two factors emerge as driving forces in the move toward analysis of sales promotion. These are improved cost accounting and availability of information on sales performance, down to the level of individual items at individual retail outlet.

Improved Cost Accounting. Improved accuracy of cost-accounting methods by both the manufacturer and the retailer now makes it possible to more accurately allocate both fixed and variable costs on a brand-by-brand, size-of-package by size-of-package basis. For example, manufacturers commonly carry a line of differentiated products within a single category, with several package sizes in each product. Each manufacturer can easily have dozens of different products in the same product category. Obviously, the addition of a differentiated product, such as a different flavor, or of a different package size, greatly aggravates the accounting problem as there are simply more items. However, the addition of each brand, extension, or size is justified on the basis of expanded sales volume, as the additions usually provide the additional consumer benefits of more product choice and greater convenience of product use.

The proliferation of items has led to difficulty in determining if all items are justified on the basis of their contribution to profit. However, with the ever-decreasing cost of collecting and processing data by computers, historical data on profit contribution can be kept at the finest level of detail. The retailer cost-accounting problem might even appear to be worse than that the manufacturer faced. A typical retail outlet in grocery, drug, or mass merchandising may handle from 15,000 to 30,000 individual items in 300 to 400 product categories. Movement of many individual items from the store may be quite small, hardly justifying individual by-hand analysis, except on an infrequent basis in making retain or drop decisions on shelf stocking. In response to this problem, retailers have adopted simple pricing formulas such as the following:

Selling Price = Purchase Price + 20%.

The simple percentage-mark-up rule is a typical method of management for many retailers. The percentage is adjusted to cover overall fixed costs, variable costs, and profit.

Markups may vary across product classes based on easily identified differential operating costs. A grocery meat department, for example, may require special processing and storage equipment and have a relatively high product loss rate due to the relatively short shelf life. Refrigerated items may require special storage and display equipment. Many produce and dairy items also have limited shelf lives. Considerations like these may dictate differential markups on a department-by-department basis.

The use of computerized techniques enables more accurate accounting and improved cost allocation, allowing for the department-by-department approach. The largest gains in allocating costs appear to be generated through analysis of operations required from the initial order of the product through the final sale to a consumer. Today certain systems can even estimate costs on an item-by-item basis.

Improved Data. Before the computer was employed at the grocery checkout lane, virtually no individual purchase data were available. The growth of automated checkout devices, or scanners, has been justified by most retailers on the basis of improved checkout productivity—reduced labor and reduced error in entering prices. The management value of the data has been generally ignored.

A by-product of such automatic checkout device installation is an accurate recording on an outlet-by-outlet basis of the prices charged and the sales volume for each item sold during time periods as short as one week. A number of syndicated data services are currently using scanner-collected data to provide to client manufacturers detailed reporting of brand-sales volume, competitive pricing, and promotional activity. Most importantly, the accumulation of very detailed historical information on an outlet-by-outlet basis provides a foundation for the statistical analysis of interactions among the pricing and promotional activities of competing brands. Also critically important is the ability to conduct experiments at the retail-outlet level to assess the probable impact of pricing and promotional activities outside the observed range of historical conditions. Previously, such information could be obtained only by manipulating pricing and promotional activity on a much broader scale, such as sales-territory level.

The A.C. Nielsen Company is a leader in using scanner data for tracking product sales and has one of the most consistent historical databases for examining the impact of pricing and promotion decisions in grocery product categories. It is these data that underlie the cases provided in later chapters and in the concluding sales promotion principles. The Nielsen data are collected using scanners in grocery, drug, and mass-merchandiser stores in selected markets around the country. The data have been collected for several years on grocery stores, providing a reasonably complete database on grocery product sales. The particular methodology will be discussed in more detail later.

Limitations. Two important factors limit the application of scanner data to sales promotion problems. The first factor is that no psychological variables are measured or recorded. The technology measures only the overt behavior of product purchase. Some questions, such as the long-term impact of sales promotion programs on the image of the brand, cannot be directly addressed. It can certainly be argued, however, that such questions are not particularly important given that sales are so well measured.

At the time of this writing, historical data on some product categories are not available. Few durable goods, for example, are recorded in commercially available databases. To date, data suppliers have concentrated on product categories sold through grocery stores, supermarkets, and drug stores. Hence, the generalizations drawn here are based upon frequently purchased nondurable package goods only. The analysis methods described, however, apply generally to scanner-collected sales data.

SALES PROMOTION DECISIONS.
Before the new data and analytic techniques can be brought to bear on any sales promotion problems, it is necessary to establish objectives for that promotion. And in order to evaluate any promotional effort, it is first necessary to understand the goals for that promotion.

Setting Objectives. The first step is always setting objectives. Objectives for sales promotion, like objectives for any marketing strategy, must be unambiguous and realistic. The objectives will be unambiguous if they provide for *measurable* outcomes. The objective of providing an "incentive to consumers," for example, is not adequate because it does not provide for an unambiguous outcome. A manager could not determine whether the promotion was a success. The objective of increasing sales by 100,000 units, however, is quite precise and measurable, assuming that the appropriate system is in place. Objectives may be stated in terms of volume sales, share of market, profitability, trial of product among previous nonusers, or changes in inventory position.

Objectives must also be realistic in terms of their potential to be fulfilled. Objectives that can never be reached should be avoided, since they make the entire process unworkable and as difficult to manage as though there are no objectives at all.

Price and Promotion. In most analyses of sales promotion activity, it is best to separate the decision about the pricing of the product from any decision about using sales promotion. A product should have an established, normal selling price that consumers expect to pay. This price is certainly influenced by both the manufacturer's and the retailer's costs, but it is not necessarily determined by them entirely. Rational manufacturers certainly would not as normal practice sell any product below its variable cost of production. Retailers sometimes sell limited numbers of items below cost when they believe that such items are influential in attracting new shoppers to the store, building overall sales volume. In cases where a product would be sold below cost, it would usually be wise to avoid incurring additional expense, such as storage costs.

There are two basic ways of determining the selling price of a particular product. The first and simplest way is to apply a simple markup rule, such as 20 percent of cost. In other words, if a mythical product costs 80 cents from the manufacturer, the retailer can then apply the markup rule, in this case 20 percent, and add 20 percent of 80 cents, or 16 cents. The selling price to the consumer is the 80 cents plus 16 cents, or 96 cents. This price would probably be psychologically adjusted to 99 cents.

The cost-plus pricing approach, in which a retailer simply applies the markup rule, has a major disadvantage: it relies on historical costs and ignores the operation of the marketplace, thus possibly ignoring maximized profits. Often a retailer may sell a product at too low a price using this method. A much better method is that borrowed from microeconomics, which uses a simple demand curve.

A demand curve is the relationship between the selling price of the product and the number of units of that product that are sold. In general, lower prices would mean higher unit sales, and higher prices would mean lower unit sales. While there are sometimes exceptions, such as special products sold on the basis of style or prestige, like perfume, lower prices usually lead to increased unit sales.

The biggest problem for both the manufacturer and retailer is being able to estimate enough of the demand curve to be able to determine the estimated sales levels at alternative selling prices. Traditional methods, such as quarterly or annual sales levels simply do not provide sufficient data, leaving subjective methods like the best-guess estimates from appropriate personnel or very expensive experimentation. Scanner-based sales reporting can provide sufficient data to do relatively inexpensive experimentation.

Because scanning records every purchase of a product instantly, comparisons can be made on virtually a day-to-day, store-by-store basis. Products then can be analyzed on a very short time interval, such as a day or a week, or over a very long time, such as months or years. Comparison of natural or promotion-induced price changes with sales volume will then provide a most reasonable estimate of the fundamental demand or price-volume curve for that product. In addition data from relatively few stores are required for experimenting with new price levels. Almost always, determining the nature of the demand or price-volume curve for the product will be the first step in analyzing any sales promotion. Figure 3.1 provides an example of a price-volume, or demand, curve.

Once the price-volume curve has been determined, costs can be directly compared. Costs usually are divided into two major components, fixed costs, and variable costs. Fixed costs do not change with sales volume and are incurred even if none of the product is sold. Variable costs change with the sale of the product and are normally directly related to the volume of the product sold. For example, gasoline requires a storage tank and pump to be sold at retail. The net expense of the pump and related equipment would be fixed cost. The electrical power needed to operate the pump and the maintenance expense would be directly related to the volume of gasoline sold and would be variable costs, as would be the cost of purchasing gasoline from the refiner or area distributor.

By converting the unit selling price to revenue and cost, a break-even chart can be prepared. Revenue results from multiplying the appropriate quantity and the selling price. Total cost is then the result of multiplying the appropriate quantity by the variable costs with the addition of all fixed costs. Total revenue and total cost curves can then be plotted against the quantity sold. When the total revenue curve is above the total cost curve, profit is earned. When the total cost curve is above the total revenue curve, there is a loss. The point where the total revenue curve and the total cost curve intersect is the break-even point. A sample break-even chart is shown in Figure 3.2.

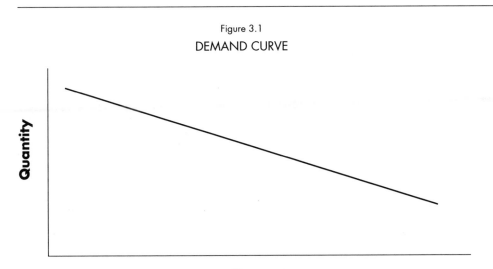

Figure 3.1
DEMAND CURVE

Quantity

Unit Selling Price

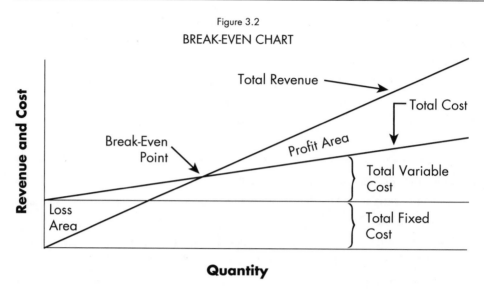

Figure 3.2
BREAK-EVEN CHART

From a marketing management perspective, the important variables are the price and the profit, not the quantity. A third graph or chart combines the demand curve and the break-even chart and compares the unit selling price with revenue and cost. A price-profit chart, as shown in Figure 3.3, is a very convenient way to assess the impact of various price levels on ultimate profit levels.

How these charts are used depends to some extent on the managerial policy of the particular organization. For example, profit can be viewed in terms of the absolute dollars or amount, or it can be viewed in terms of a percentage or rate. One price level would often result in the highest rate of profit, and another price level would result in

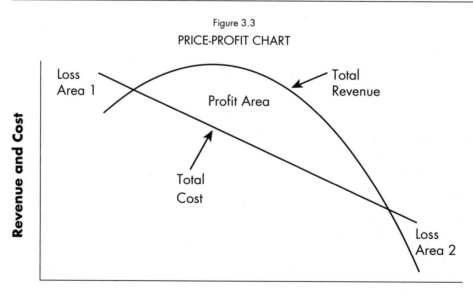

Figure 3.3
PRICE-PROFIT CHART

the greatest amount of profit. The choice, of course, would depend upon how the management of the organization views profit and rate of return.

These charts provide a convenient framework for analyzing price and promotion decisions. By holding some of the variables constant, such as the normal selling price and the cost of goods sold, the impact of promotion can easily be examined. The difficult problem is to be able to understand the impact on the sales volume; the solution normally requires research.

Evaluation and Research. Establishing the relationship between selling price and unit sales requires very careful study of product sales at the retail level. It is critically important that sales be studied at the retail level—the level where the product is ultimately sold. Examining sales at the manufacturer level can be very misleading, as the product may languish in wholesaler and retailer inventories for long periods of time before being sold to a consumer. Manufacturer shipments reflect the aggregate effects of the way the retail trade translated particular manufacturer deal offerings. The manufacturer can assess with reasonable accuracy the incremental volume and profit generated by the offer, but it seldom gains insight into the way in which alternative terms might influence volume and profit. Information on competitive manufacturers' pricing and promotional activity is difficult to incorporate in an analysis of shipments. Marketers must do substantially more than merely examine their own sales records.

Obtaining an accurate measure of retail sales is necessary to properly evaluate the effectiveness of sales promotion programs, and it requires a special research effort. Sales for most product categories can be measured in several ways at the retail level, though in certain situations some of the methods may be too expensive to be practical. Automobile sales may be the easiest to measure because the vehicle registration requirements of state governments provide a natural database describing the vehicle purchased, the purchase date, and new owner identification. Few product categories, however, have this luxury. The research required is often best performed by external specialized research organizations.

Using Research Service Organizations. For most marketers, contracting for research services with an external research company is a common practice. Few marketers possess the specialized personnel to collect the necessary data. Also, research service companies are often in a better position than marketers to contract with retailers and wholesalers for data. It is difficult for a marketer, who is generally in a continuous bargaining position with the trade, to obtain useful information on such subjects as price discounts and competitive activity.

A marketer can contract with a research service organization in two ways: on a custom basis or on a syndicated basis. With custom research, the information is collected and analyzed for only one client. With syndicated research, the same information is collected and analyzed for more than one client. Each type has advantages and disadvantages. Custom research is known only to the client and the research service organization and is therefore secret or proprietary. It is also flexible in terms of scheduling and method. The primary disadvantage of custom research is that it is more expensive than syndicated research, since one client must pay the entire bill.

Syndicated research, on the other hand, has the advantage of credibility when measures of competitive activity are being taken. If more than one competitor is paying for the research, there is less reason to suspect any particular bias. Syndicated research is also less expensive, because the cost can be shared among more than one client. The primary disadvantage of syndicated research is a lack of flexibility; it usually requires a fixed schedule and a standardized methodology. A good application of custom research would be a new product test that a marketer would not want the competitors to have any knowledge about. A good application of syndicated research is the measurement of advertising-media audiences or brand-market share over time.

MEASURING PRODUCT SALES.   Retail product sales can be measured in several ways. Various methods have evolved over the years for different product categories. The methods that have evolved and are described here are all commercial successes. They are all offered for sale by at least one commercial research service organization and, of course, are purchased by marketers.

Store Shelf Audits.   Most grocery and package good items are sold today through supermarkets that can be relatively easily monitored. By keeping counts of the movements of products on and off the shelves, an estimate of product sales can be determined for that store. Periodically counting the store's inventory and invoices and subtracting the beginning inventory from the ending inventory plus the goods shipped in provides an estimate of the sales for a given period.

The A.C. Nielsen Company has provided a service based upon this method for many years. Using a carefully selected sample of supermarkets throughout the country, Nielsen is able to provide a national estimate of retail market share for most products sold through supermarkets. Nielsen also audits drug stores and other retail outlets. Product sales can be easily estimated by brand and package size. In addition, Nielsen provides estimates of average retail prices, wholesale prices, average store inventory, promotional activity, and advertising. Special merchandising activity, such as premiums or bonus packs, may be noted as well. Nielsen audits the stores every 60 days.

Audit information such as this is available over extended periods of time, providing an indication of longer-run changes in brand or market position. It is generally available on a regional basis as well as national, allowing assessment of brand strengths and weakness by region.

There are three problems in using shelf-audit data to evaluate sales promotion programs. The first and perhaps most obvious problem is that only products sold primarily through supermarkets and drug stores can be studied. If a product has a large proportion of its sales through other outlets, examining only the supermarket portion of the sales could be misleading. Products not sold at all through supermarkets, of course, could not be studied.

A second problem is the lack of any information about the consumer. This makes it difficult to study promotional influences aimed at the individual consumer or to consider any targeted impacts on different market segments. Analysis is limited to an aggregate analysis of the entire market.

The third problem is the relatively long time period between measurements. Most promotions are designed to promote immediate response, sometimes within a single day or week. If the measurements are not taken at a frequency at least equal to the expected duration of the impact of the sales promotion program, then too many other factors can impinge on the sales of the product and dilute the effect of the specific promotion. In the mid-1980s, Nielsen introduced a scanner-based data sales monitoring service to augment store audit information. By 1992, growth in scanner usage has allowed phase-out of audit data for projecting grocery store sales, although it still remains important for channels and markets where scanner penetration is low.

Warehouse Withdrawals. Moving back a step in the distribution chain can simplify the monitoring process. Assuming that supermarkets obtain all their inventory from a few central warehouses and knowing that supermarkets tend to avoid maintaining large in-store inventories, much the same information could be obtained by inventorying the warehouses instead of the supermarkets themselves.

Selling Areas Marketing Incorporated (SAMI) used a computerized method of warehouse withdrawal to sales and distribution of products sold through supermarkets. SAMI provided data nationally and in approximately 50 individual markets. The warehouse-withdrawal method would have the same disadvantages as the shelf-audit method but would also lack the store level information. In addition, several important classes of products are generally delivered directly to the store without intermediate warehousing. These include high-turnover items justifying shipment directly from the manufacturer in truckload lots and locally produced items, often with limited shelf lives, such as bakery, dairy, or soft drink products. SAMI recently announced that it is discontinuing major portions of its business, and warehouse withdrawal information is no longer commercially available.

Mail Consumer Panels. The traditional method of collecting individual consumer-level information has been the mail consumer panel. The subjects are recruited through the mail and respond through the mail with either a purchase diary or questionnaire. The subjects generally periodically report their purchase behavior, hence the panel design. Some of the research organizations that provide this service also offer telephone service as well.

There are two types of mail-panel data collection instruments: the purchase diary and the questionnaire. The purchase diary is provided to the subject before purchases are made and is intended to be completed coincidentally with each purchase. The questionnaire method relies on the recall ability of the subjects, asking them to reconstruct their purchase behavior from memory for a specified period of time, such as a week or a month. The questionnaire method is currently the more popular method.

Several research organizations maintain pre-recruited mail panels that can easily be used to measure purchase behavior. They include National Family Opinion (NFO) and Market Facts, Incorporated. Marketing and Research Counselors, Incorporated (M/A/R/C) offers a neighborhood panel in 25 markets that can be invited to central locations for personal interviews if necessary. Most of the mail-panel research has been custom research. Mail panels have also been a very popular means of testing new products before any store placement.

Mail panels are often questioned on the representativeness of their samples and on the quality of the data obtained. Not everyone recruited agrees to participate in mail-panel research, with some estimates claiming as low as 10 percent of the initial sample agreeing to participate. The mail-panel research organizations attempt to counter this problem with very careful balancing of their panels according to geographic areas and demographic characteristics.

Anytime people are asked questions, there is the possibility of error. When recall is used, error may occur because the memory may not be entirely accurate. Comparisons of recall of product purchase versus scanner-measured purchase indicates time-compression effects. The question, "What products have you used in the last three months?" may yield responses more closely reflecting product usage in the last year. Usage of private label and generic products may be under-reported. The recording of the responses may not be complete, legible, or accurate. Therefore, the quality of the data received through a mail panel is often a problem and requires careful editing and coding.

Mail panels have an advantage, however, because they are able to collect data for virtually any product category. The product need not necessarily be sold through supermarkets or any other particular type of retail outlet. In addition, mail panels are probably still the best way to study durable goods, such as tires and major appliances.

Store Scanner Data. Perhaps the greatest technological innovation in the supermarket in recent years has been the automated checkout lane. Using the universal product bar code, a computer-controlled bar-code reader identifies the product, the appropriate price is found in a computer-maintained data base; and the customer is provided a printout receipt. Each purchase is entered into a data base for later analysis. An average supermarket may record approximately 150,000 such individual purchases in a day.

It is interesting that the supermarkets that have adopted automated checkout systems have not done so because of the value of the data they collect. Instead, the rationales for the adoption usually include the reduced clerk checkout error and increased checkout speed. Automated checkout systems have also made possible the "instant coupon," which is presented to customers at checkout time for their next purchase. Instant coupons can be awarded depending upon products purchased during the current trip. Customers could be given coupons for competing products or the same product to encourage repurchase.

The automated checkout data provides all of the characteristics of the package and brand, plus the exact price paid and the purchase quantity. This is considerably more information than is available from the shelf-audit method. The data are precisely timed so that the date and even the time of day are known.

The are two problems with scanner data alone. The first is the same as with shelf-audit data: It provides no information about the consumer making the purchase. In other words, analyses of consumer topologies still cannot be done. The other major problem with scanner data is that in most markets, not all retail outlets are scanned. A consumer may purchase products in a store that is scanned, but then go on to another store that is not. Such incomplete coverage of a market might produce very biased understanding of the market.

Several research organizations either offer scanner data or have announced projects based upon scanner data. Some of the research organizations include IRI, which has been using scanner data for household data collection since 1981, and A.C. Nielsen. Both offer a wide variety of scanner-based data service. Arbitron Scan America is currently in its test phase. There is little doubt that scanner data is revolutionizing market research.

Store Scanner Panels. One solution to the consumer problem with store scanner data is the store scanner panel. By providing individuals with special cards that can be read by the bar-code reader in the store, a selected subset of individuals can have complete recordings of all scannable purchases. This method combines the advantages of both the store-scanner data and the mail consumer panel.

Again, the problem is coverage within the geographical market area. For the system to record all the purchases of a household, all the retail outlets in the area would have to be scanning and participating. Information Resources Inc. (IRI) has minimized the problem by arranging nearly complete coverage of isolated markets where few opportunities exist for consumers to shop in non-covered outlets. The expansion of many products outside their traditional supermarket channels of distribution poses a problem for data collection based on in-store methods. A.C. Nielsen solves the coverage problem by providing each household with an in-home bar-code reader to identify products purchased. Using this method, purchasing from all channels of distribution can be monitored.

The scanner panel has been proven to be a viable alternative, and it is near the heart of rapidly expanding research services by IRI and Nielsen.

Single-Source Data. One of the goals pursued by suppliers of scanner data is "single-source" data. This means that data on all elements of the marketing mix would be collected with as much overlap of sources as possible. Retail store sales would be tracked via store scanner panel; purchases would also be tracked in a manner that allows matching to all stores in which a consumer shopped, to store causal data on brands available, and to pricing and promotion against the purchase data. Not only would coupon redemption be monitored, but records would indicate which coupons were available to households. Going beyond a simple household identification, purchases would be associated with specific family members. The TV (and VCR) viewing of each individual household member would be monitored, as would their radio listening. Usage of print media such as newspapers would also be captured. Exposure to point-of-sale materials such as shelf-talkers, grocery-cart programs, automatic coupon systems, and other in-store media would be noted. A file listing the promotional offers available to the trade would also be offered for use in assessing the reaction of retailers to different promotion terms.

All major data suppliers are working toward this ideal, though none has reached it yet. In some respects, IRI's BehaviorScan markets approach the ideal in some areas of retail food and package goods merchandising, but coverage of drug, mass-merchandiser, and convenience-store sales is less than fully complete. IRI TV monitoring captures set usage, but does not identify which members of the household are viewing. A major criticism of IRI's approach is that the small markets dictated by the outlet coverage goals may not be representative of the larger urban markets where most marketing activity is focused. Nielsen uses an in-home scanning system, which permits capture of purchases from all outlets, but relies on consumer-diary information to capture the usage of store specials and coupon usage. Both Nielsen and Arbitron are experimenting with methods of capturing TV viewing that identify specific household members. A couple of coupon clearing houses are developing information systems based on coupon offers. However, the authors know of no activity currently underway to develop a database on trade promotion offers.

One thing seems certain: Future databases will cover more types of outlets, a greater percentage of households, and more causal information as manufacturers and retailers seek greater understanding of the relations among the various elements of the marketing mix.

HISTORY OF SYNDICATED DATA SUPPLIERS. In 1923, the Procter & Gamble company established an economic research department, which soon grew to cover research on consumer acceptance of products and the effectiveness of advertising. In 1931, Procter & Gamble adopted the brand manager system of product management.

Under this system, each brand became a business center with its own budget, goals, and responsibilities for managing advertising, trade, and consumer promotions. The brand manager system, quickly adopted by many large consumer product manufacturers with multiple brands, fueled a demand for accurate data on advertising and product sales, not just for the brand manager's brand of interest, but on its competitors. Senior management needed a source of stable, consistent data on competitive products as well as on their companies' own brands in order to judge market trends and the ability of their own brand managers to expand their brands. For all but the largest companies, the cost of internally building and maintaining such a large-scale data-collection system was prohibitive.

The answer to the problems of data acquisition costs and maintenance of consistent, unbiased data reporting was found in the concept of syndicating the data collection and reporting process. An external company, with no vested interest in the apparent success or failure of any brand or subset of brands, could collect sales and advertising data on all brands in a category and in all regions of the country. These data could potentially be resold to all manufacturers of category brands. In addition, the advertising delivery media could use measurement of the audience sizes of various advertising vehicles to set advertising charges that reflected the relative efficiencies of their audiences.

A pioneer in this area was Arthur Nielsen, Sr., whose A.C. Nielsen Company began in the early 1930s to measure product sales through audits of retail store sales and to measure the effects of advertising through the use of consumer-panel diaries. From the 1930s through the 1960s, the bimonthly Nielsen sales reports provided the standard yardstick for assessing brand performance in the market. Included along with estimates of sales and share were estimates of average price. As television became an important advertising-delivery method during the 1950s, the Nielsen program ratings became the measure of program viewer drawing power and, hence the standard for establishing the relative cost of advertising on national and local television.

In the early 1960s, SAMI appeared as a competitor to Nielsen for measuring product movement. An important link in the distribution system for consumer products was the distribution warehouse, where products from many manufacturers were collected and assembled into multimanufacturer distributions to retailers. The SAMI company measured withdrawals from these warehouses on a monthly basis. Claimed benefits were that, unlike the Nielsen sample-based estimates with attendant sampling error, SAMI's sales estimates were very close to a census of all product movement and that SAMI's monthly reporting cycle allowed quicker detection of changes in sales trends and competitive sales activity.

A competitor to the Nielsen media-ratings service was Arbitron, a company that provided greater detail on local market competition in both radio and television. The growing importance of sales promotion by retailers also led to the establishment of the Majers Company, which reported on retailers' feature advertising for consumer products.

Consumer purchasing behavior was tracked over time in the 1960s, 1970s, and early 1980s by written diaries. The Market Research Company of America (later renamed MRCA Information Services) and the National Panel Diary (NPD) were the largest suppliers of such data. Consumer-panel data were generally collected along category lines defined quite similarly to Nielsen category definitions. Panel analyses of such subjects as brand switching, brand shifting, product usage, purchase quantity, and purchase cycle analyses were conducted in order to understand the consumer behavior underlying the trends and shifts observed in the Nielsen and SAMI data. Consumer behavioral analysis based on interviewing and short-span diary reporting was conducted by a number of analysis-oriented companies, in addition to the above-named companies.

In 1967, the ADTEL company introduced a diary-based service for testing new brands and testing marketing-mix variations, particularly those involving television advertising (copy, weight, and day part). In this service, towns that had cable television as their primary television source were provided with split cables. Physically adjacent households on different cables could receive different TV advertising. Written diaries recorded not only category-and-brand purchasing activity, but store- and manufacturer-coupon usage, price, and store "special" treatment. While the main focus was on the statistical analysis of test versus control TV treatments, the panel data for up to four cities was available in computer-readable form for further analysis.

The computers that were introduced into larger businesses in the late 1950s were often under the control of the accounting department, which used them to streamline the ordering, shipping, and billing processes. A by-product of the accounting operation was usually an assessment of monthly shipments. Targets for monthly shipments also became part of the brand managers' objectives. Shipment data showed a dramatic impact of retail-trade promotions. Since a trade promotion is offered to all retailers over a relatively short time and is often signaled in advance, the usual pattern was a prepromotion decline in shipments as retailers ran out of ordinarily priced products and a surge in shipments as retailers refilled depleted inventories, purchased product to meet the increased sales demand associated with retailer promotion, and stockpiled low-priced product against future demand.

At the end of a promotion, there was a clear postpromotional decrease as the stockpiled product as well as any excess ordering for the actual trade promotion was used. In the early 1960s and 1970s, most consumer-product categories showed significant growth rates in response to growth in U.S. population and increased consumption among households as real disposable income increased. Two analysis-oriented companies began providing baselining methodology for use in assessing the net impact of retail-trade promotion programs on brand sales through analysis of shipment data. These were SPAR and MDS (Management Decision Systems). While instructive in assessing the overall worth of trade promotion programs, the relative dearth of information on how the retail trade was translating the company's promotional offer into consumer-oriented marketing actions (price, features, and displays) limited the ability of the shipment data analysts to make specific recommendations on changes in promotional offer terms that would improve the performance of the trade program.

In 1979, IRI was founded. Its initial product, BehaviorScan, directly competed with ADTEL. BehaviorScan was able to assign TV advertisements to individual consumer households rather than ADTEL's neighborhood split. Instead of through a written diary, the IRI panelist had their purchasing behavior captured by the supermarket checkout scanner. In order to provide powerful covariate analysis variables for the estimation of TV advertising effects, information was collected on total sales of all products on a store-by-week basis. Causal information, such as the occurrence of in-store displays, store coupons, and store ad features, was added. Initially established in two markets, BehaviorScan was expanded to 10 markets over the next four years. In 1983, based on data from four markets, IRI introduced its *Marketing FactBook* service, which summarized across markets to give quarterly and annual measures not only on product sales and share but on the percentage of product purchased with coupons, features, displays, and price reductions. Measures of purchase-cycle length and brand loyalty were also provided. Because of the small size and isolation of the markets, the FactBook data were little used for business-tracking purposes. To address issues of the data representativeness of large markets, panels were added in New York, Chicago, and Los Angeles.

In 1986, the A.C. Nielsen Company, by then a subsidiary of Dun and Bradstreet (D&B), announced its decision to replace the bimonthly audit tracking system with scanner-based information. IRI quickly announced a competing product, and 1987 saw strong competition between the two companies for tracking data. An attempt by D&B in late 1987 to acquire IRI and merge it with the U.S. tracking business of A. C. Nielsen was rejected by the FTC, leaving Nielsen (now merged with Majers and in a joint venture with NPD on panel data), SAMI-Burke (now owned by Time Inc.), and IRI (now merged with MDS) as the three major suppliers of product-tracking data. SAMI was sold to Control Data, which merged it with ARBITRON. In late 1990, Control Data disbanded SAMI, and its clients redistributed themselves between Nielsen and IRI.

In 1988, Nielsen announced plans to collect panelists' purchase data using in-home scanning equipment to record items purchased and an auxiliary written diary system to record causal data. In 1988, Citicorp announced its decision to form a scanner-based panel-purchase tracking system. The industry started 1993 with Nielsen possessing a strong media rating division, a scanner-based tracking system for retail products in grocery, drug, and mass-merchandiser outlets, and a consumer panel based on in-home scanning with written diary recording of casuals. IRI has a media rating-service (primarily television oriented) in a number of major cities, and a cross-licensing agreement with ARBITRON, which gives access to that company's rating data. IRI controls data acquisition from about 70,000 households in 20 cities. IRI and Nielsen have also expanded tracking into drug and mass-merchandiser outlets.

INDIVIDUAL VERSUS AGGREGATE MEASUREMENT. A major requirement for data used to evaluate sales promotion programs is that they be sufficiently sensitive to detect any differences in response due to promotional activity. Data that are averaged across time may not be sufficiently sensitive because the averaging process may also be averaging away differences due to promotion.

One of the greatest difficulties is that sales promotion is always presented to consumers in a very competitive environment. Promotions are offered to consumers so frequently that the effects of one program are almost immediately countered by another. In addition, the marketplace is extremely dynamic and subject to an extraordinary number of influences.

Many studies of sales promotion programs have found that only data collected during a time period sufficiently short that pricing and promotional activity are constant are sufficiently precise to detect differences attributable to any one promotional effort. When the data are aggregated (summarized), the differences tend to disappear. Aggregate data, that is data not collected on the individual retail-outlet level on a weekly basis, generally cannot be used to evaluate sales promotion. In other words, in order to effectively evaluate sales promotion programs, the data must be collected on an *individual-store-week* basis, and not aggregated across time, stores, or markets. This point is clearly illustrated in the cases provided later in this book.

TIME PERIOD. Data can be aggregated in time. The results need to be measured on a basis consistent with the duration of the promotional event. For a weekend-special store sale, daily measurement may be required. For the typical week-long event in many grocery, drug, and mass-merchandise stores, weekly sales are usually sufficient. Consumer coupons, sweepstakes, and similar promotional events may take several months to achieve full impact. If data are collected on a less frequent basis, the impact of an individual promotion may be entirely lost in all the competing promotions that occur later in the week, or even later in the month. The same problem of aggregation exists with data summarized over several sales outlets with differing promotional conditions. Data analysis techniques that attempt to estimate promotional effects from data that has been too highly aggregated exist, but selection of the proper level of aggregation for the base data makes promotional analysis much more straightforward.

SALES AND USAGE MEASUREMENT. Sales are traditionally presented in the form of market share in marketing plans. The term market share simply refers to the sales for a given product brand divided by the total sales in the product category. When one knows a product's market share, one can compare the performance of an individual brand against competing brands. This is why it is so often used as a means of expressing product sales. When used at high levels of data aggregation, such as annual U.S. sales volume, it is a good indication of relative effectiveness.

A problem in using market share for short-run analysis is that competitive activity is included in the number. For example, if brand A runs a promotion and enjoys an increase in sales, and if brand B also runs a promotion at the same time and increases sales, brand A may have very little change in market share but significant volume-sales increases. Because market share also includes competitive activity, market share loses sensitivity to a given sales promotion program. A much better measure of sales to evaluate sales promotion, then, is sales volume, which will be demonstrated in the cases that appear later in this book. A second problem with market share is that an accurate assessment is required as to which brands or products are the appropriate market. Many product categories such as sliced lunch meats, canned soups, salted snacks, cookies, and snack crackers have a large variety of sizes, forms, and flavors. Improper specification of the items to be used as a basis for market share may materially bias analyses.

FINANCIAL ANALYSIS.
The appropriate framework for evaluating sales promotion programs is the income statement, which allows direct comparison of profit levels. The income statement can provide both a most convenient planning tool and a means of evaluation.

Income Statements. The income statement is perhaps the most fundamental of all financial statements. The income statement is sometimes referred to as a *profit or loss statement.* It shows the relationship between sales, costs, and profits. A sales promotion program, whether offered by a manufacturer or a retailer, should have impact on sales, and costs, and of course, profit.

A simplified statement (Table 3.1) shows the relationship between the manufacturer and the retailer and the source of promotional expenses. The manufacturer incurs costs with the trade allowances and promotional expenses, while the retailer incurs promotional expenses.

As discussed previously, the expense categories each contain both fixed and variable components that need to be recognized in order to determine profit. The above model simplifies the distribution channel somewhat, in that warehouses and brokers are recognized as costs to the manufacturer. Certainly promotion can be aimed at middlemen, but most of the trade promotion in this book will be assumed to be aimed at retailers.

Financial Forecasts. The format of the income statement can be readily applied as both a tool to evaluate a past sales promotion program and a means to forecast the effect of a future program. Using income statements for successive time inter-

---

Table 3.1
INCOME STATEMENT

Manufacturer	**Retailer**
Gross Sales	Gross Sales
• Discounts and Adjustments	• Returns
• Trade Allowances	———————
———————	Net Sales
Net Sales	• Cost of Goods
• Cost of Goods	———————
• Warehouse and Freight	Gross Margin
• Brokerage Fees	• Retailer Promotion
———————	• Other Expenses
Contribution to Margin	———————
• Manufacturer Promotion	Retailer Profit
• Other Expenses	
———————	
Manufacturer Profit	

vals, past sales promotion programs can be evaluated by comparing the intervals when the promotion was present to those intervals when the promotion was not.

The difficulty in comparing many time intervals is performing the repetitious computations that are necessary. This problem is easily solved by using a microcomputer with a spread-sheet program. A spread-sheet program makes the repetitious computations as simple as representing the relationship between rows and columns in terms of simple algebra. Almost any of the currently commercially available programs can be adapted to this purpose.

Once the appropriate historical data have been entered, it is then a simple matter to perform the computations with a spread-sheet program. The appropriate comparisons may be made, followed by the strategic promotional decisions. The microcomputer model may also be used as a forecasting tool, allowing the asking of fanciful "what if" questions. The analyst can enter projected values for future time periods, make reasonable assumptions from the historical data, and evaluate potential sales promotion programs. Attempting such calculations manually would be time-consuming and prone to error.

Forward Buying. Many sales promotion programs involve the shifting of purchase patterns in time. Analyzing purchase timing requires that special attention be paid to the time periods prior to, during, and after the promotional period.

A manufacturer may announce a new allowance and promotional program to the trade. The trade may also anticipate a promotional program from a manufacturer because of its experience during previous years. The trade would be expected then to defer purchase of the product from the manufacturer until the special promotional price is available. The trade would also be expected to purchase more of the product than usual to take advantage of the special price in anticipation of future sales to consumers. This phenomenon is known as forward buying. Presumably after the promotional period, the trade demand for the product would diminish until the additional quantity purchased from forward buying was sold. Not all products are suitable for forward buying, such as perishables, seasonal items, and items that would represent high cost inventory.

From the point of view of the manufacturer, forward buying moves quantities of the product from their inventory and may result in incremental sales-volume gain. From the point of view of the retailer, it affords an opportunity to obtain the product at a lower price, though this benefit needs to be carefully balanced against inventory-holding costs and lowered selling prices and margins.

TIME SERIES ANALYSIS.

Analyzing data across successive time periods, or a time series, is one of the best ways to generalize from the historical data. Sales data are naturally arrayed in a temporal sequence. One of the most common ways of analyzing time series data is linear regression, although several special problems need to be considered.

Linear Regression. A detailed discussion of linear regression can be found in any of several books dealing with statistics, but in general this term refers to a way of establishing a linear algebraic relationship between a criterion or dependent variable and one or more predictor or independent variables. The equation is in the form $Y = a + bX$, where Y is the criterion variable and X is the predictor variable. The criterion variable is the variable that is to be estimated, such as sales or profit. The predictor variable or variables are the variables that are presumed to influence the criterion variable, such as the presence or absence of a sales promotion program. In the equation, the a is referred to as the intercept and the b as the slope, or the relative change in X that is attributable to Y. The slope is also commonly referred to as the *regression coefficient.*

Linear regression, then, is an extremely useful tool for accounting for differences in a time series. The relationship, however, is limited to a straight line. If the data points in the series were plotted on a graph, they would probably not form a very good straight line. This raises the issue of fitting the best possible line through the data points. The most common method for accomplishing this is the method of least squares, or the line fit is the line that has the smallest sum of the squared distances between the actual data points and the points along the theoretical line. Sometimes this method is referred to as *ordinary least squares.*

Several computer software packages are available that can perform analyses of this type. Obviously, the appropriate manual should be consulted, as well as other books on the interpretation and application of linear regression. Some special considerations in analyzing the data appropriate to the scanner-based data will be included here.

Nonlinear Regression. When the relationship between variables is not linear, then either some form of data transformation or nonlinear regression should be considered. The use of a logarithmic transformation, as discussed in chapter 7, is a good example of how to make a variable that is not linear appear to be.

There are several nonlinear regression procedures available today. Algebraically, nonlinear relationships are much more difficult and generally require more mathematical sophistication to understand. In general, representing a nonlinear relationship as a linear one will understate the strength of the relationship. This means that if linear regression is used to analyze nonlinear data the relationships will only appear to be weaker than they actually are. From a statistical point of view, the error would be in the conservative direction if a linear analysis is applied. This in part explains why nonlinear regression has not found wider use.

Coding Variables. Linear regression has some reasonably stringent requirements for variables that can be included as either a predictor variable, such as promotional condition, or criterion variable, such as sales. Variables must be measured at least at the interval level, meaning that nominal or categorical variables are generally excluded. This means that the variable itself must be measured on a scale similar to a temperature scale, with the degrees representing equal scale intervals. Variables such as sales and price can usually be assumed to be interval variables.

Other variables, such as the presence or absence of a particular promotion, an in-store display, or an advertised price, cannot be assumed to be interval variables. The solution is the dummy coded variable, or the 0-1 variable. For those time periods when the promotion is present, a predictor variable is created that is coded a "1." When the promotion is not present the same variable is coded as a "0." This same method can be applied to a whole host of predictor variables that might have some relationship to sales, such as the day of the week or the season.

Experiments. By coding the presence of a sales promotion program using dummy variables, historical data can be analyzed as though an experiment were conducted. The control condition becomes all of those times when the promotion is not present or the dummy variable is coded "0." The non-promotion occurrences represent the "base business" for the particular brand and are defined as the average business or sales. Particular care must be taken if one effect of promotion is to cause inventory stockpiling by retailer or consumers. In this case, baselines may be artificially depressed during periods following a promotion.

While the analysis has been described here as an experiment, it is not an experiment in the strict sense. The control and experimental conditions are not strictly parallel in time, and it is always possible that conditions during the time of the promotion were unusual in some way, making them different from the average of other times. This can be partially solved by conducting experiments in different markets at different points in time. Certainly the analyst needs to be aware of the issue.

Autoregression. A particularly difficult problem with any time series analysis is the potential for autoregression. The term *autoregression* refers to selfcorrelation. A variable, such as sales, is not independent across the successive time intervals. In other words, sales in this time period are influenced by sales in the prior time period because of considerations such as the size of the business, distribution, or reputation. A large retailer or manufacturer is not expected to experience dramatic, total sales fluctuations, though individual line items may have large swings. In the absence of promotional activity, item sales in any given week will be about the same as sales of the item in the previous week, perhaps with trends and seasonal adjustments.

The problem with autoregression is that it can substantially distort the regression equation. It normally makes the relationship between the variables appear stronger than it actually is. This might give the analyst an illusion of false knowledge and lead to possible overconfidence in the estimation of the impact of a sales promotion program.

Solving the problem of autoregression is a major topic in any course in econometrics. Certainly the analyst needs to be aware of the potential of the problem. The appropriate statistical test, such as Durbin-Watson, should be run to determine whether autoregression is a problem. If it does exist, then some method, such as first differences, should be used to eliminate or control the problem. Many books on econometrics provide the necessary details, as do the manuals for statistical software packages. A reference list is provided at the end of this chapter.

INFORMATION-DENSE GRAPHICS. The problem in analyzing sales promotion data is the number of variables that need to be communicated simultaneously. Sales for a brand along with price and the presence of a newspaper feature and special display across time all need to be communicated in a single graph. This is a good example of the problem of communicating complex multivariate phenomena.

The graphs presented in this book, such as those first shown in chapter 2, show how the problem might be solved. A line graph shows the change in sales volume over time. The y-axis becomes sales volume, and the x-axis becomes time periods, usually one-week intervals. Price can be plotted on the same graph by using a second y-axis. The x-axis remains the same—that is, the one week-time intervals. To indicate the relative importance of the sales and price, sales can be represented as a solid line, which will draw the eye, and price as a dotted or broken line. To represent the presence of a promotion, feature, display, or combination, a bar chart can be created as an overlay on the line graph. For those weeks the event is present, a bar is inserted on top of the line to indicate sales. When no bar is present, and only the line shows, no special promotional condition exists. To differentiate features and displays, bars can be filled in with different colors, patterns or textures. This allows the user to see all the relevant variables at once and is a good example of what is termed *information-dense graphics.*

Depending upon the purpose of the analysis, the graphic representation could be easily tailored. Different organizations facing different decisions may want to alter the presentation. Graphical methods are one of the areas that will continue to evolve and help solve the problem of understanding and managing sales promotion.

ANALYSIS APPLICATIONS. A number of questions can be answered through the analysis of scanner-based promotion data. Perhaps the most obvious application is the evaluation of the promotional events themselves, including the critical analysis of profitability. The promotional event can be analyzed both in terms of sales volume and in terms of profitability.

Beyond the analysis of promotional events, the character of a brand itself can be analyzed. Sales volume can be divided into the base and incremental components as discussed in chapter 2. This kind of brand analysis is the first step in applying the fact-based marketing concept. Managerially the brand analysis can lead to market simulations—that is, asking "what if" questions about varying levels of marketing and promotional support along with differing promotional mixes. What would happen, for example, if an additional promotion were run? What would happen if television advertising were increased?

For the manufacturer, fact-based marketing considerably enhances the ability to gain distribution, gain promotional support, and determine the right mix of promotional activity for the brand. For the retailer, fact-based marketing helps make decisions about the reallocation of promotional resources provided by manufacturers, review marketing strategies, and evaluate manufacturer proposals and promotional programs.

Case 1: Salad Dressing

The Wondo Company has the problem of establishing the wholesale and retail prices of one of its products: salad dressing. The Wondo Company is currently marketing a very successful product that is well known by consumers throughout the country.

Wondo has conducted price testing for the product at retail prices of $1.24, $1.44, and $1.64 per unit. This product is generally priced by the retailers at cost plus 20 percent, so that a manufacturer list price of $1.20 per unit will translate to a retail shelf price of $1.44. The retailers prefer psychological pricing, so they tend to use prices that end in 4 or 9 and will adjust prices after markup to the closest such price point. The Wondo Company management believe that no change in the wholesale price should be made that would result in retail prices lower than $1.24 per unit, or higher than $1.64 per unit.

The Wondo Company conducted a national sales test manipulating the retail prices. Estimates from the test indicate that the national sales expected at various retail price levels are shown in Table 3.2.

The current national price for the product is $1.44. The decision facing Wondo management is whether this price should be changed.

The typical retailer must also be considered in this situation. A typical retailer, a supermarket chain with several stores, operates with a 20 percent-markup rule. The chain income statement is shown in Table 3.3

The normal level of sales of the Wondo Company product for this retailer are five hundred units per week when it is priced at $1.44.

Question 1. The Wondo Company is considering a change in the base retail price. The possibilities being considered are shown in Table 3.4.

Part 1. Suppose that the cost elements for the Wondo Company are $7 million in fixed operating costs and $0.30 variable cost per unit. Plot the estimated gross profit for the Wondo Company at the various wholesale prices. What price would yield maximum profit?

Table 3.2

SALAD DRESSING SALES BY PRICE

Retail Price per Unit ($)	Annual Unit Sales
1.24	13,000,000
1.44	10,000,000
1.64	7,000,000

Table 3.3

CHAIN INCOME STATEMENT

Total Annual Sales	$60,000,000 (all commodities)
Cost of Goods	50,000,000
Gross Margin	10,000,000
Fixed Operating Cost	2,500,000
Variable Operating Cost	6,250,000
Gross Profit	1,250,000

Table 3.4

CHAIN INCOME STATEMENT

Wholesale	Estimated Retail
$1.04	$1.24
1.08	1.29
1.12	1.34
1.16	1.39
1.20	1.44
1.24	1.49
1.28	1.54
1.32	1.59
1.36	1.64

Part 2. Suppose that the cost elements for the Wondo Company are $3 million in fixed operating costs and $0.70 variable cost per unit. Plot the estimated gross profit for the Wondo Company at the various wholesale prices. What price would yield maximum profit?

Question 2. The retailer in this case might want to consider using a profit-maximization rule rather than a simple markup rule to determine the retail price. Assume that the cost elements for the Wondo Company are $7 million in fixed operating cost and $0.30 variable cost per unit, and the wholesale selling price is $1.20. If the 20 percent-markup rule is used, the typical retailer would charge $1.44. Suppose, however, that the sales response for the retailer parallels the national estimates, which the retailer has determined through research. The retailer also estimates that the variable operating costs for the Wondo product are about the same as the average for the entire chain. Plot the estimated contribution to retailer profit and fixed costs over the range of retail prices from $1.24 to $1.64. What action would you recommend to the retailer?

Question 3. A natural tug-of-war exists between the manufacturer and the retailer. Assume that the Wondo Company assumptions are the same as those in question 2 and that all retailers behave in the same way as the chain previously described.

Part 1. Suppose that all retailers are profit maximizers. For the range of wholesale prices considered in question 1, what would be the expected retail prices and resulting annual sales volumes of the Wondo Company product? Plot the contribution to profit and fixed costs for (a) the Wondo Company, (b) all retailers, and (c) Wondo and the retailers combined.

Part 2. Redo part 1 assuming that all retailers operate on the 20 percent-markup rule.

Question 4. This question deals with the retailers' response to a trade price discount. Again assume that the cost characteristics for the Wondo Company are the same as they are in question 2 and that the wholesale price $1.20. Assume that all retailers operate on a 20 percent-markup rule. Retailers also normally order a two-week supply once every two weeks, and there is a 1 percent-of-purchase-price per-unit cost of carrying inventory per week.

The Wondo Company wishes to boost fourth-quarter volume, which has been lagging. It makes the following offer to all retailers: During the last two weeks of the quarter, each retailer can place on order for up to twelve times its normal weekly level of sales. The price charged will be $1.00 versus the normal $1.20. Delivery will be on the first day of the next quarter.

Assume that all sales over the amount expected for thirteen weeks of regular pricing are incremental to the brand, and are not the result of forward buying by the consumer. In other words, the consumer will use more of the product rather than stockpile it.

Part 1. Estimate the probable size of the order from a retailer who intends to maintain the base shelf price of $1.44, increasing profit through increased margin. (Hint: Develop an algebraic equation.)

Part 2. Estimate the probable size of the order from a retailer who intends to directly pass through the savings to consumers by reducing shelf price to $1.24 while the supply lasts.

Part 3. Making whatever assumptions you feel are necessary, estimate the sales of the product by the manufacturer during the two weeks of the offer and the thirteen weeks of the next quarter if (a) all retailers maintain shelf price and (b) all retailers reduce price to $1.24.

Part 4. Discuss the advantages and disadvantages to the Wondo Company that might be associated with this offer.

Part 5. The retailer has other options besides no pass through and complete pass-through of the temporary price reduction. The retailer might opt for partial pass-through to reduce the store margin in addition to the manufacturer's reduction in order to provide an extremely attractive shelf price. Assume that once the supply of specially priced product is exhausted, regular pricing of $1.44 is resumed. Plot the expected contribution to retailer profit and fixed costs for the thirteen weeks following receipt of the order versus alternative pricing points.

Case 2: Frozen Orange Juice I

The data for this case is based of grocery store sales of frozen orange juice concentrate. Trade promotion activity is fairly high in this category, with over 55 percent of annual volume moved with trade deal activity. The average price reduction on trade deal is in the range of 15 to 25 percent, although trade deal activity exists from features with no discount to deep discount two-for-the-price-of-one sales (50 percent discount). The average cost to the consumer on an equivalent ounce base is about 80 percent of "regular price". Like most frozen products, there is little in-store display activity in the frozen juice category.

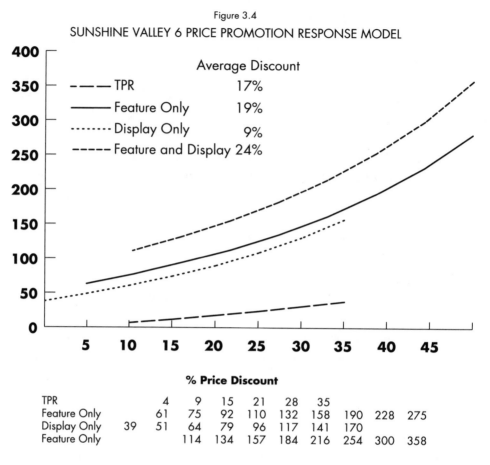

Figure 3.4

SUNSHINE VALLEY 6 PRICE PROMOTION RESPONSE MODEL

		% Price Discount								
TPR		4	9	15	21	28	35			
Feature Only		61	75	92	110	132	158	190	228	275
Display Only	39	51	64	79	96	117	141	170		
Feature Only			114	134	157	184	216	254	300	358

An analysis was conducted to determine the response to pricing and retail-promotion activity for the two major sizes of "Sunshine Valley". Figures 3.4 and 3.5 summarize the results of this analysis. Table 3.5 shows the probability of finding any Sunshine Valley size on promotion in a grocery store. The 6, 12, and 16 ounce sizes account for about 95 percent of category volume. There in little overlap in the buying of 6 ounce versus other sizes, but buyers of the 12 and 16 ounce sizes exhibit little size loyalty and switch freely among the 12 and 16 ounce sizes based on price and promotion. Sunshine

Table 3.5

FREQUENCY OF SUNSHINE VALLEY PROMOTIONS

Promotion Condition	Percent of Weeks Occurring
No Feature or Display on any size	62.5
Reduced shelf price only	26.6
Ad Feature on one or more sizes	8.1
In-store Display only on one or more sizes	0.9
Ad Feature and In-store display on one or more	1.9

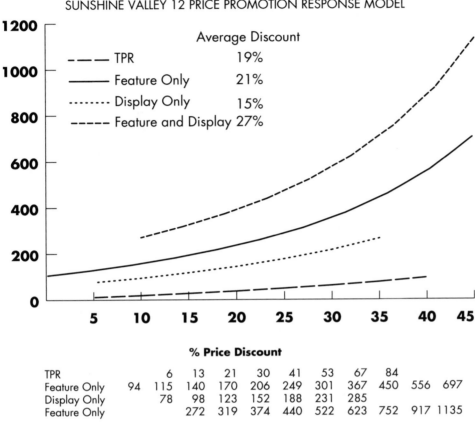

Figure 3.5

SUNSHINE VALLEY 12 PRICE PROMOTION RESPONSE MODEL

		Average Discount
– – –	TPR	19%
———	Feature Only	21%
········	Display Only	15%
– – – –	Feature and Display	27%

% Price Discount

		5	10	15	20	25	30	35	40	45
TPR			6	13	21	30	41	53	67	84	
Feature Only	94	115	140	170	206	249	301	367	450	556	697
Display Only		78	98	123	152	188	231	285			
Feature Only			272	319	374	440	522	623	752	917	1135

Valley does not have a 16 ounce size. Promotions may stimulate an appreciable increase in the product-usable rate, and most manufacturers believe that a brands promotional increases come from increased category consumption, brand switching, and from stock-piling purchases by brand loyal users. The probability of finding any Sunshine Valley size on promotion in a grocery store is shown in Table 3.5.

A common method of allocating promotional expenditures among sizes of a brand is to allocate promotion in proportion to the share that the size has of the total brand. The measure may be volume share, revenue share, or share of brand profit contribution. Make the following assumptions:

a. The average retail markup is 30 percent of manufacturer list.
b. Thirty percent of incremental sales to Sunshine Valley on promotion are incremental to the product category, the remaining 70 percent are the result of consumer sales shifted from competitive brands.
c. Seventy percent of all Sunshine Valley promotional allowance offers to retailers result in shelf price reduction only on one or both sizes, with com-

plete retailer pass-through of the promotional allowance on the size(s) promoted. The remaining 30 percent of Sunshine Valley offers result in retailer performance of feature-only, display-only, or both feature and display on one or both sizes (discounts to be described later). The base sales of the 6 ounce size are about 30 percent of total brand base sales, and the base sales of 12 ounce size are about 70 percent of total brand base sales.

d. The manufacturer of Sunshine Valley has a simple promotional program: Once every two months, the retailer is allowed to purchase at 25 percent discount from manufacturer list an amount of Sunshine Valley 12 ounce equal to five weeks base sales of the 12 ounce size. Once every three months, the retailer is allowed to purchase at 25 percent discount from manufacturer list an amount of Sunshine Valley 6 ounce size equal to five weeks base sales of the 6 ounce size.

e. The retailer never promotes both sizes of Sunshine Valley at the same time, and all feature or display promotions are one-week long. Price reduction only promotions average two weeks long. At the end of the promotion period, regular price is restored, and the retailer sells any remainder of the promotional purchase at regular price. A retailer might for example buy 100 units with a 20 cent discount from the manufacturer. If that retailer offers a 20 cent discount at retail, he is considered to have given 100 percent pass-through of the allowance, even if only one or two units of the 100 are sold with the discount. Allocation to ad-only, display-only, ad-and-display, and price-reduction-only events is the same for both sizes. If the event is price-reduction-only, the average discount is 20 percent off retailer list. The average feature-only is 25 percent off retailer list, display-only is 15 percent off retailer list, and feature-and-display is 27.5 percent off retailer list.

Question 1. A common assumption in analyzing the price and promotion response for a brand is that all sizes of the brand react similarly. The dominant size is analyzed, and the results are assumed to apply to all sizes. Discuss the similarities and differences that exist in the price and promotion responses of the two sizes.

Question 2. Use linear interpolation between the tabled values of the price and promotion responses in Figures 3.4 and 3.5. Evaluate the impact of the promotional program on the following:

a. Sunshine Valley 12 ounce volume sales.
b. Sunshine Valley 6 ounce volume sales.
c. Total Brand (6 ounce and 12 ounce) volume sales.

Question 3. Using the incremental volume estimated in question 1, estimate the cost to the manufacturer of Sunshine Valley per incremental unit obtained through promotion. Perform this estimation by size and type of retail sales promotion, both on an individual event basis, and summarized across the annual promotional program for each size.

Question 4. Suppose that an audit of retail store performance on Sunshine Valley's promotional offers indicates that, of the 70 percent of accepted offers that do not receive feature or display support, there is a 50-50 split between complete pass-through of the allowance by reduced price and the maintenance of regular shelf price with no pass-through of the allowance. Redo questions 2 and 3 with this assumption.

Question 5. Suppose Sunshine Valley's management wishes to improve retailer support via feature ad or in-store display. Since it is difficult to audit stores for shelf-price reduction, management is considering the use of a feature-audit service to assure that the brand was featured before the promotional allowance will be given. Managements assessment of the impact of this change in promotional requirements is that of the 70 percent of accepted offers that do not receive feature or display, three out of four retailers would refuse the promotional offer, and one out of four would run feature only with complete pass-through of the promotional allowance. Those accounts that currently give feature-only or feature-and-display support would not alter their behavior. Of the accounts that currently give display-only support, half would refuse the offer, and half would feature with no pass-through of the promotional allowance. There would be no change in the promotion schedule given in assumption d. Compare the estimated sales volumes and promotional costs of this program with those estimates generated in Question 4.

Question 6. Suppose that the pass-through of non-supported offers is the 50-50 split indicated in Question 4. The response to a requirement for feature support is as estimated in Question 5, and the current distribution of retail support by feature or display is split as shown in the same relative percentages as those shown in the case background. Management asks you to design an improved promotion program for the combined 6 and 12 ounce sizes of Sunshine Valley. They are not willing to provide variable cost information, but they do indicate that retailers take the same percentage markup on both sizes and that the variable costs as a percentage of manufacturer list price are the same for both sizes. Spending for stimulating retail sales by promotion is not considered as part of variable cost.

You are free to alter the number of events per year for each size subject to the following limitations:

a. Each size must have at least one promotional offer per year with at least a 7.5 percent discount from manufacturer list.
b. A size can have a maximum of nine events per year.

c. The retailer must be allowed to purchase at discount an amount equal to at least two weeks' regular sales if an offer on a size is accepted.

d. There is no inexpensive method for auditing accounts for in-store display activity, so that performance for a feature and display combination will yield the same distribution of event types as will a requirement for proof of featuring.

Management requests that you prepare proposed programs and volume estimates for the following three levels of promotional budget:

a. The current level implied by the case background.
b. Budget of 125 percent of the current level.
c. Budget of 75 percent of the current level.

Suggested Readings

Box, G. E. P., and G. M. Jenkins.
Time Series Analysis: Forecasting and Control.
Rev. Ed., San Francisco: Holden-Day, 1976.

Fuller, Wayne A.
Introduction to Statistical Time Series.
New York: John Wiley & Sons, 1976.

Nelson, C. R.
Applied Time Series for Managerial Forecasting.
San Francisco: Holden-Day, 1973.

Montgomery, D. C., and L. A. Johnson.
Forecasting and Time Series Analysis.
New York: McGraw-Hill, 1976.

Pindyck, R. S., and D. L. Rubinfeld.
Econometric Models and Economic Forecasts. Part 3.
New York: McGraw-Hill, 1976.

CHAPTER 4

CONSUMER RESPONSE
TO SALES PROMOTION

Measuring consumer response to sales promotion has always been a difficult task. Until the availability of scanner data, measuring consumer response was limited to aggregate summarizing of coupon redemptions and consumer attitude surveys. After scanner data became readily available, actual consumer shopping behavior could be easily analyzed. For products sold in grocery outlets, both the brand of product and the store itself must be considered, since not only is loyalty to a brand important, but also loyalty to a store. Additionally, the mix of items offered in a category may vary dramatically from store to store. Particularly important may be the presence of private label, or store brands, and generic products.

STORE SHOPPING LOYALTY. A 1992 study by Nielsen Marketing Research covering UPC-coded items purchased in the 52 weeks of 1991 found that consumers shopped an average of 4.8 grocery retailers during the year. Only about 10 percent of households confined their purchases to one or two retailers. Obviously, the majority of shoppers visit multiple stores, as shown in Figure 4.1

Recognition that shoppers visit more than one store in a three-month period raises the question of the influence of store promotions such as ad-features in determining consumer store choice. A 1991 study by the FMI (Food Marketing Institute), as shown in Tables 4.1 and 4.2, suggests that, while changing supermarkets due to advertised specials and shopping at discount or warehouse food stores are important factors in store choice, they are of declining importance, as are price comparisons among supermarkets, use of coupons, and reviewing the newspaper for grocery specials.

Store Characteristics. While there are many ways of classifying retail grocery outlets, one good way is weekly dollar sales volume. As might be expected, the average store loyalty changes with the size of the store.

The largest stores enjoy greater store loyalty than the smallest stores. Often they achieve this by providing a greater range of goods and services. Large stores may offer a "deli" section, a house-plant section, and an extensive section of health and beauty aids and general merchandise items. Small stores obtain more of their sales volume from shoppers who are not loyal.

Figure 4.1

NUMBER OF GROCERY RETAILERS SHOPPED IN ONE YEAR

(Percent of Households)

Average = 4.8 Retailers

* UPC-Coded Items; 52 Weeks Ending 12/91

Source: Nielsen.

Importance of Promotion.   One way of assessing the importance of sales promotion by the type of store is to examine the purchases made with a special price or deal. As might be expected, as a shopper visits more stores, he or she makes more purchases on deal. Figure 4.2 shows the relationship reported by Malec & Eskin (1984) between the number of stores visited and the proportion of purchases made on deal. Indexing the one- or two-store-visit category at 100, those visiting five or more stores are making 33 percent more purchases on deal. Clearly, price promotions seem to be related to store visits, although this does not necessarily mean that they are building store loyalty. Some shoppers may be visiting several chains weekly to take advantage of promotional prices.

BRAND SHOPPING LOYALTY. Beyond loyalty to a store, customers also show loyalty to individual brands found in the store. The issue of brand loyalty seems to be critical in determining the impact of promotion, especially price promotions. The first critical problem for the manufacturer is to understand whether a particular brand is price sensitive or promotion responsive. To determine that, the following questions need attention: How does the particular brand respond when offered on deal? How does the product respond to nonpromoted base price changes? What happens to the product category when the brand is promoted? What happens to the brand when the deal ends? Does high brand loyalty mean that the brand is promotion responsive? How a brand

Table 4.1

HOW OFTEN SHOPPERS ECONOMIZE, USE SUPERMARKET SPECIALS, COUPONS AND PRICE COMPARISONS: 1982-1991

Pretty much every time you shop %

	82	83	84	85	86	87	88	89	90	91
Use price-off coupons	39	38	39	30	39	37	40	35	37	36
Look in the newspaper for grocery specials	50	52	49	41	40		42	34	38	33
Stock up on an item when you find a bargain										24
Compare prices at different supermarkets	32	30	29	27	25	23	26	23	24	20
Buy store brands or lower priced products instead of national brands										18
Buy products on special even if you hadn't planned to buy them that day										17
Go to supermarkets other than your principle one for advertised specials	16	13	12	10	9	12	12	12	10	9
Shop at a discount or warehouse food store for grocery items										5

Source: "Trends—Consumer Attitudes and the Supermarket 1991," FMI

Table 4.2

HOW OFTEN SHOPPERS ECONOMIZE COMPARED TO ONE YEAR AGO

Frequency of Activity %

	More	Less	Same	Don't Know
Buy products on special even if you hadn't planned to buy then that day	23	13	64	1
Buy store brands or lower priced products instead of national brands	21	12	66	1
Stock up on an item when you find a bargain	18	10	71	1
Shop at a discount or warehouse food store for grocery items	12	22	64	2

Source: "Trends—Consumer Attitudes and the Supermarket 1991," FMI

Figure 4.2

IMPORTANCE OF PROMOTION BY NUMBER OF STORES VISITED
(Indexed % Purchased on Deal)

* Source: Malec and Eskin.

responds to competitive price and promotion is also critical in understanding that brand. High brand loyalty should protect a brand from sales loss due to competitive promotions. If a brand is very price sensitive, then a competitive promotion should be successful in converting sales away from the brand, and everyday price levels are also critically important.

Another problem is to understand whether a promotion results in stockpiling by current brand users, or in obtaining incremental sales from switchers who buy primarily on deal from a set of several equally acceptable brands. Understanding brand loyalty is critical to understanding the sales performance of the brand and the potential role that promotion can play.

Brand Switching. A typical brand sold through grocery retail stores can divide the source of its business into five categories. Usually the largest category is switchers, those product-category purchasers who purchase less than 70 percent to 80 percent of any one brand in the long run from the category. In contrast, most manufacturers would like the largest category to be purchasers who are exclusively loyal to the brand. A second loyal category is those who don't purchase the brand exclusively but who do purchase the brand at least 70 percent to 80 percent of the time. The two remaining categories consist of those purchasers who are loyal to another brand at least 70 percent to 80 percent of the time, and those who are infrequent category purchasers. Infrequent category purchasers have not made enough purchases to be categorized as brand-loyal buyers or as brand switchers.

Figure 4.3 shows a typical brand, Brand A, with the source of business by loyalty type. Of interest is the comparison between a nonpromoted week and a promoted

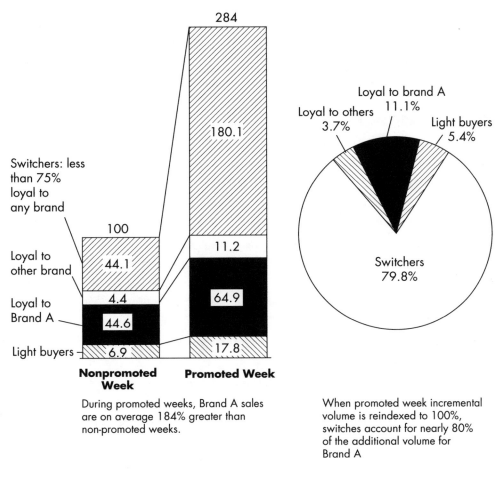

Figure 4.3

AVERAGE INCREMENTAL DUE TO PROMOTION FOR BRAND A

(By Loyalty Type)

284

180.1

Switchers: less
than 75%
loyal to
any brand

100

44.1

Loyal to
other brand

11.2

4.4

64.9

Loyal to
Brand A

44.6

Light buyers

6.9

17.8

**Nonpromoted
Week**

Promoted Week

During promoted weeks, Brand A sales
are on average 184% greater than
non-promoted weeks.

Loyal to others
3.7%

Loyal to brand A
11.1%

Light buyers
5.4%

Switchers
79.8%

When promoted week incremental
volume is reindexed to 100%,
switches account for nearly 80%
of the additional volume for
Brand A

* Source: Nielsen.

week. Overall sales for the brand increased 183 percent during the promoted week. By far the largest increase is shown in the switcher category, though all categories show some increase.

Cherry Picking. A relatively new phenomenon observable among scanner-based panel studies of shopping behavior is termed cherry picking. Cherry picking is an interesting side effect of the increased emphasis on promotion, since cherry pickers are shoppers who nearly always buy the brand that is offered on deal. This particular phenomenon has been created by both the proliferation of promotion and the training of the shoppers to wait for the next promotion, which they know is coming.

The cherry picker is not the same as the shopper who is motivated entirely by price. The lowest possible price, such as might be found with private brands and generics, is not necessarily the objective of the cherry picker. Rather, it is the best deal among a set of acceptable brands. The cherry picker may well defer purchase until a deal is offered and may also, conversely, stockpile. In product categories that are heavily promoted and frequently purchased, the cherry picker may even be brand loyal. In colas, for example, some shoppers who will only buy one brand when it is offered with a deal, shopping multiple stores to maximize exposure to deals.

PRICE SENSITIVITY. It is critically important to understand the relationship between selling price and sales volume for both the product category and the brand before any price promotion is applied. In general, the relationship would be expected to follow a general pattern of increasing sales with decreasing price as is typically depicted in demand curves. Various researchers have proposed "S-shaped" curves as more probable for accurately modeling short term deal responses than the linear or logarithmic curves typically used for long-run demand estimation.

The curves in Figure 4.4 show the results of controlled experiments conducted by Wisniewski and Blattberg (1988) for a variety of products. The results for price discount alone and price discounts with in-store display were obtained from an experimental design framework that included control stores with no promotional activity to serve as a reference. The promotion curves generally show one or more segments with distinctly different slopes.

A demand curve with major slope changes is commonly referred to as being *kinked.* A kinked demand curve means that over certain ranges, a change in price of a given increment may have a significantly different volume impact than a comparable price increment change in a different part of the price range. In bleach, for example, the first 5 percent discount yielded a 20 percent increase in sales for price reduction alone, while the next 10 percent discount, to a total of 15 percent discount, yielded only a 3 percent additional increase in sales. However, additional depth of discounts below 15 percent again produces significant increases in sales. The response curve for flour seems to be reaching a saturation level, where additional discounting below 25 percent produces little additional sales. It is believed that most products have such a saturation level of discount, although that discount level may be much deeper than ordinarily encountered. Even if the product were free, there is a limited amount that consumers could be expected to transport home and place in storage. This is particularly true for perishable items such as frozen foods.

If the demand curve is kinked for a particular product category or brand, the manager must know the promotional response function. Price discounts at the low end of the saturation level only depress sales revenue. In actual practice, most product cate-

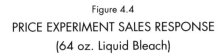

Figure 4.4
PRICE EXPERIMENT SALES RESPONSE
(64 oz. Liquid Bleach)

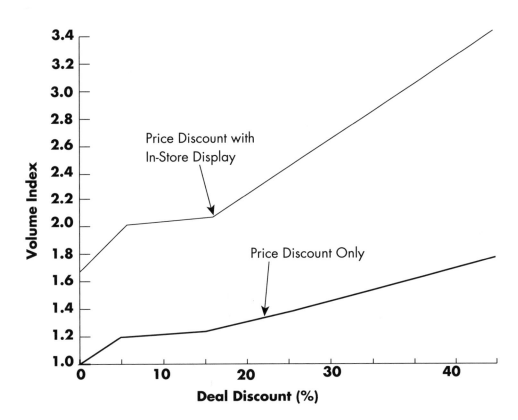

Source: Blattberg and Wisniewski.

gories that have been studied that are sold through grocery retail outlets have kinked demand curves. That makes performance of the type of analysis suggested here especially important.

PROMOTION RESPONSIVENESS.   Not only does the price make a difference in the quantity of the product sold: the presence or absence of both in-store displays and store feature advertising does as well. The price promotional response model shown in Figure 4.5 represents percentage changes in sales volume with percentage price changes for four conditions: no promotion activity, only store feature-advertising activity, only in-store display activity, and both feature advertising and in-store displays. This chart is an aggregate of many product categories sold in grocery stores and so does not reflect any particular product category or brand characteristics.

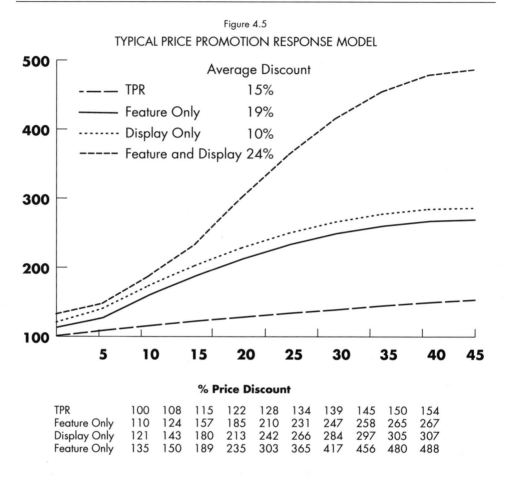

Figure 4.5
TYPICAL PRICE PROMOTION RESPONSE MODEL

Average Discount

		Average Discount
─ ─ ─	TPR	15%
────	Feature Only	19%
········	Display Only	10%
-----	Feature and Display	24%

% Price Discount

	5	10	15	20	25	30	35	40	45
TPR	100	108	115	122	128	134	139	145	150	154
Feature Only	110	124	157	185	210	231	247	258	265	267
Display Only	121	143	180	213	242	266	284	297	305	307
Feature Only	135	150	189	235	303	365	417	456	480	488

Without any change in price, feature advertising and in-store displays increase sales volume. As shown in Figure 4.5 in-store displays by themselves increase sales volume slightly more than does feature advertising by itself. Most important here is the fact that both together increase incremental sales volume more than the total of each operating alone. There is a strong synergistic effect. When price reductions are combined with in-store displays and feature advertising, sales volume can increase by as much as 400 percent, whereas a price reduction alone can only accomplish about a 40 percent volume increase.

POSTPROMOTION SALES DECLINES. Common sense would suggest that dramatic sales increases during a price promotion would be followed by at least a short period of sales decline. The actual sales data for most retail outlets, however, show little postpromotion sales decline. Figure 4.6 shows a typical example for Pepsi in 24 packs of 12 ounce cans. The solid line shows the sales volume during nonpromoted weeks as represented by the axis on the left. Sales volume on promotion is represented by the vertical bars. In the first week shown, for example, sales were in excess of 400

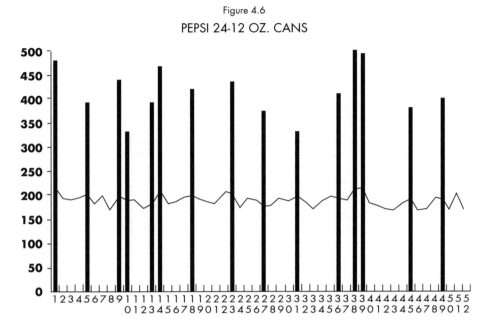

Figure 4.6

PEPSI 24-12 OZ. CANS

Source: Nielsen.

units in "Store C" with a display promotion. In the second week, with no promotion, sales fell back to approximately 200 units. Of interest is that during most of the promotion periods sales increased dramatically from the sales during the nonpromotion periods. Sales during the postpromotion periods do not appear to be lower than the period just prior to the promotion. In fact, sometimes the nonpromotion sales actually increase after the promotion ends. Figure 4.3 indicates the reason. For most promotions, the incremental volume is coming from switchers who do not purchase during nonpromotional periods. Only when loyal buyers are stockpiling is the product purchased on promotion.

It is true that Pepsi in the 24-pack of 12-ounce cans is one of the most heavily promoted products in the store. The relationship still holds true in a much less frequently promoted package size, Pepsi in the 2-liter size. Figure 4.7 can be interpreted in the same way as the previous chart. Note that no large dip in sales occurs following a promotion. Perhaps equally important is that sales seem to increase following a promotion. This again reinforces one of the main points: Sales promotion must be evaluated during the same period that the promotion occurs. In other words, the promotion will generate immediate sales but will not necessarily generate any future business after the promotion.

For the manufacturer, promotions may have quite a different effect on shipments. The manufacturer typically offers promotion to the trade from two to six times per year. Retailers must purchase sufficient inventory to minimize chances of running out of stock when the promotion is passed through to consumers. In addition, the

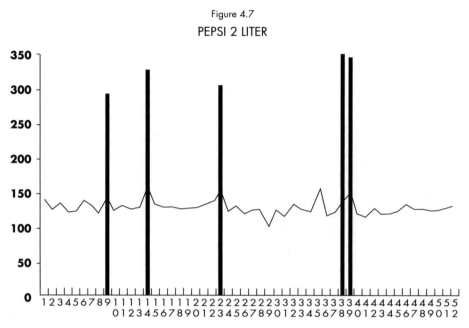

Figure 4.7
PEPSI 2 LITER

Source: Nielsen.

reduced price from the manufacturer may justify stockpiling purchases by the retailer. For example, suppose the manufacturer offers a promotional incentive to the retailer that when passed through and given advertising feature support would result in a sales increase of about three weeks extra business. Due to local variability, retailers know that 95 percent of the time the actual sales will be between one week extra and five weeks extra. Further, at this price, it is worthwhile to stockpile two weeks' worth of business. The retailer who wishes to minimize out of stocks and has stockpiled inventory might then place an order for eight weeks' worth of regular sales instead one week's worth. The manufacturer then sees a total of eight weeks increase in sales volume, which represents from the retailer one week regular volume, three weeks' incremental volume, and four weeks' safety stock and stockpiling. The manufacturer will suffer in the future a depression of about four weeks' worth of sales.

PURCHASE TIMING. A commonly discussed impact of sales promotion is the alteration of the purchase cycle. Of course, to consider any alteration of the purchase cycle it is first necessary to be able to describe it. Figure 4.8 shows how purchase timing can be quantitatively described. The normal purchase pattern without any deals is shown at the top of the figure with the average purchase volume indexed to one hundred and the average inter-purchase time indexed to one hundred. This provides a symmetrical representation of the normal purchase cycle. It is now relatively easy to distinguish alterations in purchase timing. Accelerating purchase time is shown in the second pattern, and it indicates no increase in purchase volume but a decrease in the repurchase time.

Figure 4.8

PURCHASE PATTERNS

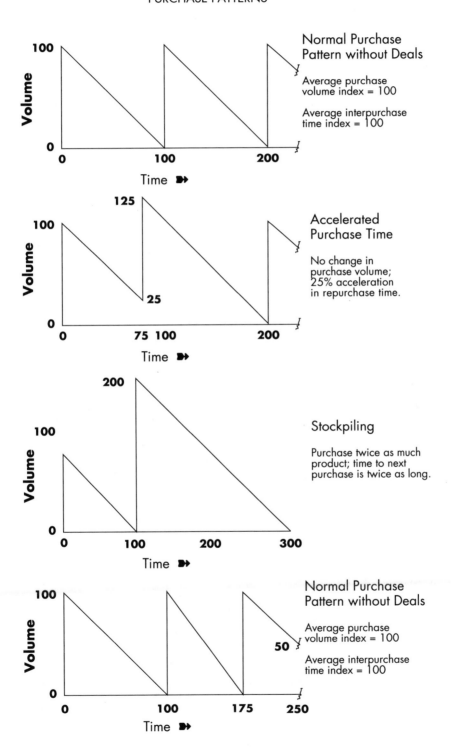

The figure shows an example of a 25 percent acceleration in repurchase time. The third pattern is stockpiling, which is purchasing more quantity and increasing the repurchase time appropriately. The figure shows an example of purchasing twice as much and then stretching the repurchase time to twice as long. The last pattern, a consumption increase, shows the normal volume purchased on each occasion, but with the repurchase time decreased, so that the consumer is back into the market faster than normal.

McAlister & Struss (1983, revised 1989) describe a partition of purchasing based on consumption that is stimulated by promotion, and consumption that is stimulated by other causes. Based on this scheme, it is possible to estimate a brands expected baseline for each segment, determine if the baseline is depressed by its own or competitive promotion, assess the brands expected promotional peak, and determine the conditions (if any) under which it is profitable to promote to the segment.

A number of authors have developed models for measuring these effects. McAlister and Totten (1985) reported on the results of modeling canned tuna purchases on subgroups of households classified as light, medium, or heavy category buyers, as brand loyal or nonloyal, and as deal sensitive or not deal sensitive. Purchases were classified as having retail deal (temporary price reduction, perhaps accompanied by ad-feature or in store display), manufacturer deal (couponing), both retail and manufacturer deal, or neither. The eight markets used in the study were classified into low, medium, and high deal availability. The study concluded that stockpiling behavior was evident in modest degree for all groups, but appeared to be strongly significant among heavy users in markets where deal availability was low. The remainder of consumers appear to adjust their purchase cycle rather than purchase quantity in order to utilize retailer promotions. Deals did appear to increase category consumption among the heavier users. Coupons appeared to expand category consumption slightly, but were not associated with purchase acceleration or increased purchase size.

Neslin, Henderson, and Quelch (1985) studied bathroom tissue and coffee in one market. Their model included coupon usage, manufacturer newspaper advertising, retailer newspaper advertising, and price discounts. Their overall conclusion was that for these two categories in the market measured, promotions have more impact on quantity than on timing. They found heavy category users to be more affected by promotion than light users. In one of the categories, they found brand loyal households accelerating their purchases to obtain deals to a larger degree than nonloyals, while in the other category both groups accelerated purchases to the same degree.

EFFECTS OF PACKAGE SIZE. Beyond the store and the brand, another important factor is package size. Different shoppers purchase different package sizes, and promotion of the wrong size might lead to failure. Hence, the package size must be considered along with the product category and brand.

Figure 4.9

QUARTERLY PEPSI SALES BY PACKAGE SIZE—MARKET A

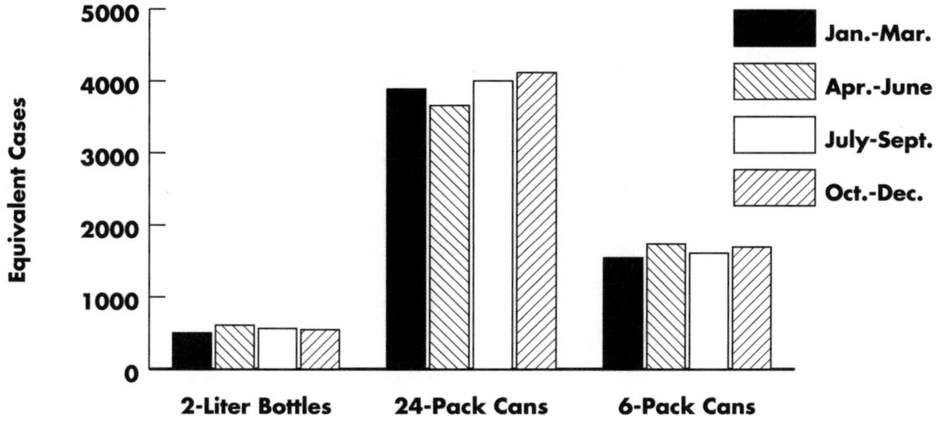

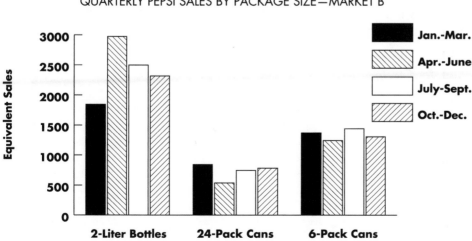

Source: Nielsen ScanPro.

Figure 4.9 shows the quarterly sales of Pepsi in Market A for three package sizes: 2-liter bottles, 24-pack cans, and 6-pack cans. Market A shows a strong dominance for 24-pack cans.

Not all markets, however, favor the same package size as Market A. Figure 4.10 shows quarterly Pepsi sales by package size for Market B. Market B seems to favor the 2-liter bottle, while the 24-pack cans drop to last place in popularity. A promotion of 24-pack cans would no doubt have a different impact in Market A than in Market B. Certainly, one promotion function does not fit all market situations or brand sizes.

Figure 4.10

QUARTERLY PEPSI SALES BY PACKAGE SIZE—MARKET B

Source: Nielsen ScanPro.

EFFECTS ON COMPETITIVE PRODUCTS. Common sense would again seem to say that when a brand is sold with a price promotion, competitive brands should suffer lessened sales. Presumably, as the brand that is promoted increases its sales volume, it takes sales from the competitors.

The data, however, show that competitive brands do not have sales declines during the promotional periods of other brands. On the contrary, competitive brands sometimes enjoy sales increases. A typical pattern can be seen in a national dairy product category. Figure 4.11 compares Store A's sales and promotion of a national brand and a private label brand in the same size package. Both brands have fairly stable prices. The

Figure 4.11
NATIONAL BRAND DAIRY PRODUCT—STORE A

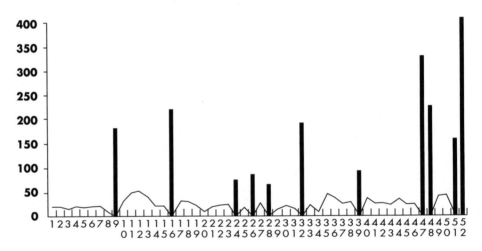

Source: Nielsen.

PRIVATE LABEL DAIRY PRODUCT—STORE A

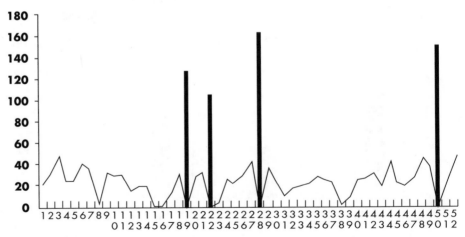

Source: Nielsen.

national brand ran promotions in weeks 9, 16, 47, and 48. Sometimes the private label dropped slightly and sometimes the volume increases as shown in week 48. Private label promotions seem to have little impact on the national brand volume. When the national brand runs a promotion, it seems to have very little impact on the private label volume, and vice versa.

In general, the effects on competitive sales are minimal, while the primary effect is on the brand that is promoted during the period of that promotion. Again, refer to the previous sources of promotional volume shown in Figure 4.3. The sales responses shown here illustrate again the impact of having a majority of incremental sales promotion response due to switchers who do not show up in the base. Over time, if both brands were to dramatically cut back on promotions, the switchers might surface in the baseline sales. Conversely, increasing promotional frequency might switch more households out of the base and into a promotion-only buying pattern.

LONG-TERM EFFECTS.

Promotion clearly generates short-term effects, but the long-term effects are less obvious. Can sales promotion help to create long-term base-level business?

The term *base-level business* is the sales level that a brand has during nonpromotional periods. It is normally the standard of comparison for the incremental sales generated by a promotion, or the level of business that should be increased if promotion were to have any long-term effect.

Frozen orange juice provides a good product category to examine. In Figures 4.12 through 4.15, the three competitive brands (disguised brand names), along with the entire category, are shown for Store A. The frozen orange juice category (Figure 4.12) had several reasonably successful promotions, but the normal base-business sales line remains almost perfectly horizontal. Sunshine Hidden Valley (Figure 4.13) is the most promoted of the three brands with several relatively successful promotions. Some others appear to have been somewhat less successful. Still the base-business line appears to be relatively flat, even though it fluctuates throughout the chart. Florida Morning (Figure 4.14) had one very successful promotion late, yet the fundamental base business did not change. The conclusion drawn is that promotion has very little, if any, impact on base business. Figure 4.15 shows the pattern for Golden Ridge with two early successful promotions. Again a relatively stable pattern for the nonpromoted base business.

If a brand reduces the promotional effort, the impact is clear: The sales volume will decrease, moving back to the base level of business. If a brand increases the promotional effort, the sales volume during the promotional period will increase. It is important to remember, however, that the sales volume changes do not necessarily mean that the profit will change as well. A reduction in promotional effort will result in sales-volume decrease, but it may result in an increase in profits because the margin is higher. Hence, a

Figure 4.12
FROZEN ORANGE JUICE CATEGORY—CHAIN A

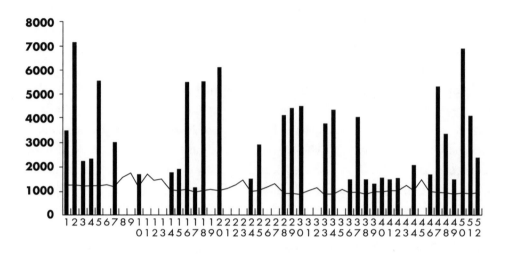

Figure 4.13
SUNSHINE HIDDEN VALLEY
CHAIN A—FROZEN ORANGE JUICE

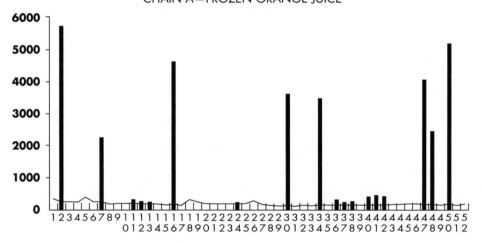

careful financial analysis should be performed for every sales promotion program to assess its profitability. Relying entirely on sales volume could be very misleading.

SEPARATING PROMOTIONAL EFFECTS. One of the more difficult tasks in understanding the marketing-communications mix is separating the impacts of various tactics such as changes in price, in-store displays, feature advertising, and television advertising. Not only do these fundamental tactics impact sales by themselves, they also work synergistically, which adds to the difficulty of understanding them.

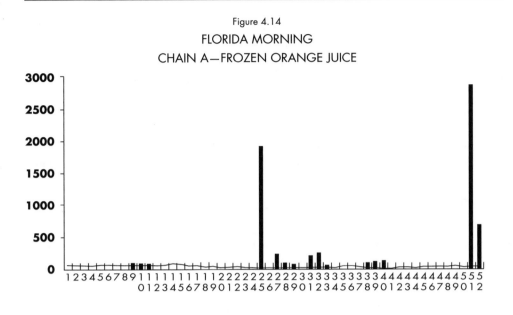

Figure 4.14
FLORIDA MORNING
CHAIN A—FROZEN ORANGE JUICE

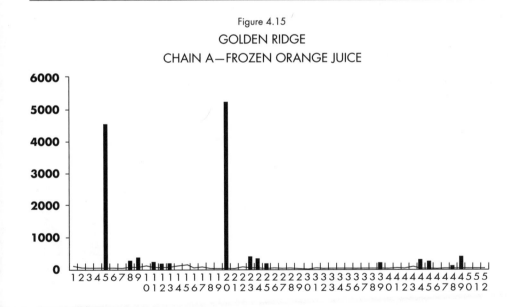

Figure 4.15
GOLDEN RIDGE
CHAIN A—FROZEN ORANGE JUICE

Another difficulty already discussed in this chapter is the particular personalities and characteristics of different product categories and different brands. What might be true for one brand may not be true at all for another. Geographic markets also respond differently and have different preferences for brands, flavors, and package sizes. Therefore, analysis must be done for each individual brand, as has been repeatedly stressed in this book.

At some risk, an aggregate picture of promotional tactics on grocery products can be presented. Based upon an analysis of U.P.C. data for 30 product categories in 50 different markets around the country, it is known that an ad feature coupled with in-store display is the most powerful marketing-communication tactic in generating brand sales, particularly when coupled with a price cut. As shown in Figure 4.16, an average 14.9 percent unadvertised shelf-price reduction on average will generate a 34 percent increase in sales. Advertising with an average price reduction of 19.2 percent in the feature advertising will generate an average 128 percent increase in sales, or nearly four times the increase with no advertising. Putting the same brand on special display, including special baskets, end-aisle and free-standing displays, with an average 10.4 percent price reduction will generate an average 134 percent increase in sales. Thus, the average display increases sales slightly more than the average feature only even though the discounts are significantly less. Combining an average 23.6 percent shelf price reduction with both feature advertising and a special display generates an average 447 percent brand sales increase, or over 12 times more than with no special display or feature advertising. The additional increment expected from feature advertising and in-store displays alone is the effect of synergy among the three promotional tactics—price reduction, advertising feature, and in-store display.

Again, the most powerful marketing-communication tactic appears to be the in-store display coupled with ad-feature. This is why it is so important for the manufac-

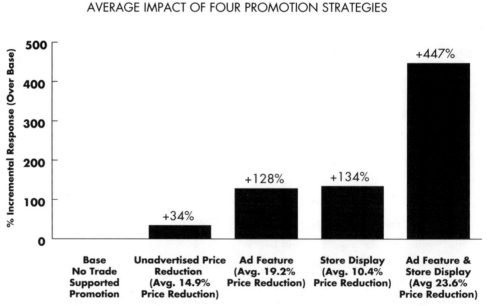

Figure 4.16
AVERAGE IMPACT OF FOUR PROMOTION STRATEGIES

Source: Nielsen ScanPro Service, 1990.

turer to get support from retailers to get in-store displays, particularly when featuring. The second most powerful tactic is the display alone, which again is in the hands of the retailer. The third most powerful tactic is the use of ad feature and price reduction, with no display support. The least powerful tactic is the unadvertised shelf-price reduction. Of course, these marketing-communication tactics are all short term, intending only to increase sales within the same one-week period in which they are administered.

ADVERTISING EFFECTS.

Usually advertising, other than feature advertising, is thought to have an impact longer than one week. One of the first questions addressed by scanner panels concerned advertising timing, including both the duration of the impact and the amount of advertising needed in a particular time interval.

The advertising question in the late 1970s become known as the "effective frequency" question, or how many exposures were necessary in what period of time to achieve the desired impact. Much of the discussion centered on the shape of the "response function" curve, or the plot of advertising impact, such as sales, against advertising exposures. Most agreed beyond some minimum number, that impact of additional exposures would diminish, so that additional effort above the minimum would generate increasingly less. The controversy was primarily around the first few exposures—whether some minimum number of exposures was necessary to achieve an impact. This issue is more commonly referred to as the three-exposure theory meaning that at least three exposures are necessary for advertising to work.

The scanner-panel data combined with household television-viewing data as described in chapter 3 seemed to provide an opportunity to answer the question. What was learned is that short-term advertising questions are very difficult and that the identification of short-term advertising effects was not as simple as first thought with regard to grocery package goods. This difficulty in finding advertising effects led some to announce that advertising, especially television advertising, doesn't work. For others, however, the difficulty in identifying short-term advertising effects from single-source scanner-based data has led to a number of important principles of how advertising works. Clearly understanding how advertising works requires knowledge of the competitive conditions of the market and all of the promotional variables.

Advertising Timing. There is no evidence for any minimum number of exposures or for the three-exposure theory. The concept of effective frequency has proven not to be very useful in planning advertising campaigns, though investigation of the concept has led to a much better understanding of the marketing-communications process.

Controlled in-market experiments have revealed that the effect of advertising is long term and probably longer than previously thought. Following the differences between control and test groups in an advertising experiment shows results as long as three years afterwards. Abraham and Lodish (1989) show in Figure 4.17 the results from

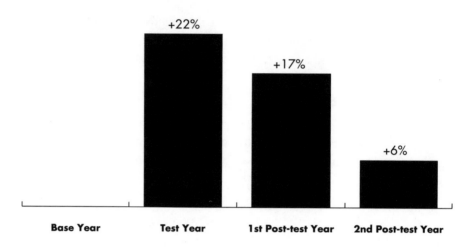

Figure 4.17
EFFECT OF ADVERTISING ON BRAND SALES

Note: Test group was exposed to 70 percent more advertising than control group in the base year.
    Advertising levels were returned to normal after the base year.

Source: Abraham and Lodish.

15 IRI advertising tests where the advertising was increased an average of 70 percent. The average sales increase was 22 percent after the advertising was returned to normal during the first, or test, year. Sales increases of 17 percent are observed in the same test group during the first post-test year after the heavier advertising, and of 6 percent during the second post-test year.

Advertising effects appear to be of very long duration, which might in part explain why short-term effects are so hard to find. This finding also reinforces the role of advertising in building base-sales volume in the fact-based marketing concept. Advertising is obviously critically important in establishing a long-term and enduring position for a brand in the marketplace.

Advertising Quality Versus Quantity. Advertising weight tests, or experiments that increase the amount of advertising spending in the test group and measure volume changes against a control group, were commonplace in the early 1970s. Their primary purpose was to help understand the relation of sales to advertising spending levels. The results, for the most part, were disappointing. A proportion of advertising weight tests tended to show no differences. Perhaps the test durations were too short, or perhaps the sales measurement was too imprecise, but the evidence has seemed to show that advertising weight or quantity is not as important as was previously thought.

The quality of the advertising message is also critical. A high-quality advertising message is one that follows a well-thought-out creative strategy and speaks directly to the target audience. Research suppliers, such as Research Systems Corporation, conduct copy tests that quantitatively measure advertising quality. Blair (1988) reports that ads that are not persuasive, that is have low advertising quality, do not increase sales, and their impact does not increase over time. The accumulated evidence shows that advertising quality is approximately three times as important as advertising quantity in generating an effect. In other words, what is said seems to be much more important than how many times it is said.

Unfortunately, advertising-message-quality measures have not been regularly combined with scanner-panel data, so many questions remain unanswered. Scanner-panel data has, however, examined the relationship between advertising weight tests and the level of dealing. The data reveal an association between much higher levels of deal activity and unsuccessful advertising tests. This finding might be explained by advertising quality. That is, manufacturers who stress deals may be less thoughtful about their advertising messages.

Competitive Effects. The importance of competing advertising messages is often overlooked. In a study of a two-brand product category, spaghetti sauce, Block and Brezen (1990) found very weak short-term effects between the two major competitors, except when one advertiser clearly dominated the other in terms of advertising weight or quantity. Clearly, then, the advertising from one competitor is cancelling the effect of the advertising from the other. This suggests a defensive role for advertising. That is, a manufacturer might advertise only to neutralize competitive advertising.

The implication is that advertising weight should be determined from competitive advertising weight and the desired position in the marketplace. Advertising should be planned with a thorough understanding of the dynamics of a brand's base and incremental volume and of the potential competitive threats. The defensive role of advertising should not be overlooked.

Advertising Targeting. There is general agreement that better-targeted advertising will result in more effective advertising. There might be some disagreement, however, in the criteria used to define and describe the targets.

Advertising media have traditionally defined their audiences in terms of demographic characteristics, such as age and gender. Media audience research suppliers, such as Simmons, have added questionnaire-based product-usage information. All these variables are regularly used to define audience targets, but they often lack sufficient precision to be able to explain sales differences.

Demographic variables are generally very weak by themselves. To use the Block and Brezen (1990) spaghetti sauce example again, variables such as income and family size predict category usage, while no demographic variable predicts brand usage. Category usage shows no advertising differences.

The first differences in the impact of advertising occur when product usage is arranged according to frequency of use or buyer-based targeting. Distinguishing heavy users from light users and one-time users begins to show differing advertising effects. The other critical variables are brand loyalty and deal proneness. These variables can best be derived from scanner-based panel data. This suggests that advertising audiences should be described in terms of real product usage, loyalty, and deal proneness using scanner data.

Case 3: Pancake Syrup

The examination of store sales generally indicates that a substantial increase in sales volume is often associated with trade-deal activity. The sources of the volume increase are usually difficult to determine from store sales data. Some possible ways to increase sales are as follows:

a. Attracting new category triers.
b. Switching buyers out of other brands.
c. Stimulating increased consumption by buyers.
d. Stockpiling by brand buyers who purchase extra items and then have longer than average times to the next purchase as they use up the excess.
e. Attracting switchers, who have a set of several brands that are acceptable and who purchase the cheapest item in the set.
f. Stimulating deal-prone buyers, who usually buy only with trade deals or manufacturer coupons.

These possibilities are not mutually exclusive. Switchers, for example, may or may not be deal prone. Stockpiling behavior might be exhibited by any buyer and can be very difficult to distinguish from increased consumption. For products that can be stored, putting a household in either a "new trier" category or a "very light user" category can be difficult. Finally, household behavior is subject to change over time. A switcher may become brand loyal. A brand-loyal household may become dissatisfied with a brand and try several other brands before returning to the previous brand or converting to some other brand. Trade dealing or manufacturer couponing activity may trigger this process.

The syrup category provides a good example to study. Syrup products can be stockpiled in the homes. However, there are several major flavors, and the dominant practice is to inventory several flavors. Syrup is not a major cost item for most consumers, and a large number of coupons and trade deals are available. Hence, only limited stockpiling behavior is expected.

The category is dominated by maple flavor syrup, with significant sales also in butter flavor. A small fraction of sales are in flavored syrups (blueberry, etc). In a year, about 60 percent of all households purchase syrup at least once, with an average time between purchases of about 120 days. About 30 percent of category volume is sold with some form of deal. The trade deals are predominately presented to consumers in the form of featured prices in store advertising. About 15 percent of total volume is moved with trade deal. Consumer coupons (both manufacturer and retailer) are an important element of the marketing mix in this category, and about 20 percent of volume is moved with coupon usage. The predominant size is 24 ounces, and most deals occur on this size, although many coupons are good on any size and may be used on the 12 or 36 ounce sizes which make up the major portion of the remaining sizes.

The data used in this case study are detailed purchasing histories collected from a 3,000 household sample in a major market. Table 4.3 provides a summary of a single year's purchasing by the panel, including nonbuyers. Table 4.4 gives detailed purchase history on a number of selected individual households. Table 4.5 gives a breakdown on the volume of Jemima, one of the major brands in the syrup category, based on a purchasing behavior classification scheme. One-time and light buyers purchased only one to three times in the year, high-deal groups purchased a much higher than expected proportion of their volume on deal, while brand loyals concentrated 80 percent or more of their purchases in one brand.

Table 4.3

SYRUP CATEGORY PURCHASING

Brand	Volume Purchased (Pounds)	Percent Volume Purchased with		
		Trade Deal Only	Coupon Only	Both Trade & Coupon
Market Total	152034.5	11.5	16.2	3.4
Butterworth	44494.8	18.5	20.5	7.7
Jemima	36932.4	6.0	15.5	1.5
Log Cabin	26624.4	15.9	13.3	4.0
PL/Generic	20838.8	6.6	3.2	0.6
All Other	23144.1	6.1	22.1	2.1

Table 4.4

PANCAKE SYRUP PURCHASE HISTORIES - SELECTED PANELISTS

PANELNUM = 6008345

YR	MO	DA	CHAIN	BRAND	SIZE	FLAVOR	UNIT	TOT$	NET$ UNIT	CPN VAL	M	S	R
91	06	10	IND	ALL/OTH	24	MAPLE	01	0164	164	.	.	.	Y
91	09	01	1	PL/GENERIC	24	ALL/OTH	01	0229	129	100	.	Y	.
91	11	13	1	BUTTERWORTH	24	BUTTER	02	0630	141	349	Y	Y	.
92	03	16	1	JEMIMA	24	MAPLE	01	0289	289	.	.	.	Y

YR	MO	DA	CHAIN	BRAND	SIZE	FLAVOR	UNIT	TOT$	NET$ UNIT	CPN VAL	M	S	R
PANELNUM = 6017687													
91	06	23	IND	JEMIMA	24	MAPLE	01	0319	319		.	.	.	.
91	06	23	1	PL/GENERIC	24	MAPLE	01	0189	189		.	.	.	.
91	09	23	IND	LOG CABIN	24	MAPLE	01	0168	168		.	.	.	Y
92	02	21	IND	BUTTERWORTH	24	BUTTER	01	0248	248		.	.	.	.
92	03	30	IND	BUTTERWORTH	24	BUTTER	01	0248	248		.	.	.	.
92	05	12	IND	BUTTERWORTH	24	BUTTER	01	0248	248		.	.	.	.
PANELNUM = 6018705													
91	06	14	IND	BUTTERWORTH	24	BUTTER	01	0274	274		.	.	.	.
91	08	28	IND	BUTTERWORTH	24	BUTTER	01	0327	327		.	.	.	.
91	08	28	IND	BUTTERWORTH	24	BUTTER	01	0327	327		.	.	.	.
91	10	02	IND	BUTTERWORTH	36	BUTTER	01	0324	289	035	Y	.	.	.
92	03	11	IND	BUTTERWORTH	12	BUTTER	01	0200	200		.	.	.	.
92	04	08	IND	BUTTERWORTH	36	BUTTER	01	0359	359		.	.	.	.
PANELNUM = 6020678													
91	08	25	2	PL/GENERIC	24	MAPLE	01	0219	219		.	.	.	.
91	10	06	1	PL/GENERIC	24	ALL/OTH	01	0179	179		.	.	.	Y
91	12	17	1	PL/GENERIC	24	ALL/OTH	01	0179	179		.	.	.	.
92	05	26	2	PL/GENERIC	24	MAPLE	01	0149	149		.	.	.	.
PANELNUM = 6021535													
91	07	06	5	ALL/OTH	16	ALL/OTH	01	0143	143		.	.	.	.
91	07	06	5	ALL/OTH	24	MAPLE	01	0279	259	020	Y	.	.	.
91	09	02	5	LOG CABIN	24	MAPLE	01	0185	185		.	.	.	Y
91	11	23	5	LOG CABIN	36	MAPLE	01	0365	340	025	.	Y	.
92	01	11	5	LOG CABIN	24	BUTTER	01	0183	183		.	.	.	Y
92	02	10	1	LOG CABIN	24	MAPLE	01	0229	159	070	.	Y	.
92	03	21	5	JEMIMA	24	MAPLE	01	0263	243	020	Y	.	.
PANELNUM = 6028839													
91	06	29	1	ALL/OTH	24	MAPLE	01	0285	285		.	.	.	.
91	07	06	1	ALL/OTH	24	MAPLE	01	0299	239	060	Y	.	.
91	07	22	1	LOG CABIN	24	MAPLE	01	0199	199		.	.	.	Y
91	07	28	1	LOG CABIN	24	MAPLE	01	0275	275		.	.	.	Y
91	08	16	1	LOG CABIN	24	MAPLE	02	0398	037	325	Y	Y	.
91	10	26	1	BUTTERWORTH	36	BUTTER	01	0399	264	135	Y	Y	.
91	11	09	IND	ALL/OTH	16	ALL/OTH	01	0159	159		.	.	.	.
91	12	01	1	ALL/OTH	24	MAPLE	01	0295	220	075	Y	.	.
91	12	17	2	ALL/OTH	12	MAPLE	01	0311	311		.	.	.	Y
92	01	24	1	BUTTERWORTH	24	BUTTER	01	0199	049	150	Y	Y	Y
92	02	12	1	LOG CABIN	24	MAPLE	01	0299	149	150	Y	Y	.
92	03	09	1	BUTTERWORTH	24	BUTTER	01	0279	229	050	Y	.	.
92	03	20	1	BUTTERWORTH	24	BUTTER	01	0279	229	050	Y	.	.
PANELNUM = 6057690													
91	09	03	2	LOG CABIN	24	MAPLE	01	0319	269	050	Y	.	.
91	09	13	2	ALL/OTH	12	MAPLE	01	0159	159		.	.	.	.

YR	MO	DA	CHAIN	BRAND	SIZE	FLAVOR	UNIT	TOT$	NET$ UNIT	CPN VAL	M	S	R
91	10	12	IND	ALL/OTH	08	MAPLE	01	0139	139	.	.	.	.
91	11	16	2	JEMIMA	24	BUTTER	01	0315	255	060	Y	.	.
91	11	30	2	ALL/OTH	16	ALL/OTH	01	0153	153	.	.	.	.
92	01	04	2	JEMIMA	24	MAPLE	01	0319	319	.	.	.	.
92	03	23	1	JEMIMA	24	BUTTER	01	0319	319	.	.	.	.
92	04	10	IND	JEMIMA	24	BUTTER	01	0179	179	.	.	.	Y
92	04	26	IND	JEMIMA	24	BUTTER	01	0299	299	.	.	.	.
92	05	22	2	JEMIMA	24	MAPLE	01	0315	315	.	.	.	.

PANELNUM = 6300798

YR	MO	DA	CHAIN	BRAND	SIZE	FLAVOR	UNIT	TOT$	NET$ UNIT	CPN VAL	M	S	R
92	02	25	1	ALL/OTH	12	MAPLE	01	0199	159	040	Y	.	.
92	03	18	IND	BUTTERWORTH	24	BUTTER	01	0279	179	100	Y	.	Y
92	04	25	IND	LOG CABIN	12	MAPLE	01	0199	041	158	.	Y	.
92	05	16	IND	JEMIMA	12	MAPLE	01	0199	174	025	Y	.	.
92	05	20	IND	BUTTERWORTH	24	BUTTER	01	0309	259	050	Y	.	.

PANELNUM = 7003000

YR	MO	DA	CHAIN	BRAND	SIZE	FLAVOR	UNIT	TOT$	NET$ UNIT	CPN VAL	M	S	R
91	06	17	IND	ALL/OTH	24	MAPLE	01	0239	139	100	Y	Y	.
91	07	28	IND	LOG CABIN	24	MAPLE	01	0219	149	070	Y	Y	.
91	09	06	IND	PL/GENERIC	24	MAPLE	01	0098	098	.	.	.	Y
91	10	04	IND	PL/GENERIC	24	MAPLE	01	0089	089	.	.	.	Y
91	11	04	IND	LOG CABIN	24	MAPLE	01	0299	099	200	Y	Y	.
91	11	29	IND	LOG CABIN	12	MAPLE	01	0185	085	100	Y	Y	.
91	12	07	IND	ALL/OTH	16	ALL/OTH	01	0125	125	.	.	.	Y
92	04	25	IND	BUTTERWORTH	12	BUTTER	01	0198	118	080	Y	Y	.
92	04	25	IND	LOG CABIN	12	MAPLE	01	0199	099	100	Y	Y	.

PANELNUM = 7013260

YR	MO	DA	CHAIN	BRAND	SIZE	FLAVOR	UNIT	TOT$	NET$ UNIT	CPN VAL	M	S	R
91	08	16	1	LOG CABIN	24	MAPLE	01	0199	199	.	.	.	Y
91	11	12	1	ALL/OTH	12	MAPLE	01	0345	345	.	.	.	Y
92	01	02	2	JEMIMA	24	MAPLE	01	0335	310	025	Y	.	.
92	02	27	2	PL/GENERIC	24	MAPLE	01	0139	139	.	.	.	Y
92	03	25	2	JEMIMA	12	MAPLE	01	0199	164	035	Y	.	.
92	04	29	2	ALL/OTH	24	MAPLE	01	0315	260	055	Y	.	.

PANELNUM = 9061427

YR	MO	DA	CHAIN	BRAND	SIZE	FLAVOR	UNIT	TOT$	NET$ UNIT	CPN VAL	M	S	R
91	07	01	2	PL/GENERIC	36	MAPLE	01	0289	289	.	.	.	.
91	08	15	2	ALL/OTH	16	ALL/OTH	01	0155	155	.	.	.	.
91	08	15	2	ALL/OTH	16	ALL/OTH	01	0155	155	.	.	.	.
91	09	06	2	JEMIMA	24	MAPLE	01	0305	305	.	.	.	.
91	10	02	2	LOG CABIN	36	MAPLE	01	0353	353	.	.	.	.
91	12	21	2	PL/GENERIC	36	MAPLE	01	0289	289	.	.	.	.
92	01	17	2	LOG CABIN	36	MAPLE	01	0425	425	.	.	.	.
92	04	17	2	JEMIMA	36	MAPLE	01	0415	415	.	.	.	.

PANELNUM = 9061473

YR	MO	DA	CHAIN	BRAND	SIZE	FLAVOR	UNIT	TOT$	NET$ UNIT	CPN VAL	M	S	R
91	10	18	2	BUTTERWORTH	36	BUTTER	01	0299	299	.	.	.	Y
91	11	10	5	BUTTERWORTH	24	BUTTER	02	0598	299	.	.	.	.
91	11	16	5	BUTTERWORTH	36	BUTTER	01	0324	324	.	.	.	.
91	11	16	5	LOG CABIN	36	MAPLE	01	0365	365	.	.	.	.

YR	MO	DA	CHAIN	BRAND	SIZE	FLAVOR	UNIT	TOT$	NET$ UNIT	CPN VAL	M	S	R
91	11	16	5	LOG CABIN	24	MAPLE	01	0188	188	.	.	.	Y
92	03	06	5	BUTTERWORTH	36	BUTTER	01	0324	274	050	Y	.	.
92	03	06	5	LOG CABIN	36	MAPLE	03	1065	355	.	.	.	.

PANELNUM = 9086944

YR	MO	DA	CHAIN	BRAND	SIZE	FLAVOR	UNIT	TOT$	NET$ UNIT	CPN VAL	M	S	R
91	06	23	1	LOG CABIN	36	MAPLE	01	0409	409	.	.	.	Y
91	07	03	1	PL/GENERIC	24	ALL/OTH	01	0199	199	.	.	.	.
91	10	11	IND	LOG CABIN	24	MAPLE	01	0145	145	.	.	.	Y
91	10	11	IND	ALL/OTH	16	ALL/OTH	01	0177	177	.	.	.	.
91	11	07	NON	ALL/OTH	24	MAPLE	01	0179	124	055	Y	.	Y
91	11	14	NON	BUTTERWORTH	24	BUTTER	01	0209	209	.	.	.	.
91	11	14	NON	ALL/OTH	24	MAPLE	01	0179	124	055	Y	.	.
92	02	23	NON	ALL/OTH	24	MAPLE	01	0189	189	.	.	.	.
92	02	26	NON	BUTTERWORTH	24	BUTTER	01	0189	189	.	.	.	Y
92	03	21	NON	ALL/OTH	24	MAPLE	01	0177	122	055	Y	.	.
92	05	25	1	ALL/OTH	24	MAPLE	01	0299	299	.	.	.	.

PANELNUM = 9094820

YR	MO	DA	CHAIN	BRAND	SIZE	FLAVOR	UNIT	TOT$	NET$ UNIT	CPN VAL	M	S	R
91	07	11	1	LOG CABIN	24	MAPLE	01	0335	285	050	Y	.	.
91	09	19	1	JEMIMA	24	MAPLE	01	0299	274	025	Y	.	.
91	10	24	1	ALL/OTH	24	MAPLE	01	0299	224	075	Y	.	.
91	11	07	1	ALL/OTH	08	MAPLE	01	0266	266	.	.	.	.
91	11	14	1	JEMIMA	24	MAPLE	01	0335	285	050	Y	.	.
91	12	11	2	ALL/OTH	24	MAPLE	01	0289	239	050	Y	.	.
92	01	16	2	LOG CABIN	24	MAPLE	01	0315	280	035	Y	.	.
92	02	27	2	ALL/OTH	24	MAPLE	01	0273	173	100	Y	.	.

PANELNUM = 9110598

YR	MO	DA	CHAIN	BRAND	SIZE	FLAVOR	UNIT	TOT$	NET$ UNIT	CPN VAL	M	S	R
91	08	23	1	LOG CABIN	12	MAPLE	01	0199	199	.	.	.	.
91	09	18	1	LOG CABIN	12	MAPLE	01	0199	199	.	.	.	.
91	11	30	3	LOG CABIN	12	MAPLE	01	0185	185	.	.	.	.
92	01	04	3	LOG CABIN	12	MAPLE	01	0185	185	.	.	.	.
92	05	03	3	LOG CABIN	12	MAPLE	01	0185	185	.	.	.	.

PANELNUM = 9115250

YR	MO	DA	CHAIN	BRAND	SIZE	FLAVOR	UNIT	TOT$	NET$ UNIT	CPN VAL	M	S	R
91	10	25	4	JEMIMA	12	MAPLE	02	0430	190	050	Y	.	.
91	11	07	4	LOG CABIN	24	MAPLE	01	0199	199	.	.	.	Y
91	11	16	4	ALL/OTH	24	MAPLE	02	0596	233	130	Y	Y	.
92	01	09	4	JEMIMA	12	MAPLE	01	0215	215	.	.	.	.
92	03	14	4	ALL/OTH	12	MAPLE	01	0190	190	.	.	.	.

PANELNUM = 9115269

YR	MO	DA	CHAIN	BRAND	SIZE	FLAVOR	UNIT	TOT$	NET$ UNIT	CPN VAL	M	S	R
91	07	16	1	ALL/OTH	24	MAPLE	01	0275	275	.	.	.	.
91	07	27	1	ALL/OTH	24	MAPLE	01	0275	275	.	.	.	.
91	08	25	1	JEMIMA	24	MAPLE	01	0335	300	035	Y	.	.
91	09	16	1	JEMIMA	24	MAPLE	01	0335	335	.	.	.	.
91	10	15	IND	ALL/OTH	24	MAPLE	01	0279	279	.	.	.	.
91	11	27	1	ALL/OTH	08	MAPLE	01	0249	249	.	.	.	.
91	12	20	1	BUTTERWORTH	24	BUTTER	01	0289	289	.	.	.	.
92	01	08	1	ALL/OTH	12	MAPLE	01	0349	349	.	.	.	Y

YR	MO	DA	CHAIN	BRAND	SIZE	FLAVOR	UNIT	TOT$	NET$ UNIT	CPN VAL	M	S	R
92	01	22	1	BUTTERWORTH	24	BUTTER	01	0199	199	.	.	.	Y
92	02	24	1	LOG CABIN	24	MAPLE	01	0259	259	.	.	.	Y
92	04	04	1	BUTTERWORTH	24	BUTTER	01	0315	315	.	.	.	.
92	05	30	1	JEMIMA	24	MAPLE	01	0200	200	.	.	.	Y
PANELNUM = 9164289													
91	06	08	IND	JEMIMA	36	MAPLE	01	0399	399	.	.	.	.
91	07	12	IND	JEMIMA	36	MAPLE	01	0385	385	.	.	.	.
91	08	08	IND	JEMIMA	36	MAPLE	01	0289	289	.	.	.	.
91	08	31	IND	JEMIMA	36	MAPLE	01	0399	399	.	.	.	.
91	09	27	5	JEMIMA	36	MAPLE	01	0399	399	.	.	.	.
91	10	12	5	JEMIMA	36	MAPLE	01	0399	399	.	.	.	.
91	10	26	5	JEMIMA	36	MAPLE	01	0399	399	.	.	.	.
91	11	08	5	JEMIMA	36	MAPLE	01	0399	399	.	.	.	.
91	11	29	5	JEMIMA	36	MAPLE	01	0399	399	.	.	.	.
91	12	07	5	JEMIMA	36	MAPLE	01	0399	399	.	.	.	.
92	01	18	5	JEMIMA	36	MAPLE	01	0399	399	.	.	.	.
92	02	15	5	JEMIMA	36	MAPLE	01	0399	399	.	.	.	.
92	03	13	5	JEMIMA	36	MAPLE	01	0399	399	.	.	.	.
92	04	04	5	JEMIMA	36	MAPLE	01	0399	399	.	.	.	.
92	04	18	5	JEMIMA	36	MAPLE	01	0399	399	.	.	.	.
92	05	01	5	JEMIMA	36	MAPLE	01	0332	332	.	.	.	.
92	05	16	5	JEMIMA	24	MAPLE	01	0268	268	.	.	.	.
92	05	29	5	JEMIMA	36	MAPLE	01	0399	399	.	.	.	.
PANELNUM = 9169344													
91	06	28	IND	BUTTERWORTH	24	BUTTER	01	0274	274	.	.	.	.
91	06	28	IND	PL/GENERIC	24	MAPLE	01	0179	179	.	.	.	.
91	07	10	IND	PL/GENERIC	24	MAPLE	01	0179	179	.	.	.	.
91	07	29	IND	JEMIMA	24	BUTTER	01	0229	189	040	Y	.	Y
91	08	06	IND	JEMIMA	24	BUTTER	01	0229	229	.	.	.	Y
91	08	06	IND	LOG CABIN	24	MAPLE	01	0299	299	.	.	.	.
91	09	28	IND	BUTTERWORTH	36	BUTTER	01	0360	210	150	Y	.	Y
91	10	23	IND	LOG CABIN	24	MAPLE	01	0299	299	.	.	.	.
91	10	26	IND	BUTTERWORTH	36	BUTTER	01	0299	199	100	Y	Y	.
91	11	04	IND	LOG CABIN	36	MAPLE	01	0399	399	.	.	.	.
91	12	21	IND	ALL/OTH	24	MAPLE	02	0516	221	075	Y	.	.
92	01	13	IND	ALL/OTH	24	MAPLE	01	0249	224	025	Y	.	.
92	01	18	IND	ALL/OTH	24	MAPLE	01	0259	209	050	Y	.	.
92	01	28	IND	LOG CABIN	24	MAPLE	01	0295	295	.	.	.	Y
92	01	30	NON	JEMIMA	24	MAPLE	01	0288	288	.	.	.	.
92	02	13	NON	JEMIMA	24	BUTTER	01	0288	248	040	Y	.	.
92	02	13	NON	LOG CABIN	24	MAPLE	01	0288	248	040	Y	.	Y
92	02	20	IND	ALL/OTH	24	MAPLE	01	0255	205	050	Y	.	.
92	03	01	NON	BUTTERWORTH	36	BUTTER	01	0359	324	035	Y	.	.
92	03	07	IND	LOG CABIN	36	MAPLE	01	0365	365	.	.	.	.
92	03	25	IND	BUTTERWORTH	24	BUTTER	02	0315	000	315	.	Y	.

YR	MO	DA	CHAIN	BRAND	SIZE	FLAVOR	UNIT	TOT$	NET$ UNIT	CPN VAL	M	S	R
92	03	27	IND	LOG CABIN	24	MAPLE	01	0288	288	.	.	.	Y
92	04	08	IND	LOG CABIN	24	MAPLE	01	0299	249	050	Y	.	.
92	04	18	IND	LOG CABIN	24	MAPLE	01	0299	299	.	.	.	.
92	04	23	1	LOG CABIN	24	MAPLE	01	0160	000	160	.	Y	Y
92	05	22	IND	BUTTERWORTH	36	BUTTER	01	0359	304	055	Y	.	.

PANELNUM =   9170971

YR	MO	DA	CHAIN	BRAND	SIZE	FLAVOR	UNIT	TOT$	NET$ UNIT	CPN VAL	M	S	R
91	06	02	1	ALL/OTH	08	MAPLE	01	0143	143	.	.	.	.
91	06	21	1	ALL/OTH	24	MAPLE	01	0259	259	.	.	.	.
91	06	27	2	BUTTERWORTH	24	BUTTER	01	0287	287	.	.	.	.
91	07	05	IND	ALL/OTH	24	MAPLE	02	0178	089	.	.	.	.
91	07	15	1	LOG CABIN	24	MAPLE	01	0195	195	.	.	.	Y
91	07	31	1	LOG CABIN	24	MAPLE	01	0202	202	.	.	.	Y
91	08	22	1	BUTTERWORTH	24	BUTTER	01	0299	299	.	.	.	.
91	09	06	1	LOG CABIN	24	MAPLE	01	0315	315	.	.	.	.
91	09	13	IND	ALL/OTH	24	MAPLE	01	0169	169	.	.	.	.
91	09	18	1	PL/GENERIC	24	ALL/OTH	01	0179	179	.	.	.	.
91	09	20	1	PL/GENERIC	24	ALL/OTH	02	0358	179	.	.	.	Y
91	10	02	IND	PL/GENERIC	24	ALL/OTH	02	0334	167	.	.	.	.
91	11	22	1	ALL/OTH	24	MAPLE	01	0275	275	.	.	.	.
91	12	06	1	PL/GENERIC	24	ALL/OTH	01	0179	179	.	.	.	.
91	12	09	1	PL/GENERIC	24	ALL/OTH	01	0179	179	.	.	.	.
92	01	07	1	JEMIMA	24	MAPLE	01	0315	315	.	.	.	.
92	01	22	1	PL/GENERIC	24	ALL/OTH	01	0189	189	.	.	.	.
92	01	29	IND	PL/GENERIC	24	MAPLE	01	0159	159	.	.	.	.
92	02	21	1	LOG CABIN	36	MAPLE	01	0349	349	.	.	.	.
92	03	06	1	PL/GENERIC	24	ALL/OTH	01	0157	157	.	.	.	.
92	03	20	1	PL/GENERIC	24	ALL/OTH	02	0314	157	.	.	.	.
92	04	07	1	BUTTERWORTH	36	BUTTER	01	0409	409	.	.	.	.
92	04	23	1	PL/GENERIC	24	ALL/OTH	01	0155	155	.	.	.	.
92	05	01	1	PL/GENERIC	24	ALL/OTH	01	0155	155	.	.	.	.

Table 4.5

LOG CABIN SYRUP VOLUME SOURCES BY BUYER GROUPING

Buyer Group	**Volume Sales in Pounds**			
	Total	With Trade Deal Only	With Coupon	With Trade & Coupon
Total L/C Purchases	26624.4	4233.3	3531.0	1065.0
L/C Loyal-High Deal	1184.4	257.6	288.7	67.5
L/C Loyal-Low Deal	9910.3	868.1	988.3	151.1
Other Loyal-High Deal	447.0	110.4	142.6	61.6
Other Loyal-Low Deal	529.7	68.2	73.1	45.5
Nonloyal-High Deal	6726.5	1999.2	1241.8	580.9
Nonloyal -Low Deal	6538.2	535.8	699.2	88.0
One Time & Light	1288.3	394.0	97.4	70.4

Question 1. Butterworth and Log Cabin made heavy use of trade deal, while all brands except Pl/generic made extensive use of coupons. Using Table 4.3, what interactions do you find between purchasing with coupons and purchasing with trade deals?

Question 2. Some of the trade deal volume is incremental to the category, the rest is reshuffling among the brands. Using Table 4.3, estimate what the impact on Log Cabin and its competitors would have been if only Log Cabin trade dealing had been eliminated for each of the following assumptions:

   a. All trade deal volume for Log Cabin is incremental to both the brand and the category.
   b. None of the trade deal volume is incremental to the category, and the Log Cabin trade deal volume would be redistributed across all brands in the category, including Log Cabin, in proportion to their total sales.
   c. None of the trade deal volume is incremental to the category, and the Log Cabin trade deal volume would be redistributed across all brands in the category, excluding Log Cabin, in proportion to their trade deal sales.
   d. Since Butterworth accounts for nearly all sales of butter flavored syrup, while the remaining brands are primarily maple or all/other flavors, assume that none of the trade deal volume is incremental to the category, and the Log Cabin deal volume would be redistributed across all brands in the category, excluding Butterworth but including Log Cabin, in proportion to their total sales.
   e. Since Butterworth accounts for nearly all sales of butter flavored syrup, while the remaining brands are primarily maple or all/other flavors, assume that none of the trade deal volume is incremental to the category, and the Log Cabin deal volume would be redistributed across all brands in the category, excluding Butterworth but including Log Cabin, in proportion to their trade deal sales.

Question 3. Repeat question 2 using Jemima instead of Log Cabin.

Question 4. Contrast the results obtained from questions 2 and 3.

Question 5. Review the individual panelist purchasing histories given in Table 4.4. Comment on the differing types of purchase behavior shown, the apparent importance of trade dealing and coupons in the purchase decisions, and the stability of purchase behavior over time.

Question 6. Using Table 4.5 as the basis, discuss the importance of each buyer group to:

   a. Log Cabin sales without trade deal or coupon.
   b. Log Cabin sales with trade deal.

    c. Log Cabin sales with coupon.

    d. Log Cabin total sales.

Question 7. Discuss the probable impact on Log Cabin sales in this market of:

    a. Eliminating manufacturer coupon drops for Log Cabin; or

    b. Eliminating trade dealing activity for Log Cabin.

Question 8 (Optional). The method of constructing the buyer groups defined in Table 4.5 carries the potential for generating biased results. Since brand loyalty was defined as 75 percent or more of total volume in a single brand, these households are severely restricted in the amount of volume they can contribute to other brands. In categories with very frequent purchases, an alternative is to classify households during some base period, and then analyze their purchasing behavior in a subsequent time period. Discuss other potential sources of bias with either analysis procedure.

Households were classified as one-time or light buyers if they purchased syrup three times or less.

Households purchasing four or more times were classified on two dimensions:

Deal sensitivity — Low deal sensitivity if their volume purchased with trade deal and coupon was less than the market average. High deal sensitivity if their volume purchased with trade deal and coupon was market average or more.

Brand Loyalty — Brand loyal if at least 75 percent of their purchase volume was in one specific brand, and nonloyal if no one brand accounted for at least 75 percent of total purchase volume. Households loyal to brands other than Log Cabin were combined into the "loyal to other brands" group.

Suggested Readings

Abraham, Magid and Leonard Lodish.
Advertising Works.
Chicago: Information Resources, Inc. (1989)

Blair, Margaret Henderson.
"An Empirical Investigation of Advertising Wearin and Wearout."
Journal of Advertising Research 27 (January 1988).
Block, Martin and Tamara Brezen.
**"A New Media Planning Concept Using Database
   Analysis to Segment Media Audiences,"**
Journal of Media Planning (Spring 1990).

McAlister, Leigh and Rudolph W. Struss III.
**"Promotion Response Patterns and Their
   Implications for Manufacturers,"**
Unpublished Paper. (1983 and Revised 1989).

McAlister, Leigh and John C. Totten.
**"Decomposing the Promotional Bump: Switching,
   Stockpiling and Consumption Increase,"**
Unpublished Paper. Presented at ORSA/TIMS Joint Meeting (1985).

Malec, John and Gerald Eskin.
**"Consumer and Retailer Dynamics as
   Viewed Through the Scanner,"**
Unpublished Paper. Presented at the Food Marketing Institute
   Conference (1984).

Neslin, Scott A., Caroline Henderson and John Quelch,
"Consumer Promotions and the Acceleration of Product Purchases,"
Marketing Science 4 (Spring 1985) 147-165.

Wisnieski, Kenneth J., and Robert C. Blattberg,
**"Analysis of Consumer Response to Retail
   Price Dealing Styrategies",**
University of Chicago, April 1988, Final Report under NSF Grant SES8421165.

CHAPTER 5

MANUFACTURER–CONTROLLED STRATEGIES

S ales promotion programs can come from two sources: the manufacturer and the retailer. Promotion programs that originate from the retailer are considered in the next chapter. Promotion programs that originate from the manufacturer are always aimed at the final consumer, though their approach may be either indirect or direct. An indirect manufacturer-controlled promotion strategy is aimed at the trade–wholesalers and retailers–with the hope that, as a result, they will influence the final consumer through their selling efforts. A direct manufacturer-controlled promotion program is aimed at the final consumer.

CORPORATE STRATEGY. A manufacturer's corporate strategy generally involves a set of decisions that are beyond either the brand manager or the sales manager. The first corporate strategy decision involves the determination of product-line pricing. The fundamental product line pricing decision needs to be made according to the line's position in the marketplace. Is the product line intended to compete on the basis of any product benefit or uniqueness? Is it intended to compete on the basis of quality? Does the product line have any image or ego-enhancing benefits? Is it intended to compete on the basis of price? What is the distribution strategy? All these questions need to be resolved in order to establish the product line's regular price and market niche.

A second corporate-level strategy decision involves the allocation of available marketing funds to product lines and brands. Especially in complex multiline and multibrand enterprises, the decision on how much each brand should be supported needs to be made at the corporate level. This decision should be made using careful analysis of the product category and substitutable product categories.

A third corporate-level strategy decision involves the support of product research and development. Ability to maintain unique product benefits impacts the ability to compete on product attributes other than price. The alternative to product research and development is intensive price competition. However, product research and development are long-term processes that involve some risk. Competitive new products or product improvements may not result from this direct effort, as a competitor may realize an innovation first.

BRAND MANAGER'S STRATEGY. There are several strategy decisions that brand managers typically make. These decisions generally concern everything about marketing the brand except direct control of the sales force. Depending upon the size of the organization, the brand manager may have support personnel such as specialized sales promotion staff to assist in the preparation of a sales promotion strategy. In most organizations the brand manager is probably the one with primary responsibility for brand promotion strategy. Eight brand-manager promotion decisions are discussed bellow.

Brand Pricing. Preparing the wholesale price list for the brand in all of its package sizes and varieties is normally a fundamental responsibility. Pricing needs to reflect a careful analysis of the marketplace and an understanding of the fundamental demand curve for the product. How the product will be sold against competition is also a critical consideration. Often, the list price may not be the actual selling price; instead, the list price merely begins a negotiation process with the retailer. How price lists are used is certainly an important consideration for the brand manager.

Allocation of Funds to Trade Promotion. Dividing the promotion budget between trade promotion and consumer promotion is another fundamental responsibility of the brand manager. Depending on how the product is sold and how it is positioned in the marketplace, the brand manager must decide what portion of the budget to allocate to trade promotion. The brand manager knows that trade promotion, almost always in the form of trade allowances, is vital in obtaining in-store display, feature advertising space, and shelf-price reductions, and that these things are the only vehicles that build short-term sales volume. The brand manager should also know that increasing trade promotion places more control for the marketing of the brand in the hand of the retailer and may diminish the long-term value of the brand.

Allocation of Funds to Consumer Promotion. Not only must consumer promotion compete with trade promotion, it must also compete with other forms of consumer-marketing communication, such as advertising. As discussed in chapter 1, consumer promotion takes many forms and choices. These programs are often the territory of the sales promotion agency, whose business depends on the ability to sell these programs to manufacturers. The consideration of consumer-sales promotion programs may occupy more of the brand manager's time than consideration of the budget. Other considerations might be corporate-consumer promotion programs that might provide an individual brand with a special opportunity. The decisions about the allocation of budget to a consumer promotion program should obviously be made only after careful analysis of the marketplace for the product.

Trade Promotion Programs. Developing trade promotion programs is another major responsibility of the brand manager. Ongoing programs, such as forward buying arrangements, may also occupy valuable time of the brand manager. In addition, support materials, such as displays and artwork for feature advertising, need to be readily available.

Trade contests may also be effective, and trade premiums can sometimes be very helpful in obtaining special displays. Trade advertising can develop directly from the analysis of scanner-based promotion data. Note the following examples of trade advertising which contain performance claims that are directly supported by the analysis of IRI data.

Gaining Distribution. A critical marketing problem occurs when new products gain new distribution. A key to gaining this distribution is trade promotion that provides the retailer with the incentive to stock and sell the product. It is commonplace for retailers to charge manufacturers to place new products on the shelves. Slotting allowances were first established because of the software modifications necessary in the store-scanning equipment to accommodate new product codes. These allowances now are viewed as the cost of obtaining shelf space.

The typical supermarket stocks more items than it probably would like. Generally retailers do not meet new products with the same enthusiasm as do manufacturers, who see the new products as a way of expanding their volume. Retailers see the new products as adding to their inventory-management problem and not increasing either their store traffic or their sales volume. This conflict makes expanding distribution one of the more difficult and expensive problems faced by the brand manager.

Optimizing Product Size Mix. Most brands come in a variety of flavors, types, and package sizes. As discussed in chapter 3, different package sizes have different promotion responsiveness in different markets. Too few package sizes can lead a potential buyer to a competitor that has the right package size. Too many can contribute to out-of-stocks of the right package size. Having too few sizes or the wrong sizes can lead to less shelf space. Too many sizes may lead to retailer resistance and, perhaps, retailer selection of sizes. Again, based upon careful analysis of the category and brand, the brand manager should determine what the most profitable mix of package sizes should be for the brand.

Targeting Specific Competitors. By monitoring the retail sales activity of a specific competitor, a brand manager can develop a strategy aimed at that competitor. Understanding the market dynamics of a competitor—the portion of a competitor's sales volume that is base and incremental—makes it much easier to plot appropriate strategy against it.

Exploiting Peak Seasonal Demand Periods. Understanding the seasonal-demand characteristics of a product category and brand is critical for the brand manager. Seasonal-demand characteristics, such as the critical week before Easter for vinegar, are not always obvious and require careful analysis to be detected. Traditional analyses have often aggregated away seasonal characteristics by combining too many markets across time periods that are too long. Also many seasonal characteristics, such as those driven by holidays, vary in time from year to year. This kind of detail must be retained in any analysis.

SALES MANAGER'S STRATEGY. A sales manager differs from a brand manager in that the sales manager has responsibility for managing a sales force. The sales manager is concerned directly with meeting the needs of the prospect, usually the retailer. In addition, the sales manager is normally faced with the responsibility of selling a number of brands, sometimes even competing brands, in the same product category of one manufacturer. This situation can create an interesting relationship between the sales manager and the brand manager.

Regional Marketing. One of the first decisions faced by the sales manager is the allocation of sales support among brands. The sales manager must develop a strategy that optimizes overall corporate sales, despite the best efforts of individual brand managers. The sales manager must also make decisions about the allocation of funds among geographic regions. The sales manager must be keenly aware of competitive activity and local market conditions.

Different geographic markets clearly respond differently to promotion. This can be partially explained by different retail environments with different promotion histories. In addition, different geographic markets contain different types of consumers with different lifestyles, preferences, and tastes. Any given promotion program should be expected to perform differently across markets. The geographic-market case at the end of this chapter strongly illustrates this concept. Certainly the best way for the sales manager to distinguish geographic markets is to do scanner-based sales promotion analysis in the same way that the corporate planner and the brand manager do.

Key Accounts. Another strategy option for the sales manager is the development of special programs for key accounts. Key accounts are usually large chains that account for a substantial portion of the manufacturer's sales volume. An advantage of a key-account program is that it begins a marketing partnership between the manufacturer and retailer. Key-account programs can clearly recognize the differences between various retailers and their own individual marketing strategies. The analysis of scanner-based sales data can also provide the sales manager with the means of optimizing the product size mix by account. This kind of analysis benefits both the manufacturer and the retailer.

PROMOTION TO THE CONSUMER. A manufacturer has perhaps the widest range of choices in the type of promotion to use when aiming directly at the final consumer. A manufacturer may use virtually any type of price promotion, including coupons, price-offs, rebates, and bonus packs. In addition, a manufacturer may use any of the interest promotions, such as premiums, contests, and sweepstakes. The only form of sales promotion that the manufacturer can't use directly to the consumer is the trade allowance.

Consumer promotions can be difficult to manage for several reasons. The first problem is getting the promotion distributed to the consumer. The manufacturer has a wide variety of choices, including paid mass-media delivery through such vehicles as newspaper free standing inserts, in-store displays with tear-off pads, or on- or in-package delivery. Each method has its own special problems. Media delivery has the problems of relatively high cost and waste circulation. In-store displays need the cooperation of the retailer, which may require a supporting trade promotion. On- or in-package delivery may not reach nonpurchasers or purchasers of other brands. Delivery of the promotion to the consumer is usually a major component of the cost of the promotional effort.

A second problem involves redemption or fulfillment. A price-off pack avoids this problem, but it is very expensive because it gives the special price to all purchasers of the product, including those who would have purchased the product without the benefit of the promotion. Redeeming coupons involves not only the cost of the face value of the coupon, but also the cost of handling the coupon. Redemption rate can also be a very important issue, especially if it is much higher than expected. If a free-in-the-mail or self-liquidating premium is used, then fulfillment, or getting the premium delivered to the consumer, is an important issue. The same is true for both contests and sweepstakes.

A third problem is high cost. A manufacturer promoting directly to the consumer most likely will pay the highest delivery rates. A retailer enjoys the lower local-newspaper media rate, whereas a manufacturer would most likely have to pay the higher national rate. This is because a manufacturer engaged in a direct consumer promotion does not benefit from any cost sharing with retailers. One exception is manufacturer coupons, which may be combined with local retailer support in double or triple coupon value promotions.

Consumer promotions do have a major advantage despite their difficulties in administration. For example, the manufacturer has complete control over the timing and method of promotion and doesn't depend on the whim of the retailer. The manufacturer can be certain of the form and method of promotion as well as the critical issue of timing. In essence, the manufacturer in direct promotion does not relinquish any control of the promotional program, while it may with an indirect promotional program.

PROMOTION TO THE TRADE. Indirect promotions are designed to influence wholesalers and retailers, who in turn will influence the final consumer. The first problem with promotion to the trade is that the linkage just described works with varying levels of efficiency. Sometimes the retailer decides to take full advantage of a trade promotion offered by a manufacturer and to add considerably more to it, making the indirect trade promotion far more effective than an equivalent direct consumer promotion. On the other hand, sometimes a retailer ignores the trade promotion altogether and makes no changes in the pricing, display, or store advertising of the product. Other times, the retailer does something in between these two extremes.

Probably the most pervasive form of trade promotion is the trade allowance, which is simply a short-term reduction in the selling price to the trade. Presumably, this incentive will induce the trade to promote the particular product over competing products, or perhaps even over other product categories. Trade promotion may also include coupons, contests, and other vehicles as discussed before.

Perhaps more important than implementing a temporary reduction in price to the final consumer is the use of trade promotion to gain the cooperation of the retailer in support of other promotional and marketing programs. Getting a retailer to use in-store displays or to provide valuable shelf space may be critically important to the success of a marketing program and may only be accomplished through the use of effective trade promotion.

The major disadvantage of trade promotion from the perspective of the manufacturer is the loss of managerial control. Retailers may or may not take advantage of the promotion, and they may alter the promotion as well. While it might seem a simple solution to establish stringent criteria for the retailer's use of the promotion, such criteria are often difficult to enforce. This is especially true of large retailers, who represent substantial sales volume and are in an extremely competitive environment.

Despite any problems, trade promotions are a necessary part of business for most manufacturers. In fact, it is quite difficult for a manufacturer to implement any marketing strategy without a trade promotion component.

Distribution-Channel Management. Ideally, the manufacturer would like to be the dominant force in the distribution channel, which includes the manufacturer, wholesalers, and retailers. The manufacturer should be able to maximize profitability with strong brands that consumers demand, thereby forcing the trade to comply with the strategies of the manufacturer in order to have products to sell. Unfortunately, from the perspective of the manufacturer, this type of channel control rarely exists.

Trade promotion is one tool the manufacturer can use to gain cooperation from the trade, but it may be diminishing in its effectiveness. As retailers increase in their concentration, or become part of larger chains, their marketplace power increases. Moreover, the trend toward increased retail concentration will probably continue in the future. This may mean that the retailer, not the manufacturer, will be the dominant force in the distribution channel. Thus, the giant retail chain with its access to the final consumer may well be in a position to dictate its marketing strategy to the manufacturer. Certainly, the relative strength of the retail chain contributes to the importance of trade promotion.

One result of increasing retail concentration is a substantially more sophisticated retailer. This is especially apparent in food retailing. The larger chains are beginning to view their shelf space on a profit-center basis and are employing increasingly sophisticated models in its allocation. Obviously, manufacturers must increase their sophistication to remain competitive.

BRAND-FAMILY MANAGEMENT. Most manufacturers have both multiple lines within a single brand and multiple brands. The obvious consideration in the promotion of any single brand or line is the impact that its promotion may have on other lines and brands. The manufacturer needs to decide how to allocate promotional dollars most efficiently across both brands and lines to maximize profit.

The critical question is how much of the promotion of one brand or of one line benefits others. Most evidence suggests that while there might be some benefit, it is probably minimal. The seeming inability of sales promotion for established brands to produce increased long-term sales volume after a promotion, and the differential effects of package size, suggest sales promotion would have a minimal sales impact on other brands in the family. However, there might be some negative impact on related brands and lines if one is so heavily promoted that the brand image is damaged. Although the degree of impact on related brands and other lines is not clearly understood, there may well be some effect. The manager should certainly examine the profitability for each member of the entire brand family to assess this potential impact.

COMPETITIVE ACTIVITY. An interesting finding from the examination of scanner data is that the direct effects on competition from a single promotional effort are minimal. In other words, the promotional program of one brand at one point in time does not appear to have much impact on the level of business of competing brands. In addition, when competing promotions take place within the same product category, they tend to reduce the impact of both in terms of incremental business.

In the short term, at least, sales promotion does not seem to have much impact on the base level of business, but it certainly has considerable impact on incremental business and, hence, on overall market share. If one brand does not promote and another promotes heavily, the heavily promoted brand should enjoy a higher share. There is, then, pressure to meet competitive promotional levels to maintain market share.

A brand must maintain the promotional levels established by the competing brands within a product category in order to maintain the status quo. This means that manufacturers must continuously monitor competing promotions to be certain that they do not lose the competitive edge.

MANUFACTURER DECISIONS. A manufacturer must make a number of critical decisions each time it considers a promotional program. The decisions for the most part cross the boundaries of both consumer and trade promotions. These decisions are summarized in the following six categories.

Feature Promotion. Probably the first decision is whether to include a promotion in the advertising program. For example, coupons might be included in magazine advertisements. Other promotions, such as contests or sweepstakes, premiums, or special packages also might be featured in the national advertising program.

The manufacturer may also attempt to influence the retailer to feature a promotion in its advertising through cooperative advertising offers. Making available the appropriate advertising copy and a sufficiently attractive cooperative agreement would certainly increase the likelihood that the retailer would feature the promotion. The evidence clearly demonstrates that featuring a promotion in supporting advertising greatly enhances its impact. Generally, the manufacturer can manipulate the ratios in a cooperative advertising program, including both the proportion of the advertising expense it is willing to reimburse the retailer, and the maximum proportion of sales it is willing to reimburse. For example, a manufacturer may reimburse up to 50 percent of the cost of the advertising space or time purchased by the retailer up to a maximum of 3 percent of the gross purchases the retailer makes from the manufacturer during some specified period of time. Increasing the proportion of the advertising expense the manufacturer will reimburse the retailer or increasing the proportion of sales should be considered as part of the profitability analysis of the promotion.

Displays. Like advertising, the use of in-store displays clearly enhances the impact of a promotion. Displays alone generate more sales, but not nearly as many as displays with a special price. So, in general, if a display can be used, it will substantially improve sales. For most product categories, an in-store display without feature advertising generates a higher level of sales than an advertising feature without an in-store display at the same price.

A manufacturer may prepare and distribute display materials to the retailer. This can represent a substantial expense, depending on the complexity and the nature of the display. A hidden cost in the use of displays is the additional promotional support needed to get the retailer to use the display.

Most retailers receive many more displays or display offers than they can possibly use. Hence, manufacturers must also offer trade price promotion support to gain the necessary cooperation. The high-traffic areas within the store are most desirable, and thus especially in demand. Some special positions, such as front-aisle ends, require a direct payment to the retailer. Again, all the costs should be included in a profitability analysis against the increased sales volume the display should generate.

Additional Allowances for the Retailer. How much of a trade allowance to provide the retailer is always an important consideration. Presumably, the greater the allowance, the greater the likelihood of obtaining retailer cooperation. Additional allowances may also increase the chance that the retailer will provide additional effort in the promotion. Again, based upon past experience, the increase in trade allowance should be carefully evaluated in terms of potential profitability.

Raised Shelf Price. Another possible strategy is to raise shelf price. If the brand is strong, an announced higher shelf price may have the same effect as an increased trade allowance, as it makes the current price lower than the future price. Of course, considerations in this decision are the relative position of the brand and competitive conditions within the product category. A key consideration is probable competitive reaction.

Promotion Duration. The length of time the promotion should be in effect is another critical manufacturer decision. On one hand, the manufacturer wants to be certain that consumers have enough time to respond; on the other hand, the promotion should not last so long that it becomes accepted as the normal selling condition. An important consideration would be the normal purchase cycle, or average length of time between purchases. Retailers are also likely to cooperate for only limited periods of time.

The type of promotion being used should also affect promotion duration. Contests and sweepstakes, for example, should probably last longer than the purchase cycle for most grocery store products. The same is true for manufacturer-distributed coupons, because the consumer needs time to take advantage of the offer during the normal purchase cycle. As a practical matter, stores are likely to cooperate for periods much longer than a week, except in highly seasonal categories.

Package Size. Selecting the proper package size to promote to a target market is critical in the success of a promotional program. As discussed before, different geographic markets, even different demographic segments, purchase different package sizes. The decision of which package size or sizes to promote should be carefully considered in terms of the marketing objectives.

INTRODUCING NEW PRODUCTS.

A special marketing problem is the introduction of new products. A new product has two unique problems when compared to established products: no shelf space and no consumer experience. Sales promotion can be used to help remedy both problems.

Projecting Sales from Test Markets. New products pose especially difficult problems for most manufacturers. The overwhelming majority of new products do not succeed in the marketplace; thus a manufacturer must be able to distinguish the winning products from the others. A typical method used to experiment with new products is the test market. A test market is simply a representative single market area in which the performance of a new product is evaluated. This approach involves a minimum of investment in the product itself and in associated marketing expenses.

Measuring the results from the test market and controlling the various marketing variables that influence the success or failure of the product are the traditional problems with test markets. For example, an excellent product may appear to fail because competitive advertising and promotion overwhelm it.

A solution to some of these problems has been the introduction of the electronic test market, complete with scanner panels and targetable television. These sophisticated systems have greatly enhanced the ability to discriminate between successful and unsuccessful products. The electronic test markets have also reduced the time necessary to make the judgment from the test. Perhaps one shortcoming of these test facilities is their inability to test trade reaction. The access through the trade to the consumer is forced, with the focus of the test on consumer reaction to the product.

Product categories that are not sold through grocery or drug outlets may not be easily tested using electronic test markets. However, testing capabilities are generally being expanded to include other types of outlets, including general-merchandise stores. The selection and design of test-market experiments are complex subjects, which are made considerably more complex when the models and procedures for projecting sales from them are also included. Whenever possible, the same high-quality data should be employed to evaluate new products as are used to evaluate sales promotion programs.

Obtaining Distribution. Getting access to valuable shelf space for any product, new or established, is a difficult task. Convincing retailers that existing products should be taken off the shelf to make room for a new one without any sales history is not easy. As retailers become more sophisticated, the task may become even more difficult.

Sales promotion, in the form of trade promotion, is a virtual necessity in obtaining trade cooperation. The trade requires additional incentive to accept the risk to its profit that a new product poses. The requirements for trade promotion in the introduction of a new product add considerably to the cost of introducing that new product.

Getting Trial. Once the manufacturer obtains distribution, it must get the consumer to try the product. Several sales promotion methods can be used for the purpose, including sampling and coupons. Providing free samples of the new product or attractive price offers can be very expensive. The manufacturer is faced not only with substantial trade-promotion expense, but also with substantial consumer-promotion expense.

Encouraging Repeat Purchasing. Sales promotion can be quite effective in getting the initial consumer experience with the new product, but success is still not guaranteed. Most products, new or established, find themselves in an extremely competitive environment. Competitors continue with their promotional programs, and they likely have the advantage of more than one trial experience. A new product must also be promoted to encourage repeat purchasing, even after a trial has been obtained.

Additional couponing and other promotional efforts must continue to be employed to encourage repeat purchasing. A new product introduction then requires trade promotion to obtain distribution, consumer promotion to obtain consumer trial, and more consumer promotion to encourage repeat product purchasing in the competitive environment where most products are found.

Case 4: Colas I

Reviewing trade promotional activity on an event-by-event basis usually leads to the conclusion that more promotion generates more volume and, consequently, more revenue. As long as the promoted products are sold at prices above the variable cost of production and distribution, they contribute to profit and overhead. In this case, the consequences of an increasing rate of promotion in a market will be examined.

Cola sales in all major grocery outlets in a market were collected using supermarket scanners. Information about the type of trade promotion was collected to determine sales with in-store display only, feature ad only, and combination of feature ad with in-store display. Tables 5.1 and 5.2 show volume movements and prices under these various conditions for the dominant pack sizes of Brand B (Table 5.1) and Brand A (Table 5.2). These pack sizes account for about 80 percent of cola sales in the city. Prices are given on a standard unit basis, and not on the actual shelf prices of the dominant package size. In Tables 5.3 and 5.4, volumes have been normalized for differences in overall store sales that occur from cell to cell and week to week (volume per $1,000 of all commodity volume) for Brand B (Table 5.3) and Brand A (Table 5.4).

Tables 5.5 and 5.6 give four-week moving averages for several key variables in the case for Brand B (Table 5.5) and Brand A (Table 5.6). Refer to case 7 in chapter 6 for the general background on the cola product category.

Tables 5.1 and 5.2 give city volume by promotion type. This table will indicate the contribution of promotional activity to city sales, but since it is not adjusted for the size of the stores promoting in any given week, it provides little insight into the impact of promotional activity compared to base sales.

Tables 5.3 and 5.4 are normalizations of Tables 5.1 and 5.2, obtained by dividing the volume numbers in each column by a measure of the total store activity (shopper counts or total store sales) for stores running each promotional type. Tables of this type are useful for comparing the relative impact of any promotion type versus base sales, but they do not indicate the overall importance of promotion to total brand sales.

Tables 5.5 and 5.6 provide some four-week moving averages of key variables. The column headed *Promotion Opportunity* indicates the degree of market coverage by promotion. For example, Brand B (Table 5.5) shows a 68.75 in week 4 under Promotion Opportunity. This means that in the first four weeks, 68.75 percent of all grocery-store-dollars spending (all commodities) took place in stores that had an advertising feature, in-store display, or both on Brand B.

The *Adjusted Dollar Sales* column indicates the total retail sales revenue generated on the brand across all stores in the market. The three volume columns are adjusted for store sizes and can be considered as proportional to brand volume sales per $1,000 spent in the market in stores with the promotional conditions indicated.

Question 1. Without the aid of any computer statistical analysis techniques, trends and changes in these trends may be difficult to determine in the highly variable week-to-week scanner data. Two methods used to overcome this difficulty are moving averages and summarization over longer time periods.

a. Plot the percentage of market covered by promotion for Brand A from the four-week moving averages (Table 5.6).
b. Plot the percentage of market covered by promotion for Brand A from the four-week moving averages, but use only those weeks that are evenly divisible by four.

Contrast the results from these two plots in their ability to illustrate the degree of change over time in the data, and in their ease of interpretation.

Question 2. Both Brand A and Brand B exhibit significant variation in the percentage of market covered across the time period considered. Plot from Table 5.5 the normalized volume on feature-only events versus percentage coverage of market by promotion for the brand (promotion opportunity). How does increasing the promotion frequency in this market affect the average sales on feature-only events?

Question 3. Using Tables 5.5 and 5.6, plot for both Brand A and Brand B the normalized volume from nonpromoting stores versus the percentage promotion coverage of the market by the brand. How does increasing the promotion frequency in this market affect the average sales in nonpromoting stores?

Question 4. For Brand A from Table 5.4, plot normalized nonpromoted volume versus the nonpromoted price. Plot the feature-only volume versus the feature-only price. Discuss the relationship between price and volume shown in these plots.

Question 5. Plot from Table 5.6 the total normalized volume and total sales revenue for Brand A versus the percentage promotion coverage of the market. Repeat the plot for Brand B (Table 5.5). What do these graphs suggest about the relation between promotion coverage and total sales volume, and about total retailer revenue from the brands?

Question 6. For students who have access to computerized regression analysis. Consider Brand A from Tables 5.4 and 5.6, and use regression techniques to do the following:

a. Relate nonpromotion sales to nonpromotion price.
b. Relate nonpromotion sales to promotion coverage.
c. Relate nonpromotion sales to both nonpromotion price and promotion coverage.
d. Relate feature-only sales to feature-only price.
e. Relate feature-only sales to promotion coverage.
f. Relate feature-only sales to both feature-only price and promotion coverage.

Question 7. From the results in question 6, compare Brand A sales from Table 5.4 for the display-only events and the combination feature and display events to your best estimates of feature-only volume and nonpromoted volume under similar conditions of pricing and promotion coverage. Discuss the results.

Table 5.1

CITY SALES OF DOMINANT COLA PACKS BY WEEK
Price Is Volume Weighted Average
Sales by Promotional Type

Brand B
(12 Pack–Indianapolis)

Week	No Promotion Vol	Price	Price Reduction Vol	Price	Feature Only Vol	Price	Display Only Vol	Price	Feature & Display Vol	Price
1 DEC 08	2735	5.00	1591	4.07	5834	5.02	6157	4.41	13538	4.59
2 DEC 15	4023	5.22	2260	3.88	1461	4.39	12127	4.55	6270	4.55
3 DEC 22	2474	5.17	3084	4.08	2711	2.65	15420	4.36	17506	3.48
4 DEC 29	746	5.04	4218	4.23	1015	3.99	15264	4.29	6867	3.99
5 JAN 05	1363	5.13	682	3.59	5463	4.09	8073	4.39	11838	4.24
6 JAN 12	5151	5.27	0	.	1874	4.22	6109	5.10	14996	4.24
7 JAN 19	2853	4.75	970	4.16	3254	5.32	11287	4.57	2569	5.19
8 JAN 26	4961	5.19	795	3.99	4746	4.28	9626	4.90	2918	4.31
9 FEB 02	2110	4.86	427	3.98	2886	3.75	7153	4.83	16865	3.59
10 FEB 09	1918	5.08	839	4.16	3006	5.27	10681	4.63	6761	4.41
11 FEB 16	6948	4.97	0	.	660	4.73	9741	4.91	6109	4.16
12 FEB 23	2272	5.15	0	.	3875	5.09	8586	4.57	5431	4.67
13 MAR 02	3701	5.18	4087	3.88	838	4.25	11228	4.74	1871	4.01
14 MAR 09	1708	5.42	0	.	6207	4.55	2183	4.80	20596	4.16
15 MAR 16	5326	5.19	2956	3.78	0	.	11471	4.77	0	.
16 MAR 23	3140	5.14	18	3.94	2232	4.24	7582	4.68	17524	3.88
17 MAR 30	1082	4.86	1423	3.98	7803	3.99	7594	4.33	19487	4.05
18 APR 06	696	5.19	817	4.01	18569	3.93	7709	4.45	19443	4.07
19 APR 13	2921	5.33	1994	4.89	977	4.17	11140	4.55	7819	4.17
20 APR 20	1196	4.85	1178	4.15	4349	3.90	7765	4.38	13824	3.67
21 APR 27	1687	5.25	3893	4.17	592	4.32	8001	4.41	5905	4.25
22 MAY 04	464	5.33	2505	4.53	6370	3.32	5551	4.69	27601	3.04
23 MAY 11	702	5.55	3390	3.93	2873	3.23	12005	4.38	6958	2.66
24 MAY 18	2160	5.11	437	4.12	2981	2.94	8274	4.63	21707	2.88
25 MAY 25	3936	4.70	347	4.11	3655	2.85	11380	4.58	20149	2.88
26 JUN 01	1798	4.53	1173	3.51	1956	5.06	11993	4.41	12251	3.72
27 JUN 08	5062	5.19	349	4.32	4121	3.93	7358	4.11	13198	3.35
28 JUN 15	3082	4.91	412	3.96	22345	2.89	3873	4.07	34052	3.12
29 JUN 22	5989	4.94	4289	4.18	0	.	14245	4.11	1196	4.65
30 JUN 29	3835	4.57	4085	4.26	2548	2.39	18257	4.00	16758	2.39

Week	No Promotion		Price Reduction		Feature Only		Display Only		Feature & Display	
	Vol	Price	Vol	Price	Vol	Price	Vol	Price	Vol	Price
31 JUL 06	2808	4.84	3013	4.15	2459	2.39	9291	4.08	21512	2.48
32 JUL 13	3076	4.77	762	4.96	1329	3.85	13101	4.41	11581	3.40
33 JUL 20	2034	4.58	1865	3.99	3179	3.86	13060	4.14	3661	4.02
34 JUL 27	4324	4.75	1400	4.36	2506	4.05	4157	4.40	18990	3.67
35 AUG 03	1529	4.43	1901	3.99	2618	4.00	11781	4.26	27048	3.76
36 AUG 10	3733	4.80	2533	4.08	1247	3.85	18652	4.28	911	3.97
37 AUG 17	3818	4.77	2216	3.99	3256	4.74	4311	4.09	17577	4.19
38 AUG 24	624	3.99	1565	3.99	77349	2.75	3785	4.43	52003	3.52
39 AUG 31	5286	4.94	2853	4.10	3210	2.65	15554	4.43	28163	2.75
40 SEP 07	6327	4.65	2060	4.48	3409	4.02	9310	4.35	19424	3.45
41 SEP 14	2969	4.92	2645	4.21	6862	4.03	10303	4.18	26435	2.89
42 SEP 21	4692	4.53	328	4.11	3997	4.63	11199	4.21	13051	3.67
43 SEP 28	6846	4.98	0	.	3130	4.40	13079	4.16	7859	4.20
44 OCT 05	7834	5.08	410	5.32	212	4.39	12878	4.56	22581	3.82
45 OCT 12	1426	4.56	449	4.65	3574	3.52	15681	4.23	31305	2.72
46 OCT 19	3291	4.79	0	.	430	4.65	18380	4.97	17051	4.17
47 OCT 26	1892	4.82	0	.	3307	4.29	22009	4.78	1954	3.99
48 NOV 02	1981	4.69	0	.	1622	4.41	4118	4.55	49615	3.87
49 NOV 09	4772	4.88	531	5.72	4919	4.19	5277	4.37	32134	4.14
50 NOV 16	7273	5.09	12818	3.99	0	.	18356	4.53	0	.
51 NOV 23	5364	5.26	1527	4.48	2570	4.35	32087	4.07	10727	4.49
52 NOV 30	4220	4.79	355	5.33	5383	3.72	5782	4.56	43194	3.08

Table 5.2

CITY SALES OF DOMINANT COLA PACKS BY WEEK
Price Is Volume Weighted Average
Sales by Promotional Type

Brand A
(12 Pack—Indianapolis)

Week	No Promotion		Price Reduction		Feature Only		Display Only		Feature & Display	
	Vol	Price	Vol	Price	Vol	Price	Vol	Price	Vol	Price
1 DEC 8	5031	4.98	1343	3.91	35	3.29	8235	4.68	121	3.31
2 DEC 15	3703	5.01	1210	4.44	2661	2.88	7306	4.84	4823	2.79
3 DEC 22	1041	5.37	1917	4.19	9248	2.70	4698	4.07	47217	2.57
4 DEC 29	880	5.28	2194	4.16	2011	2.51	9654	4.26	7267	2.93
5 JAN 5	2566	5.29	3143	4.25	0	.	10990	4.24	533	4.65
6 JAN 12	2700	5.17	1227	4.39	1262	3.32	10594	4.69	6414	3.66
7 JAN 19	3692	5.16	1343	4.39	1140	4.49	6591	4.61	11452	4.03
8 JAN 26	3145	5.29	1297	4.38	5313	4.01	3896	4.95	16763	4.11

Week	No Promotion		Price Reduction		Feature Only		Display Only		Feature & Display	
	Vol	Price	Vol	Price	Vol	Price	Vol	Price	Vol	Price
9 FEB 2	5020	5.08	1651	4.55	0	.	9046	4.70	2583	4.49
10 FEB 9	4300	5.10	0	.	3469	4.55	4762	5.05	4609	4.41
11 FEB 16	3636	5.08	774	4.59	8114	4.48	3728	4.62	7517	3.63
12 FEB 23	4044	4.91	875	4.66	2937	4.68	4727	5.15	5729	4.28
13 MAR 2	1630	4.61	1444	4.75	12836	4.43	865	3.94	10100	4.38
14 MAR 9	3527	5.07	2625	4.32	0	.	7688	4.85	0	.
15 MAR 16	908	5.11	1167	4.96	15471	4.26	454	4.52	13623	4.22
16 MAR 23	1391	4.79	2597	4.30	2922	4.86	5365	4.71	5162	4.24
17 MAR 30	2187	5.09	1445	4.77	10522	3.66	7368	4.78	1105	4.02
18 APR 6	2113	4.94	3281	4.37	5611	4.20	4294	4.93	14395	4.29
19 APR 13	910	5.02	1559	4.24	9465	3.87	5372	4.42	5996	4.64
20 APR 20	2383	5.18	1657	4.39	3789	2.67	6943	4.63	15758	2.74
21 APR 27	1720	5.13	606	4.01	2383	4.37	7542	4.34	5421	4.41
22 MAY 4	3306	4.96	1430	4.43	0	.	7821	4.46	5051	2.65
23 MAY 11	2321	5.04	1364	4.70	2380	3.97	3987	4.40	10764	3.90
24 MAY 18	3102	5.16	2452	4.29	986	2.64	6785	4.45	12617	3.21
25 MAY 25	1232	5.11	748	3.95	15251	2.97	4437	4.55	29220	2.64
26 JUN 1	2022	5.12	2280	3.47	2081	4.12	3126	4.82	14797	3.74
27 JUN 8	922	4.58	0	.	14220	3.45	11956	4.08	18124	3.53
28 JUN 15	3587	4.97	2822	3.52	0	.	15887	4.24	8533	2.99
29 JUN 22	922	4.92	899	4.42	15497	3.30	2906	4.05	19365	3.26
30 JUN 29	3053	4.76	9801	3.50	0	.	12784	4.05	0	.
31 JUL 6	4464	4.56	1794	4.23	11171	3.23	12285	3.93	1767	3.85
32 JUL 13	2177	4.20	0	.	5132	3.97	6794	3.86	22752	4.00
33 JUL 20	3495	4.93	282	3.84	7876	3.54	8454	4.54	11167	3.91
34 JUL 27	4010	4.33	466	3.45	2214	3.99	8521	4.25	19451	3.96
35 AUG 3	4648	5.15	1113	3.45	8334	3.72	8536	4.46	9635	4.08
36 AUG 10	3254	4.51	0	.	5473	4.03	3755	3.95	30641	3.78
37 AUG 17	4707	5.03	0	.	9930	3.14	18043	4.36	4908	2.65
38 AUG 24	4814	4.77	1135	3.99	0	.	11295	4.42	1203	3.59
39 AUG 31	3668	4.57	583	3.72	7553	3.00	11938	4.27	29113	2.73
40 SEP 7	3289	4.30	279	3.83	5711	4.83	11079	4.22	9381	4.69
41 SEP 14	3176	4.77	9611	3.49	1247	3.99	12852	4.35	4324	3.97
42 SEP 21	4667	4.79	751	5.36	852	3.98	8457	4.45	5827	4.21
43 SEP 28	4120	4.49	106	3.99	5240	3.82	6494	4.37	27851	2.67
44 OCT 5	4507	4.53	0	.	3043	4.83	7820	4.39	9995	4.50
45 OCT 12	3465	4.87	9675	3.84	346	4.39	3425	4.89	5562	4.28
46 OCT 19	4319	4.58	0	.	3567	4.79	5251	4.55	6385	4.37
47 OCT 26	2763	4.87	0	.	8261	4.30	1444	4.58	9255	4.62
48 NOV 2	5916	4.98	0	.	1052	4.39	10041	4.68	0	.
49 NOV 9	5342	5.03	0	.	9965	3.67	7878	4.70	3077	3.59
50 NOV 16	3409	5.12	742	4.25	3039	5.13	4372	4.27	11968	4.53
51 NOV 23	4322	4.81	0	.	7154	3.89	8765	4.30	22671	3.70
52 NOV 30	7689	5.09	930	4.26	868	4.25	13613	4.63	554	4.25

Table 5.3, Part 1

CITY SALES OF DOMINANT COLA PACKS BY WEEK

Price Is Volume Weighted Average/Normalized Sales by Promotional Type

Brand B (12 Pack—Indianapolis)

Week	TPACV	Volume No Promo	Price No Promo	Volume Price Only	Price Price Only	Volume Feature Only
DEC 08	101	184.16	5.00	123.61	4.07	245.51
DEC 15	106	177.68	5.22	199.63	3.88	193.58
DEC 22	100	164.93	5.17	181.41	4.08	1355.50
DEC 29	100	124.33	5.04	183.39	4.23	507.50
JAN 05	100	272.60	5.13	97.43	3.59	248.32
JAN 12	99	203.98	5.27	.	.	154.61
JAN 19	99	141.22	4.75	137.19	4.16	292.86
JAN 26	99	175.41	5.19	157.41	3.99	939.71
FEB 02	106	172.05	4.86	90.52	3.98	203.94
FEB 09	102	113.22	5.08	222.86	4.16	245.68
FEB 16	105	253.31	4.97	.	.	120.31
FEB 23	106	100.35	5.15	.	.	194.48
MAR 02	105	155.69	5.18	298.01	3.88	458.28
MAR 09	109	161.61	5.42	.	.	227.34
MAR 16	110	179.49	5.19	225.81	3.78	.
MAR 23	107	145.82	5.14	3.34	3.94	207.31
MAR 30	106	99.56	4.86	157.12	3.98	615.42
APR 06	113	91.03	5.19	160.28	4.01	840.66
APR 13	111	177.76	5.33	144.10	4.89	188.28
APR 20	106	93.35	4.85	128.73	4.15	297.03
APR 27	98	121.74	5.25	218.51	4.17	119.62
MAY 04	98	117.20	5.33	158.18	4.53	429.04
MAY 11	96	86.85	5.55	167.75	3.93	473.90
MAY 18	99	137.78	5.11	55.75	4.12	380.31
MAY 25	101	180.70	4.70	43.81	4.11	922.89
JUN 01	100	128.43	4.53	117.30	3.51	150.46
JUN 08	99	161.66	5.19	345.51	4.32	407.98
JUN 15	100	385.25	4.91	412.00	3.96	798.04
JUN 22	100	239.56	4.94	306.36	4.18	.
JUN 29	99	199.82	4.57	202.21	4.26	420.42
JUL 06	100	108.00	4.84	273.91	4.15	614.75
JUL 13	100	118.31	4.77	152.40	4.96	265.80
JUL 20	100	113.00	4.58	621.67	3.99	176.61
JUL 27	99	203.85	4.75	173.25	4.36	275.66
AUG 03	102	141.78	4.43	646.34	3.99	534.07
AUG 10	99	184.78	4.80	417.95	4.08	617.27
AUG 17	101	214.23	4.77	559.54	3.99	274.05
AUG 24	102	90.93	3.99	532.10	3.99	4383.11
AUG 31	101	254.23	4.94	360.19	4.10	1621.05
SEP 07	100	275.09	4.65	343.33	4.48	681.80
SEP 14	101	187.42	4.92	333.93	4.21	364.77
SEP 21	103	178.99	4.53	84.46	4.11	257.31
SEP 28	100	228.20	4.98	.	.	240.77
OCT 05	100	244.81	5.08	205.00	5.32	106.00
OCT 12	101	205.75	4.56	226.75	4.65	277.67
OCT 19	100	205.69	4.79	.	.	215.00
OCT 26	97	187.27	4.82	.	.	409.16
NOV 02	101	222.31	4.69	.	.	182.02
NOV 09	100	280.71	4.88	265.50	5.72	307.44
NOV 16	100	242.43	5.09	2563.60	3.99	.
NOV 23	100	157.76	5.26	305.40	4.48	428.33
NOV 30	100	191.82	4.79	177.50	5.33	897.17

Table 5.3, Part 2

CITY SALES OF DOMINANT COLA PACKS BY WEEK

Price Is Volume Weighted Average/Normalized Sales by Promotional Type

Brand B (12 Pack—Indianapolis)

Week	Price Feature Only	Volume Display Only	Price Display Only	Volume Feature & Display	Price Feature & Display
DEC 08	5.02	518.21	4.41	369.55	4.59
DEC 15	4.39	367.27	4.55	246.16	4.55
DEC 22	2.65	275.36	4.36	1750.60	3.48
DEC 29	3.99	254.40	4.29	763.00	3.99
JAN 05	4.09	336.38	4.39	281.86	4.24
JAN 12	4.22	232.61	5.10	412.39	4.24
JAN 19	5.32	219.10	4.57	254.33	5.19
JAN 26	4.28	194.48	4.90	240.74	4.31
FEB 02	3.75	315.92	4.83	364.83	3.59
FEB 09	5.27	241.46	4.63	359.18	4.41
FEB 16	4.73	259.86	4.91	238.63	4.16
FEB 23	5.09	278.83	4.57	239.87	4.67
MAR 02	4.25	223.28	4.74	292.34	4.01
MAR 09	4.55	247.86	4.80	417.59	4.16
MAR 16	.	215.47	4.77	.	.
MAR 23	4.24	272.61	4.68	574.47	3.88
MAR 30	3.99	270.49	4.33	551.72	4.05
APR 06	3.93	274.97	4.45	586.82	4.07
APR 13	4.17	322.02	4.55	301.36	4.17
APR 20	3.90	223.30	4.38	539.52	3.67
APR 27	4.32	224.54	4.41	238.64	4.25
MAY 04	3.32	207.71	4.69	774.60	3.04
MAY 11	3.23	220.02	4.38	860.78	2.66
MAY 18	2.94	241.27	4.63	692.33	2.88
MAY 25	2.85	212.85	4.58	1565.42	2.88
JUN 01	5.06	315.61	4.41	490.04	3.72
JUN 08	3.93	331.11	4.11	373.31	3.35
JUN 15	2.89	193.65	4.07	791.91	3.12
JUN 22	.	254.38	4.11	239.20	4.65
JUN 29	2.39	516.41	4.00	873.18	2.39
JUL 06	2.39	299.71	4.08	768.29	2.48
JUL 13	3.85	247.19	4.41	1052.82	3.40
JUL 20	3.86	277.87	4.14	261.50	4.02
JUL 27	4.05	146.98	4.40	569.70	3.67
AUG 03	4.00	250.35	4.26	788.26	3.76
AUG 10	3.85	279.78	4.28	180.38	3.97
AUG 17	4.74	217.71	4.09	377.72	4.19
AUG 24	2.75	227.10	4.43	930.58	3.52
AUG 31	2.65	270.85	4.43	2370.39	2.75
SEP 07	4.02	358.08	4.35	485.60	3.45
SEP 14	4.03	495.53	4.18	721.60	2.89
SEP 21	4.63	320.42	4.21	672.13	3.67
SEP 28	4.40	421.90	4.16	302.27	4.20
OCT 05	4.39	357.72	4.56	806.46	3.82
OCT 12	3.52	287.96	4.23	1317.42	2.72
OCT 19	4.65	367.60	4.97	532.84	4.17
OCT 26	4.29	302.56	4.78	276.29	3.99
NOV 02	4.41	189.05	4.55	821.49	3.87
NOV 09	4.19	277.74	4.37	698.57	4.14
NOV 16	.	282.40	4.53	.	.
NOV 23	4.35	1234.12	4.07	369.90	4.49
NOV 30	3.72	304.32	4.56	846.94	3.08

Table 5.4, Part 1

CITY SALES OF DOMINANT COLA PACKS BY WEEK

Price Is Volume Weighted Average/Normalized Sales by Promotional Type

Brand A (12 Pack—Indianapolis)

Week		TPACV	Volume No Promo	Price No Promo	Volume Price Only	Price Price Only	Volume Feature Only
DEC	08	101	141.58	4.98	107.57	3.91	7.29
DEC	15	106	147.56	5.01	90.01	4.44	269.92
DEC	22	95	130.13	5.37	147.46	4.19	1027.56
DEC	29	96	111.16	5.28	130.42	4.16	677.39
JAN	05	95	171.07	5.29	142.86	4.25	.
JAN	12	97	112.50	5.17	306.75	4.39	631.00
JAN	19	98	138.15	5.16	452.28	4.39	143.97
JAN	26	112	134.49	5.29	499.19	4.38	408.97
FEB	02	118	123.41	5.08	243.52	4.55	.
FEB	09	107	119.82	5.10	.	.	214.80
FEB	16	130	123.09	5.08	174.69	4.59	392.42
FEB	23	117	154.02	4.91	177.73	4.66	198.86
MAR	02	128	135.83	4.61	213.93	4.75	342.29
MAR	09	106	114.54	5.07	144.92	4.32	.
MAR	16	125	107.48	5.11	217.08	4.96	387.39
MAR	23	109	101.89	4.79	190.24	4.30	171.24
MAR	30	106	80.41	5.09	149.73	4.77	999.40
APR	06	105	113.60	4.94	205.80	4.37	422.33
APR	13	97	55.83	5.02	147.82	4.24	705.15
APR	20	104	164.78	5.18	107.84	4.39	349.34
APR	27	102	186.64	5.13	54.80	4.01	161.61
MAY	04	103	121.05	4.96	75.92	4.43	.
MAY	11	110	146.23	5.04	85.93	4.70	158.76
MAY	18	99	197.87	5.16	125.13	4.29	335.44
MAY	25	114	108.04	5.11	56.85	3.95	915.06
JUN	01	111	112.22	5.12	168.72	3.47	144.37
JUN	08	105	80.68	4.58	.	.	1148.54
JUN	15	99	208.89	4.97	349.22	3.52	.
JUN	22	104	159.81	4.92	93.50	4.42	671.54
JUN	29	110	115.80	4.76	539.05	3.50	.
JUL	06	101	204.94	4.56	164.72	4.23	1611.82
JUL	13	102	201.87	4.20	.	.	523.46
JUL	20	103	179.99	4.93	145.23	3.84	579.45
JUL	27	105	200.50	4.33	69.90	3.45	387.45
AUG	03	100	202.09	5.15	159.00	3.45	833.40
AUG	10	102	207.44	4.51	.	.	429.42
AUG	17	100	188.28	5.03	.	.	1655.00
AUG	24	100	160.47	4.77	126.11	3.99	.
AUG	31	101	154.36	4.57	84.12	3.72	1271.42
SEP	07	102	167.74	4.30	71.15	3.83	448.09
SEP	14	102	147.25	4.77	1225.40	3.49	423.98
SEP	21	100	186.68	4.79	187.75	5.36	170.40
SEP	28	101	143.49	4.49	35.69	3.99	661.55
OCT	05	102	183.89	4.53	.	.	258.65
OCT	12	99	103.95	4.87	532.13	3.84	171.27
OCT	19	99	158.36	4.58	.	.	168.16
OCT	26	103	91.80	4.87	.	.	531.80
NOV	02	104	143.08	4.98	.	.	182.35
NOV	09	104	132.28	5.03	.	.	1480.51
NOV	16	106	116.57	5.12	262.17	4.25	201.33
NOV	23	105	137.52	4.81	.	.	938.96
NOV	30	105	192.23	5.09	195.30	4.26	303.80

Table 5.4, Part 2
CITY SALES OF DOMINANT COLA PACKS BY WEEK
Price Is Volume Weighted Average/Normalized Sales by Promotional Type
Brand A (12 Pack—Indianapolis)

Week		Price Feature Only	Volume Display Only	Price Display Only	Volume Feature & Display	Price Feature & Display
DEC	08	3.29	209.14	4.68	25.20	3.31
DEC	15	2.88	209.02	4.84	413.96	2.79
DEC	22	2.70	313.20	4.07	944.34	2.57
DEC	29	2.51	232.28	4.26	282.44	2.93
JAN	05	.	207.36	4.24	106.60	4.65
JAN	12	3.32	179.56	4.69	801.75	3.66
JAN	19	4.49	237.82	4.61	361.56	4.03
JAN	26	4.01	187.44	4.95	450.12	4.11
FEB	02	.	209.30	4.70	277.09	4.49
FEB	09	4.55	183.02	5.05	256.86	4.41
FEB	16	4.48	162.85	4.62	407.17	3.63
FEB	23	4.68	169.44	5.15	258.60	4.28
MAR	02	4.43	144.17	3.94	299.26	4.38
MAR	09	.	163.25	4.85	.	.
MAR	16	4.26	197.05	4.52	341.12	4.22
MAR	23	4.86	179.66	4.71	275.00	4.24
MAR	30	3.66	195.30	4.78	139.94	4.02
APR	06	4.20	167.17	4.93	738.75	4.29
APR	13	3.87	200.11	4.42	231.63	4.64
APR	20	2.67	219.47	4.63	726.43	2.74
APR	27	4.37	233.82	4.34	202.84	4.41
MAY	04	.	169.49	4.46	1072.69	2.65
MAY	11	3.97	196.58	4.40	359.02	3.90
MAY	18	2.64	168.90	4.45	677.74	3.21
MAY	25	2.97	219.92	4.55	757.06	2.64
JUN	01	4.12	144.58	4.82	456.24	3.74
JUN	08	3.45	246.15	4.08	656.21	3.53
JUN	15	.	266.58	4.24	563.18	2.99
JUN	22	3.30	151.11	4.05	457.72	3.26
JUN	29	.	230.53	4.05	.	.
JUL	06	3.23	225.60	3.93	297.45	3.85
JUL	13	3.97	223.54	3.86	464.14	4.00
JUL	20	3.54	223.27	4.54	410.79	3.91
JUL	27	3.99	248.53	4.25	583.53	3.96
AUG	03	3.72	266.75	4.46	344.11	4.08
AUG	10	4.03	212.78	3.95	568.25	3.78
AUG	17	3.14	273.38	4.36	1636.00	2.65
AUG	24	.	205.36	4.42	200.50	3.59
AUG	31	3.00	344.50	4.27	1013.94	2.73
SEP	07	4.83	251.12	4.22	478.43	4.69
SEP	14	3.99	247.34	4.35	275.66	3.97
SEP	21	3.98	211.43	4.45	224.12	4.21
SEP	28	3.82	204.97	4.37	969.98	2.67
OCT	05	4.83	227.90	4.39	339.83	4.50
OCT	12	4.39	178.46	4.89	203.94	4.28
OCT	19	4.79	192.54	4.55	263.38	4.37
OCT	26	4.30	148.73	4.58	207.23	4.62
NOV	02	4.39	189.87	4.68	.	.
NOV	09	3.67	160.65	4.70	800.02	3.59
NOV	16	5.13	193.10	4.27	396.44	4.53
NOV	23	3.89	270.68	4.30	793.49	3.70
NOV	30	4.25	280.27	4.63	145.43	4.25

Table 5.5
CITY SALES OF DOMINANT COLA PACKS BY WEEK
Four-Week Moving Averages
Brand B

Week	Promotion Opportunity	Adjusted Dollar Sales	Total Volume	No Promotion Volume	Feature Only Volume
1	72.2772	1387.68	298.55	156.045	353.21
2	70.7174	1340.37	289.26	164.440	340.95
3	66.5283	1300.77	299.05	182.296	357.78
4	68.7500	1501.92	379.24	173.104	472.93
5	75.2500	1181.84	279.37	171.081	314.99
6	84.6869	1204.90	275.97	184.254	292.55
7	74.2424	1222.97	263.31	187.091	289.75
8	71.2121	1021.39	214.61	149.586	240.90
9	70.7547	1112.08	246.45	169.301	278.33
10	81.0877	1166.48	281.64	144.705	311.88
11	73.6134	1135.08	242.38	169.957	264.40
12	69.7682	1116.71	235.78	220.305	241.59
13	69.6474	1009.14	214.11	138.544	242.70
14	65.2435	1124.47	249.66	203.794	271.28
15	77.3825	1288.37	291.24	180.019	318.00
16	57.1983	1067.27	233.74	180.430	269.90
17	70.8320	1409.77	335.62	118.990	412.59
18	77.8708	1706.04	415.11	124.495	482.76
19	78.8749	1803.84	433.73	138.014	497.94
20	68.0567	1170.41	267.18	151.800	314.98
21	72.6099	1096.32	270.65	130.196	317.84
22	68.2959	1053.65	264.76	171.657	303.88
23	75.0801	1371.34	395.36	148.256	467.51
24	69.9025	1070.20	292.12	137.217	352.17
25	72.6879	1298.70	373.77	120.441	461.12
26	71.7228	1354.90	368.93	139.865	459.24
27	73.9192	1200.43	294.00	137.304	349.29
28	73.5076	1396.61	385.07	186.157	456.76
29	83.5000	1804.79	542.53	314.545	587.58
30	60.9015	1221.95	306.60	247.797	344.35
31	61.2045	1463.76	438.83	190.622	596.16
32	64.5000	1225.87	367.75	150.007	487.59
33	71.5000	1149.67	283.37	135.202	342.42
34	76.9268	1045.33	256.93	188.758	277.38
35	74.5989	1378.25	347.52	202.767	396.81
36	83.1402	1617.61	404.27	245.496	436.46
37	74.8575	1207.56	281.01	246.912	292.47
38	81.2124	2056.49	572.15	270.005	642.05
39	85.4688	3641.17	1152.61	253.008	1305.56

Week	Promotion Opportunity	Adjusted Dollar Sales	Total Volume	No Promotion Volume	Feature Only Volume
40	71.2153	1844.04	514.32	284.909	607.05
41	72.3094	1631.55	427.01	277.847	484.13
42	74.6539	1637.23	452.27	215.635	532.61
43	69.9272	1359.66	326.79	182.108	389.01
44	69.0000	1484.45	341.64	232.113	390.85
45	72.2723	1839.32	460.45	239.895	545.07
46	89.3168	1744.83	491.14	208.646	524.93
47	84.9742	1700.73	368.39	202.485	396.75
48	88.6950	1613.77	367.57	195.231	386.62
49	88.5668	2211.57	549.10	245.907	588.24
50	77.0000	1951.65	453.37	391.304	471.90
51	64.0000	1847.10	419.04	466.417	392.39
52	64.7500	2192.09	539.40	179.064	735.56
53	76.0000	2016.28	589.34	190.625	715.25

Table 5.6

CITY SALES OF DOMINANT COLA PACKS BY WEEK

Four-Week Moving Averages

Brand A

Week	Promotion Opportunity	Adjusted Dollar Sales	Total Volume	No Promotion Volume	Feature Only Volume
1	48.9802	715.10	152.216	132.737	171.314
2	50.8507	747.35	165.798	131.629	196.472
3	60.8467	1105.45	324.289	129.541	433.602
4	73.0651	1626.13	564.129	136.176	692.605
5	67.1953	840.70	219.079	134.249	254.181
6	60.7500	849.76	193.437	151.468	217.444
7	68.5765	1022.91	234.044	147.906	269.746
8	68.2341	1164.25	265.639	169.880	306.009
9	66.3990	1234.85	280.159	159.461	337.147
10	54.4348	867.38	181.919	136.390	219.193
11	60.5918	908.92	195.805	122.217	238.807
12	62.7282	1029.05	233.383	136.369	284.840
13	67.9279	985.92	213.049	158.796	235.470
14	69.7111	1101.94	246.003	146.202	283.639
15	55.8648	873.60	190.477	127.886	235.444
16	78.0563	1278.07	294.766	148.499	326.985
17	63.3107	897.10	201.446	131.327	234.329
18	56.7275	1127.93	262.298	112.275	358.226
19	60.3815	1325.35	302.108	142.948	388.086
20	65.6592	1080.45	269.265	103.721	338.829

Week	Promotion Opportunity	Adjusted Dollar Sales	Total Volume	No Promotion Volume	Feature Only Volume
21	66.5612	1046.38	290.590	131.620	356.123
22	68.0077	807.45	186.343	109.508	216.556
23	54.4544	773.43	189.794	105.140	255.934
24	64.3727	930.21	227.809	127.263	278.771
25	65.1551	1154.42	329.192	142.983	422.346
26	73.6961	1382.91	442.425	97.343	565.593
27	73.4942	1145.12	295.350	130.424	354.831
28	85.1154	1547.03	416.237	154.103	462.078
29	77.2145	1241.05	330.190	230.936	359.479
30	77.3252	1259.50	361.012	201.953	407.655
31	58.4226	1052.40	270.987	269.497	272.048
32	72.7990	1260.63	328.245	192.557	378.944
33	86.5720	1421.94	354.598	191.912	379.831
34	77.3139	1314.65	321.210	174.193	364.349
35	72.5000	1398.17	340.630	174.445	403.666
36	73.5784	1439.41	349.802	194.320	405.635
37	81.9853	1622.53	417.392	200.794	464.986
38	71.5000	1304.31	328.027	176.053	388.605
39	63.0767	1042.94	270.490	149.621	341.243
40	71.0978	1623.93	470.760	141.175	604.741
41	75.0000	1317.99	301.067	234.910	323.120
42	70.6912	1180.10	285.460	373.428	248.988
43	70.3292	1044.09	263.682	172.560	302.126
44	70.1102	1348.51	391.995	143.736	497.834
45	68.7389	1097.95	246.420	213.212	261.522
46	54.5455	941.89	217.352	240.564	198.009
47	72.0212	910.99	200.723	140.463	224.132
48	67.0906	940.36	205.445	107.910	253.288
49	58.8942	886.28	193.222	140.430	230.069
50	61.6927	1109.21	255.790	131.678	332.856
51	68.0863	1243.30	283.755	131.409	355.163
52	65.2381	1555.73	380.975	155.235	501.260
53	55.2381	1122.14	236.540	192.552	272.185

Case 5: Hot Cereals I

The hot cereal category is a somewhat seasonal product category. It is dominated by one brand, Grannies. Tastimeal has traditionally competed on price and has made relatively heavy use of trade promotion in the past. Golden Prairie is the only other significant national brand. Private label hot cereals have just recently been introduced in some stores. The historical brands shares in the category are shown in Table 5.7.

Table 5.7
HOT CEREAL BRAND SHARES

	Brand Share
Grannies	61%
Tastimeal	21
Golden Prairie	13
Private Labels	5

In Table 5.8, five stores were selected from one market. Two years of data (104 weeks) that show weekly sales volume (standardized for package size), selling price and promotional condition. A zero means no promotion, 1 means a temporary shelf price reduction, 2 means a feature ad, 3 means a display, and 4 means both a feature and display. Two of the stores do not sell any private label hot cereals. One store, 550, has sold a private label hot cereal for the entire two period. Two stores have recently introduced a private label. Store 163 introduced a private label during week 7 and store 2253 introduced a private label during week 86.

Table 5.8
HOT CEREAL VOLUME AND SELLING PRICE BY BRAND
in Selected Stores—104 weeks

		Grannies			**Golden Prairie**			**Tastimeal**			**Private**		
Store	Week	Vol.	Prc.	Pm.	Vol.	Prc.	Pm.	Vol.	Prc.	Pm.	Vol.	Prc.	Pm.
155	1	22	2.59	0	15	1.80	0	4	1.65	1	0	0	0
155	2	27	2.49	0	11	1.80	0	21	1.65	1	0	0	0
155	3	24	2.49	0	8	1.80	0	16	1.65	1	0	0	0
155	4	49	2.49	2	13	1.75	0	11	1.65	1	0	0	0
155	5	22	2.49	0	10	1.75	0	11	1.80	0	0	0	0
155	6	44	2.49	2	19	1.75	0	9	1.80	0	0	0	0
155	7	20	2.59	0	12	1.80	0	12	1.80	0	0	0	0
155	8	23	2.59	0	4	1.80	0	17	1.80	0	0	0	0
155	9	26	2.59	0	14	1.80	0	11	1.80	0	0	0	0
155	10	31	2.59	0	15	1.80	0	16	1.80	0	0	0	0
155	11	21	2.59	0	11	1.80	0	13	1.80	0	0	0	0
155	12	22	2.59	0	13	1.80	0	3	1.80	0	0	0	0
155	13	25	2.59	0	9	1.80	0	9	1.80	0	0	0	0
155	14	26	2.59	0	10	1.71	0	12	1.67	1	0	0	0
155	15	26	2.59	0	9	1.71	0	17	1.67	1	0	0	0
155	16	35	2.59	0	13	1.71	0	20	1.67	1	0	0	0
155	17	31	2.59	0	13	1.80	0	12	1.67	1	0	0	0
155	18	19	2.59	0	9	1.80	0	15	1.80	0	0	0	0
155	19	30	2.59	0	5	1.80	0	17	1.67	1	0	0	0
155	20	21	2.59	0	9	1.80	0	16	1.67	1	0	0	0

Store	Week	Grannies			Golden Prairie			Tastimeal			Private		
		Vol.	Prc.	Pm.	Vol.	Prc.	Pm.	Vol.	Prc.	Pm.	Vol.	Prc.	Pm.
155	21	21	2.59	0	8	1.80	0	13	1.67	1	0	0	0
155	22	21	2.59	0	6	1.80	0	8	1.67	1	0	0	0
155	23	19	2.59	0	7	1.98	0	3	1.67	1	0	0	0
155	24	24	2.59	0	18	1.98	2	10	1.80	0	0	0	0
155	25	25	2.59	0	5	1.98	0	12	1.80	0	0	0	0
155	26	21	2.59	0	4	1.98	0	11	1.80	0	0	0	0
155	27	19	2.78	0	7	1.98	0	14	1.80	0	0	0	0
155	28	17	2.78	0	6	1.98	0	11	1.80	0	0	0	0
155	29	22	2.78	0	6	1.98	0	8	1.80	0	0	0	0
155	30	17	2.78	0	5	1.98	0	12	1.80	0	0	0	0
155	31	17	2.78	0	5	2.12	0	10	1.80	0	0	0	0
155	32	19	2.78	0	8	2.12	0	6	1.80	0	0	0	0
155	33	25	2.78	0	3	2.12	0	7	1.80	0	0	0	0
155	34	18	2.78	0	5	2.12	0	13	1.80	0	0	0	0
155	35	11	2.78	0	8	2.12	0	13	1.80	0	0	0	0
155	36	16	2.78	0	9	2.12	0	15	1.80	0	0	0	0
155	37	20	2.78	0	6	2.12	0	11	1.80	0	0	0	0
155	38	16	2.78	0	3	2.12	0	10	1.80	0	0	0	0
155	39	17	2.85	0	5	2.17	0	7	1.80	0	0	0	0
155	40	13	2.85	0	9	2.17	0	13	1.80	0	0	0	0
155	41	13	2.85	0	2	2.17	0	10	1.80	0	0	0	0
155	42	10	2.85	0	4	2.17	0	14	1.80	0	0	0	0
155	43	17	2.85	0	2	2.17	0	10	1.80	0	0	0	0
155	44	12	2.85	0	5	2.17	0	8	1.66	1	0	0	0
155	45	10	2.85	0	4	2.17	0	14	1.66	1	0	0	0
155	46	15	2.85	0	6	2.14	0	10	1.66	1	0	0	0
155	47	16	2.85	0	3	2.17	0	16	1.80	0	0	0	0
155	48	15	2.85	0	2	2.17	0	15	1.80	0	0	0	0
155	49	21	2.85	0	8	2.17	0	15	1.80	0	0	0	0
155	50	17	2.85	0	11	2.17	2	20	1.80	0	0	0	0
155	51	20	2.85	0	17	2.17	2	19	1.80	0	0	0	0
155	52	29	2.85	0	9	2.17	0	14	1.80	0	0	0	0
155	53	21	2.85	0	16	2.07	0	20	1.65	1	0	0	0
155	54	30	2.85	0	9	2.07	0	22	1.65	1	0	0	0
155	55	35	2.50	3	12	2.07	0	20	1.65	1	0	0	0
155	56	41	2.50	3	8	2.07	0	15	1.65	1	0	0	0
155	57	31	2.50	1	16	2.07	0	13	1.80	0	0	0	0
155	58	29	2.50	1	11	2.17	0	17	1.80	0	0	0	0
155	59	23	2.50	1	6	2.17	0	15	1.65	1	0	0	0
155	60	25	2.85	0	16	2.17	0	15	1.65	1	0	0	0
155	61	23	2.85	0	14	2.17	0	19	1.80	0	0	0	0
155	62	25	2.85	0	14	2.17	0	15	1.80	0	0	0	0
155	63	14	2.85	0	9	2.17	0	13	1.80	0	0	0	0
155	64	32	2.85	0	12	2.17	0	20	1.80	0	0	0	0
155	65	49	2.85	0	14	2.17	0	17	1.80	0	0	0	0

Store	Week	Grannies			Golden Prairie			Tastimeal			Private		
		Vol.	Prc.	Pm.	Vol.	Prc.	Pm.	Vol.	Prc.	Pm.	Vol.	Prc.	Pm.
155	66	28	2.85	0	15	2.17	0	20	1.80	0	0	0	0
155	67	31	2.85	0	13	2.17	0	12	1.80	0	0	0	0
155	68	23	2.85	0	9	2.17	0	15	1.80	0	0	0	0
155	69	29	2.85	0	8	2.17	0	19	1.80	0	0	0	0
155	70	21	2.85	0	12	2.17	0	16	1.80	0	0	0	0
155	71	22	2.85	0	3	2.17	0	16	1.80	0	0	0	0
155	72	22	2.85	0	12	2.17	0	11	1.97	0	0	0	0
155	73	27	2.85	0	7	2.17	0	12	1.97	0	0	0	0
155	74	24	2.85	0	11	2.17	0	12	1.81	1	0	0	0
155	75	15	3.03	0	9	2.17	0	17	1.81	1	0	0	0
155	76	14	3.03	0	9	2.17	0	18	1.81	1	0	0	0
155	77	17	3.03	0	10	2.17	0	18	1.81	1	0	0	0
155	78	20	3.03	0	6	2.17	0	7	1.97	0	0	0	0
155	79	11	3.03	0	5	2.17	0	13	1.97	0	0	0	0
155	80	13	3.03	0	8	2.17	0	19	1.97	0	0	0	0
155	81	15	3.03	0	3	2.17	0	13	1.97	0	0	0	0
155	82	20	3.03	0	7	2.17	0	13	1.97	0	0	0	0
155	83	9	3.03	0	4	2.17	0	11	1.97	0	0	0	0
155	84	13	3.03	0	10	2.17	0	13	1.97	0	0	0	0
155	85	12	3.03	0	7	2.17	0	9	1.97	0	0	0	0
155	86	13	3.03	0	8	2.17	0	10	1.97	0	0	0	0
155	87	13	3.03	0	8	2.17	0	10	1.97	0	0	0	0
155	88	10	3.03	0	8	2.17	0	12	1.97	0	0	0	0
155	89	10	3.03	0	3	2.17	0	5	1.97	0	0	0	0
155	90	10	3.03	0	4	2.19	0	12	1.99	0	0	0	0
155	91	10	3.03	0	4	2.19	0	5	2.15	0	0	0	0
155	92	14	3.03	0	6	2.19	0	8	2.15	0	0	0	0
155	93	6	3.03	0	6	2.19	0	8	2.15	0	0	0	0
155	94	10	3.03	0	6	2.19	0	12	2.15	0	0	0	0
155	95	14	3.03	0	5	2.19	0	19	1.99	3	0	0	0
155	96	8	3.03	0	3	2.19	0	9	1.99	1	0	0	0
155	97	7	3.03	0	9	2.19	0	12	1.99	1	0	0	0
155	98	7	3.03	0	6	2.19	0	11	1.99	1	0	0	0
155	99	17	3.03	0	3	2.19	0	7	2.08	0	0	0	0
155	100	14	3.03	0	3	2.19	0	17	2.08	0	0	0	0
155	101	15	3.03	0	2	2.19	0	9	2.08	0	0	0	0
155	102	11	3.03	0	7	2.19	0	16	2.08	0	0	0	0
155	103	12	3.03	0	7	2.19	0	10	2.25	0	0	0	0
155	104	16	3.03	0	4	2.19	0	15	2.08	1	0	0	0

Table 5.8 (continued)

HOT CEREAL VOLUME AND SELLING PRICE BY BRAND

in Selected Stores—104 weeks

Store	Week	Grannies			Golden Prairie			Tastimeal			Private		
		Vol.	Prc.	Pm.	Vol.	Prc.	Pm.	Vol.	Prc.	Pm.	Vol.	Prc.	Pm.
163	1	23	2.67	0	14	2.03	0	8	1.79	0	0	0	0
163	2	87	2.19	4	59	1.79	5	14	1.79	0	0	0	0
163	3	42	2.19	3	22	1.79	4	10	1.79	0	0	0	0
163	4	34	2.19	1	12	1.79	1	11	1.79	0	0	0	0
163	5	32	2.19	1	11	1.79	1	10	1.79	0	0	0	0
163	6	26	2.67	0	11	2.03	0	6	1.79	0	0	0	0
163	7	24	2.67	0	7	2.03	0	6	1.79	0	11	1.97	0
163	8	37	2.67	0	10	2.03	0	13	1.79	0	15	1.97	0
163	9	31	2.67	0	12	2.03	0	5	1.79	0	13	1.97	0
163	10	28	2.67	0	11	2.03	0	12	1.79	0	17	1.97	0
163	11	24	2.67	0	14	2.03	0	7	1.79	0	12	1.97	0
163	12	23	2.67	0	12	2.03	0	10	1.79	0	10	1.97	0
163	13	34	2.67	0	8	2.03	0	7	1.79	0	10	1.97	0
163	14	34	2.67	0	8	2.03	0	7	1.79	0	10	1.97	0
163	15	33	2.67	0	20	1.79	5	7	1.79	0	10	1.97	0
163	16	24	2.67	0	16	1.79	4	11	1.79	0	11	2.03	0
163	17	27	2.67	0	10	2.03	0	9	1.65	1	12	2.03	0
163	18	22	2.67	0	10	2.03	0	11	1.65	1	10	2.03	0
163	19	26	2.67	0	11	2.03	0	8	1.65	1	9	2.03	0
163	20	26	2.65	0	11	2.03	0	4	1.65	1	11	2.03	0
163	21	20	2.65	0	12	2.03	0	16	1.65	1	14	2.03	0
163	22	21	2.65	0	9	2.03	0	36	1.39	5	5	2.03	0
163	23	20	2.85	0	3	2.19	0	28	1.39	4	9	2.03	0
163	24	15	2.85	0	7	2.03	1	21	1.39	4	2	2.03	0
163	25	18	2.85	0	4	2.03	1	4	1.79	0	15	2.03	0
163	26	14	2.85	0	7	2.03	1	12	1.79	0	6	2.03	0
163	27	13	2.85	0	8	2.03	1	5	1.79	0	15	2.03	0
163	28	13	2.85	0	9	2.03	1	10	1.98	0	12	2.03	0
163	29	17	2.85	0	3	2.03	1	6	1.98	0	8	2.03	0
163	30	17	2.85	0	7	2.03	1	8	1.98	0	12	2.03	0
163	31	20	2.85	0	14	2.03	0	9	1.98	0	12	2.03	0
163	32	10	2.85	0	2	2.03	0	3	1.98	0	12	2.03	0
163	33	10	2.85	0	2	2.03	0	3	1.98	0	11	2.03	0
163	34	12	2.85	0	5	2.03	0	6	1.98	0	14	2.03	0
163	35	15	2.85	0	4	2.03	0	5	1.98	0	18	2.03	0
163	36	15	2.85	0	4	2.03	0	3	1.98	0	7	2.03	0
163	37	19	2.85	0	8	2.03	0	7	1.98	0	8	2.03	0
163	38	14	2.85	0	4	2.03	0	9	1.98	0	10	2.03	0
163	39	17	2.85	0	6	2.03	0	4	1.98	0	15	2.03	0
163	40	14	2.85	0	6	2.03	0	8	1.98	0	10	2.03	0

Store	Week	Grannies			Golden Prairie			Tastimeal			Private		
		Vol.	Prc.	Pm.	Vol.	Prc.	Pm.	Vol.	Prc.	Pm.	Vol.	Prc.	Pm.
163	41	14	2.85	0	3	2.03	0	4	1.84	1	13	2.03	0
163	42	14	2.85	0	3	2.03	0	4	1.84	1	12	2.03	0
163	43	14	2.85	0	4	2.03	0	7	1.84	1	8	2.03	0
163	44	13	2.85	0	5	2.03	0	4	1.84	1	11	2.03	0
163	45	10	2.85	0	5	2.03	0	3	1.98	0	16	2.03	0
163	46	18	2.85	0	3	2.03	0	7	1.98	0	13	2.03	0
163	47	14	2.85	0	4	2.03	0	7	1.98	0	6	2.03	0
163	48	22	2.85	0	6	2.03	0	5	1.98	0	16	2.03	0
163	49	17	2.85	0	11	2.03	0	5	1.98	0	15	2.03	0
163	50	34	2.85	0	9	2.03	0	7	1.98	0	23	2.03	0
163	51	27	2.85	0	10	2.03	0	8	1.98	0	23	2.03	0
163	52	34	2.85	0	7	2.03	0	9	1.98	0	23	2.03	0
163	53	31	2.85	0	12	2.03	0	6	1.98	0	6	2.03	0
163	54	29	2.85	0	7	2.03	0	5	1.98	0	25	2.03	0
163	55	40	2.85	0	10	2.03	0	14	1.98	0	17	2.03	0
163	56	26	2.85	0	16	2.03	0	5	1.98	0	15	2.03	0
163	57	18	2.85	0	12	2.03	0	6	1.98	0	16	2.03	0
163	58	28	2.85	0	10	2.03	0	9	1.98	0	12	2.03	0
163	59	28	2.85	0	14	2.03	0	12	1.98	0	23	2.03	0
163	60	26	2.85	0	10	2.03	0	12	1.98	0	18	2.03	0
163	61	23	2.85	0	8	2.03	0	8	1.98	0	16	2.03	0
163	62	42	2.85	0	6	2.03	0	9	2.25	0	16	2.03	0
163	63	28	2.85	0	7	2.03	0	9	2.25	0	14	2.03	0
163	64	30	2.85	0	9	2.03	0	6	2.25	0	19	2.03	0
163	65	32	2.85	0	14	2.03	0	8	2.25	0	20	2.03	0
163	66	26	2.85	0	10	2.03	0	6	2.25	0	17	2.03	0
163	67	29	2.85	0	15	2.21	0	5	2.25	0	24	2.03	0
163	68	33	2.85	0	20	2.21	0	5	2.25	0	25	2.03	0
163	69	25	2.85	0	11	2.21	0	6	2.25	0	19	2.03	0
163	70	24	2.85	0	10	2.21	0	6	2.25	0	18	2.03	0
163	71	20	2.93	0	14	2.23	0	5	2.25	0	21	2.03	0
163	72	15	3.15	0	10	2.23	0	0	0.00	0	16	2.03	0
163	73	15	3.15	0	6	2.23	0	6	2.25	0	23	2.15	0
163	74	16	3.15	0	9	2.23	0	7	2.25	0	6	2.15	0
163	75	20	3.15	0	9	2.23	0	9	2.25	0	11	2.15	0
163	76	16	3.15	0	7	2.23	0	2	2.25	0	12	2.15	0
163	77	19	3.15	0	3	2.23	0	6	2.25	0	12	2.15	0
163	78	21	3.15	0	3	2.23	0	6	2.25	0	13	2.15	0
163	79	14	3.13	0	11	2.23	0	7	2.25	0	10	2.15	0
163	80	11	3.13	0	6	2.23	0	3	2.25	0	12	2.15	0
163	81	21	3.13	0	9	2.23	0	5	2.25	0	14	2.15	0
163	82	8	3.13	0	8	2.23	0	10	2.25	0	13	2.15	0
163	83	6	3.13	0	7	2.23	0	7	2.25	0	11	2.15	0
163	84	6	3.13	0	5	2.23	0	5	2.25	0	8	2.15	0
163	85	7	3.13	0	13	2.23	0	6	2.25	0	12	2.15	0

Store	Week	Grannies			Golden Prairie			Tastimeal			Private		
		Vol.	Prc.	Pm.	Vol.	Prc.	Pm.	Vol.	Prc.	Pm.	Vol.	Prc.	Pm.
163	86	13	3.13	0	1	2.23	0	11	2.25	0	7	2.15	0
163	87	10	3.13	0	2	2.23	0	2	2.25	0	8	2.15	0
163	88	8	3.13	0	3	2.23	0	3	2.25	0	7	2.15	0
163	89	4	3.13	0	10	2.23	0	7	2.25	0	9	2.15	0
163	90	9	3.13	0	4	2.23	0	5	2.25	0	10	2.15	0
163	91	13	3.13	0	1	2.23	0	2	2.25	0	10	2.15	0
163	92	13	3.13	0	4	2.23	0	5	2.25	0	10	2.15	0
163	93	3	3.13	0	0	0.00	0	6	2.25	0	11	2.15	0
163	94	7	3.13	0	2	2.23	0	5	2.25	0	4	2.15	0
163	95	14	3.13	0	9	2.23	0	0	0.00	0	8	2.15	0
163	96	13	3.13	0	5	2.23	0	8	2.25	0	9	2.15	0
163	97	11	3.13	0	6	2.23	0	5	2.25	0	13	2.15	0
163	98	10	3.13	0	4	2.23	0	2	2.25	0	5	2.15	0
163	99	15	3.13	0	6	2.23	0	7	2.25	0	5	2.15	0
163	100	16	3.13	0	5	2.23	0	3	2.25	0	11	2.15	0
163	101	18	3.13	0	7	2.23	0	6	2.25	0	14	2.15	0
163	102	22	3.13	0	12	2.23	0	6	2.25	0	12	2.15	0
163	103	15	3.13	0	3	2.23	0	5	2.25	0	19	2.15	0
163	104	25	3.13	0	2	2.31	0	15	2.31	0	10	2.15	0

Table 5.8 (continued)

HOT CEREAL VOLUME AND SELLING PRICE BY BRAND

in Selected Stores—104 weeks

Store	Week	Grannies			Golden Prairie			Tastimeal			Private		
		Vol.	Prc.	Pm.	Vol.	Prc.	Pm.	Vol.	Prc.	Pm.	Vol.	Prc.	Pm.
550	1	145	2.29	0	0	0.00	0	79	1.58	0	51	1.66	0
550	2	162	2.29	0	0	0.00	0	71	1.58	0	54	1.66	0
550	3	191	2.29	0	0	0.00	0	64	1.29	1	9	1.66	0
550	4	163	2.19	0	0	0.00	0	60	1.29	1	24	1.66	0
550	5	182	2.19	0	85	1.75	0	60	1.29	1	72	1.66	0
550	6	195	2.19	0	106	1.75	0	64	1.29	1	69	1.66	0
550	7	171	2.09	1	75	1.69	0	64	1.58	0	51	1.66	0
550	8	200	2.09	1	88	1.69	0	75	1.58	0	60	1.66	0
550	9	220	2.09	3	93	1.69	0	56	1.58	0	63	1.66	0
550	10	211	2.09	0	79	1.69	0	42	1.58	0	66	1.66	0
550	11	165	2.09	0	132	1.79	3	53	1.58	0	60	1.66	0
550	12	113	2.09	0	64	1.79	0	34	1.58	0	34	1.66	0
550	13	128	2.09	0	81	1.79	0	58	1.58	0	47	1.66	0
550	14	146	2.09	0	27	1.79	0	68	1.39	1	32	1.66	0
550	15	119	2.09	1	66	1.79	0	69	1.39	1	41	1.66	0
550	16	113	2.09	1	64	1.69	1	42	1.39	1	30	1.66	0
550	17	103	2.09	1	68	1.69	1	79	1.39	1	41	1.66	0

		Grannies			Golden Prairie			Tastimeal			Private		
Store	Week	Vol.	Prc.	Pm.	Vol.	Prc.	Pm.	Vol.	Prc.	Pm.	Vol.	Prc.	Pm.
550	18	172	2.29	0	74	1.69	1	39	1.39	1	30	1.66	0
550	19	144	2.29	1	46	1.69	1	37	1.39	1	35	1.66	0
550	20	144	2.29	1	46	1.69	0	37	1.39	1	35	1.66	0
550	21	137	2.18	0	65	1.79	0	44	1.58	0	25	1.66	0
550	22	138	2.18	0	81	1.79	0	65	1.58	0	41	1.67	0
550	23	100	1.98	1	45	1.79	0	53	1.39	1	27	1.67	0
550	24	102	1.98	1	48	1.79	0	62	1.39	1	3	1.67	0
550	25	96	1.98	1	43	1.92	0	47	1.39	1	0	0.00	0
550	26	98	1.98	1	67	1.92	0	52	1.58	0	0	0.00	0
550	27	103	1.98	1	56	1.92	0	41	1.58	0	0	0.00	0
550	28	70	1.98	1	19	1.92	0	26	1.58	0	5	1.67	0
550	29	71	1.98	1	22	1.92	0	33	1.74	0	21	1.67	0
550	30	98	1.98	0	36	1.92	0	25	1.74	0	37	1.67	0
550	31	97	1.98	0	36	1.92	0	25	1.74	0	37	1.67	0
550	32	79	1.98	0	38	1.92	0	39	1.74	0	29	1.67	0
550	33	67	1.98	0	34	1.92	0	43	1.74	0	35	1.67	0
550	34	63	1.98	0	26	1.92	0	25	1.74	0	44	1.67	0
550	35	76	1.98	0	30	1.92	0	40	1.74	0	25	1.67	0
550	36	76	1.98	0	30	1.92	0	40	1.74	0	25	1.67	0
550	37	59	2.46	0	23	1.92	0	21	1.74	0	26	1.67	0
550	38	48	2.46	0	30	1.92	0	33	1.74	0	31	1.67	0
550	39	73	2.46	0	31	1.92	0	21	1.74	0	29	1.67	0
550	40	76	2.46	0	44	1.92	0	30	1.74	0	44	1.67	0
550	41	57	2.46	0	19	1.92	0	31	1.74	0	31	1.67	0
550	42	60	2.46	0	29	1.92	0	28	1.74	0	16	1.67	0
550	43	67	2.46	0	32	1.92	0	31	1.74	0	18	1.67	0
550	44	78	2.46	0	54	1.92	0	40	1.74	0	28	1.67	0
550	45	69	2.46	0	44	1.92	0	40	1.74	0	31	1.67	0
550	46	69	2.46	0	39	1.92	0	48	1.59	1	38	1.67	0
550	47	81	2.46	0	37	1.92	0	55	1.59	1	27	1.67	0
550	48	79	2.46	0	36	1.92	0	54	1.59	1	26	1.67	0
550	49	83	2.46	0	38	1.92	0	57	1.59	1	27	1.67	0
550	50	111	2.46	0	62	1.92	0	38	1.74	0	38	1.66	0
550	51	81	2.46	0	42	1.92	0	46	1.74	0	42	1.66	0
550	52	130	2.46	0	100	1.92	3	45	1.74	0	29	1.66	0
550	53	199	2.46	2	100	1.92	2	47	1.74	0	35	1.66	0
550	54	137	2.46	0	68	1.92	0	42	1.74	0	47	1.66	0
550	55	169	2.35	0	59	1.92	0	52	1.59	1	33	1.66	0
550	56	166	2.35	0	76	1.92	0	37	1.59	1	41	1.66	0
550	57	208	2.35	2	91	1.92	0	58	1.74	0	38	1.66	0
550	58	207	2.35	2	125	1.92	2	36	1.58	1	45	1.66	0
550	59	137	2.35	0	61	1.92	0	38	1.58	1	30	1.66	0
550	60	130	2.46	0	76	1.92	0	29	1.58	1	44	1.66	0
550	61	173	2.46	0	77	1.92	0	52	1.58	1	55	1.66	0

Store	Week	Grannies			Golden Prairie			Tastimeal			Private		
		Vol.	Prc.	Pm.	Vol.	Prc.	Pm.	Vol.	Prc.	Pm.	Vol.	Prc.	Pm.
550	62	156	2.46	0	87	1.92	0	59	1.58	1	42	1.66	0
550	63	149	2.46	0	83	1.92	0	56	1.58	1	40	1.66	0
550	64	82	2.46	0	40	1.92	0	52	1.58	1	0	0.00	0
550	65	158	2.46	0	83	1.92	0	34	1.74	0	0	0.00	0
550	66	154	2.46	0	85	1.92	0	43	1.74	0	0	0.00	0
550	67	150	2.46	0	82	1.92	0	42	1.74	0	0	0.00	0
550	68	127	2.46	0	70	1.92	0	58	1.74	0	0	0.00	0
550	69	130	2.46	0	71	1.92	0	59	1.74	0	0	0.00	0
550	70	124	2.46	0	67	1.92	0	56	1.74	0	0	0.00	0
550	71	109	2.46	0	69	1.92	0	41	1.97	0	0	0.00	0
550	72	117	2.46	0	49	1.92	0	44	1.97	0	0	0.00	0
550	73	114	2.46	0	30	2.05	0	51	1.97	0	0	0.00	0
550	74	137	2.63	0	48	2.05	0	47	1.85	1	0	0	0
550	75	97	2.63	0	45	2.05	0	1	1.85	1	0	0	0
550	76	89	2.63	0	42	2.05	0	37	1.85	1	0	0	0
550	77	70	2.63	0	24	2.05	0	49	1.79	1	0	0	0
550	78	84	2.63	0	37	2.05	0	46	1.79	1	0	0	0
550	79	95	2.63	0	34	2.05	0	42	1.97	0	0	0	0
550	80	71	2.65	0	37	2.05	0	39	1.97	0	0	0	0
550	81	85	2.65	0	18	2.05	0	27	1.97	0	0	0	0
550	82	92	2.65	0	29	2.05	0	45	1.97	0	0	0	0
550	83	75	2.65	0	26	2.05	0	37	1.97	0	0	0	0
550	84	77	2.65	0	26	2.05	0	35	1.97	0	0	0	0
550	85	54	2.65	0	19	2.05	0	27	1.97	0	0	0	0
550	86	50	2.65	0	13	2.05	0	21	1.97	0	0	0	0
550	87	72	2.65	0	19	2.05	0	44	1.97	0	0	0	0
550	88	68	2.65	0	33	2.05	0	27	1.97	0	0	0	0
550	89	49	2.65	0	26	2.05	0	23	1.97	0	0	0	0
550	90	53	2.65	0	21	2.05	0	40	1.97	0	0	0	0
550	91	81	2.65	0	31	2.05	0	30	1.97	0	0	0	0
550	92	74	2.65	0	27	2.05	0	31	1.97	0	0	0	0
550	93	53	2.65	0	25	2.05	0	19	1.97	0	0	0	0
550	94	45	2.65	0	16	2.05	0	18	1.97	0	0	0	0
550	95	72	2.65	0	18	2.04	0	56	1.97	0	0	0	0
550	96	100	2.65	3	36	2.04	0	25	1.77	1	0	0	0
550	97	68	2.65	0	31	1.96	0	53	1.77	1	0	0	0
550	98	59	2.65	0	27	1.96	0	40	1.77	1	0	0	0
550	99	91	2.65	0	14	2.04	0	30	1.77	1	0	0	0
550	100	111	2.65	0	49	2.04	0	35	1.77	1	0	0	0
550	101	113	2.65	0	50	2.04	0	36	1.77	1	0	0	0
550	102	109	2.65	0	48	2.04	0	35	1.77	1	0	0	0
550	103	108	2.65	0	48	2.04	0	35	1.77	0	0	0	0
550	104	132	2.65	0	71	1.93	1	61	1.77	0	0	0	0

Table 5.8 (continued)

HOT CEREAL VOLUME AND SELLING PRICE BY BRAND

in Selected Stores—104 weeks

		Grannies			Golden Prairie			Tastimeal			Private		
Store	Week	Vol.	Prc.	Pm.	Vol.	Prc.	Pm.	Vol.	Prc.	Pm.	Vol.	Prc.	Pm.
2253	1	60	2.13	0	42	1.83	0	33	1.59	0	0	0	0
2253	2	83	2.05	0	32	1.79	0	37	1.59	0	0	0	0
2253	3	109	2.05	0	13	1.79	0	35	1.59	0	0	0	0
2253	4	97	2.05	0	33	1.79	0	23	1.59	0	0	0	0
2253	5	68	2.05	0	24	1.79	0	28	1.59	0	0	0	0
2253	6	70	2.05	0	22	1.83	0	27	1.59	0	0	0	0
2253	7	65	2.05	0	31	1.83	0	30	1.59	0	0	0	0
2253	8	82	2.13	0	31	1.83	0	33	1.59	0	0	0	0
2253	9	99	2.13	0	35	1.83	0	37	1.59	0	0	0	0
2253	10	73	2.13	0	28	1.83	0	40	1.59	0	0	0	0
2253	11	76	2.13	0	28	1.83	0	28	1.59	0	0	0	0
2253	12	63	2.13	0	26	1.83	0	32	1.59	0	0	0	0
2253	13	72	2.13	0	20	1.83	0	31	1.59	0	0	0	0
2253	14	42	2.13	0	26	1.79	0	42	1.43	1	0	0	0
2253	15	43	2.13	0	24	1.79	0	32	1.43	1	0	0	0
2253	16	45	2.13	0	24	1.79	0	22	1.43	1	0	0	0
2253	17	58	2.13	0	23	1.79	2	33	1.43	1	0	0	0
2253	18	67	2.13	0	31	1.79	0	39	1.43	1	0	0	0
2253	19	60	2.13	0	20	1.83	0	29	1.43	1	0	0	0
2253	20	74	1.99	1	17	1.83	0	27	1.43	1	0	0	0
2253	21	56	1.99	1	23	1.83	0	41	1.43	0	0	0	0
2253	22	61	1.99	1	16	1.83	0	35	1.43	0	0	0	0
2253	23	33	2.15	0	32	1.83	0	25	1.43	0	0	0	0
2253	24	48	2.15	0	18	1.83	0	43	1.43	0	0	0	0
2253	25	51	2.15	0	22	1.83	0	38	1.59	0	0	0	0
2253	26	36	2.15	0	21	1.83	0	25	1.59	0	0	0	0
2253	27	32	2.15	0	21	1.83	0	28	1.59	0	0	0	0
2253	28	36	2.15	0	16	1.83	0	23	1.59	0	0	0	0
2253	29	35	2.29	0	10	1.83	0	15	1.75	0	0	0	0
2253	30	23	2.29	0	28	1.83	0	22	1.75	0	0	0	0
2253	31	29	2.29	0	14	1.83	0	22	1.75	0	0	0	0
2253	32	35	2.29	0	16	1.83	0	20	1.75	0	0	0	0
2253	33	37	2.29	0	14	1.83	0	22	1.75	0	0	0	0
2253	34	34	2.29	0	14	1.83	0	23	1.75	0	0	0	0
2253	35	23	2.29	0	20	1.83	0	13	1.75	0	0	0	0
2253	36	22	2.29	0	15	1.83	0	16	1.75	0	0	0	0
2253	37	16	2.29	0	11	1.83	0	12	1.75	0	0	0	0
2253	38	29	2.29	0	14	1.83	0	12	1.75	0	0	0	0
2253	39	21	2.29	0	12	1.83	0	24	1.75	0	0	0	0
2253	40	27	2.29	0	13	1.83	0	9	1.75	0	0	0	0

Store	Week	Grannies			Golden Prairie			Tastimeal			Private		
		Vol.	Prc.	Pm.	Vol.	Prc.	Pm.	Vol.	Prc.	Pm.	Vol.	Prc.	Pm.
2253	41	24	2.29	0	13	1.83	0	20	1.75	0	0	0	0
2253	42	22	2.29	0	12	1.83	0	18	1.75	0	0	0	0
2253	43	29	2.29	0	15	1.83	0	20	1.65	1	0	0	0
2253	44	30	2.29	0	28	1.83	0	19	1.65	1	0	0	0
2253	45	26	2.29	0	20	1.83	0	30	1.65	1	0	0	0
2253	46	24	2.29	0	11	1.83	0	18	1.65	1	0	0	0
2253	47	26	2.29	0	13	1.83	0	18	1.75	0	0	0	0
2253	48	17	2.29	0	17	1.83	0	32	1.75	0	0	0	0
2253	49	58	2.29	0	27	1.83	0	33	1.75	0	0	0	0
2253	50	60	2.29	0	28	1.83	0	34	1.75	0	0	0	0
2253	51	65	2.29	0	28	1.83	0	28	1.75	0	0	0	0
2253	52	55	2.29	0	43	1.78	0	27	1.65	1	0	0	0
2253	53	87	2.19	0	39	1.78	0	34	1.65	1	0	0	0
2253	54	87	2.19	0	44	1.78	0	35	1.65	1	0	0	0
2253	55	79	2.19	0	40	1.83	0	29	1.65	1	0	0	0
2253	56	97	2.19	0	32	1.83	0	25	1.65	0	0	0	0
2253	57	107	2.19	0	31	1.83	0	44	1.65	0	0	0	0
2253	58	89	2.35	0	43	1.83	0	29	1.65	0	0	0	0
2253	59	67	2.35	0	49	1.83	0	29	1.65	0	0	0	0
2253	60	73	2.35	0	40	1.83	0	32	1.75	0	0	0	0
2253	61	99	2.35	0	32	1.83	0	45	1.75	0	0	0	0
2253	62	43	2.35	0	19	1.83	0	16	1.75	0	0	0	0
2253	63	49	2.35	0	17	1.83	0	16	1.99	0	0	0	0
2253	64	44	2.35	0	18	1.83	0	20	1.99	0	0	0	0
2253	65	65	2.35	0	36	1.83	0	23	1.99	0	0	0	0
2253	66	63	2.35	0	27	1.83	0	18	1.99	0	0	0	0
2253	67	80	2.35	0	44	1.83	0	23	1.99	0	0	0	0
2253	68	74	2.35	0	24	1.83	0	27	1.99	0	0	0	0
2253	69	65	2.35	0	27	1.83	0	27	1.99	0	0	0	0
2253	70	41	2.35	0	27	1.83	0	8	1.99	0	0	0	0
2253	71	47	2.35	0	20	1.83	0	14	1.99	0	0	0	0
2253	72	53	2.35	0	19	1.83	0	19	1.99	0	0	0	0
2253	73	38	2.35	0	21	1.99	0	18	1.83	1	0	0	0
2253	74	36	2.49	0	17	1.99	0	20	1.83	1	0	0	0
2253	75	38	2.49	0	13	1.99	0	19	1.83	1	0	0	0
2253	76	33	2.49	0	22	1.99	0	17	1.83	1	0	0	0
2253	77	20	2.49	0	13	1.99	0	13	1.83	1	0	0	0
2253	78	26	2.49	0	11	1.99	0	12	1.99	0	0	0	0
2253	79	35	2.49	0	16	1.99	0	24	1.99	0	0	0	0
2253	80	34	2.49	0	18	1.99	0	18	1.99	0	0	0	0
2253	81	30	2.49	0	14	1.99	0	13	1.99	0	0	0	0
2253	82	28	2.49	0	24	1.99	0	22	1.99	0	0	0	0
2253	83	30	2.49	0	18	1.99	0	9	1.99	0	0	0	0
2253	84	26	2.49	0	10	1.99	0	13	1.99	0	0	0	0
2253	85	15	2.49	0	9	1.99	0	9	1.99	0	0	0	0

		Grannies			Golden Prairie			Tastimeal			Private		
Store	Week	Vol.	Prc.	Pm.	Vol.	Prc.	Pm.	Vol.	Prc.	Pm.	Vol.	Prc.	Pm.
2253	86	24	2.49	0	9	1.99	0	11	1.99	0	3	1.89	0
2253	87	25	2.49	0	10	1.99	0	15	1.99	0	7	1.89	0
2253	88	22	2.49	0	11	1.99	0	12	1.99	0	6	1.89	0
2253	89	23	2.49	0	6	1.99	0	10	1.99	0	5	1.89	0
2253	90	30	2.49	0	8	1.99	0	17	1.99	0	10	1.89	0
2253	91	16	2.49	0	8	1.99	0	11	1.99	0	7	1.89	0
2253	92	18	2.49	0	9	1.99	0	11	1.99	0	7	1.89	0
2253	93	32	2.53	0	4	1.99	0	15	1.99	0	5	1.89	0
2253	94	26	2.53	0	9	1.99	0	13	1.99	0	7	1.89	0
2253	95	22	2.53	0	5	1.99	0	10	1.99	0	7	1.39	1
2253	96	23	2.53	0	11	1.99	0	23	1.99	0	9	1.39	1
2253	97	26	2.53	0	8	1.95	0	15	1.99	0	8	1.39	1
2253	98	21	2.53	0	21	1.95	0	18	1.99	0	13	1.39	1
2253	99	31	2.53	0	9	1.99	0	23	1.89	1	13	1.39	1
2253	100	26	2.53	0	8	1.99	0	23	1.89	1	16	1.39	1
2253	101	31	2.53	0	6	1.99	0	16	1.89	1	8	1.39	1
2253	102	44	2.53	0	22	1.99	0	30	1.89	1	10	1.39	0
2253	103	34	2.53	0	36	1.99	0	19	1.99	0	11	1.39	0
2253	104	40	2.53	0	50	1.99	0	31	1.95	0	18	1.39	0

Table 5.8 (continued)

HOT CEREAL VOLUME AND SELLING PRICE BY BRAND

in Selected Stores—104 weeks

		Grannies			Golden Prairie			Tastimeal			Private		
Store	Week	Vol.	Prc.	Pm.	Vol.	Prc.	Pm.	Vol.	Prc.	Pm.	Vol.	Prc.	Pm.
7901	1	6	2.93	0	9	2.23	0	5	1.65	1	0	0	0
7901	2	6	2.93	0	2	2.23	0	6	1.65	1	0	0	0
7901	3	6	2.93	0	2	2.23	0	6	1.65	1	0	0	0
7901	4	4	2.93	0	5	2.23	0	4	1.65	1	0	0	0
7901	5	11	2.93	3	6	2.23	0	9	1.65	1	0	0	0
7901	6	8	2.93	0	3	2.23	0	5	1.65	1	0	0	0
7901	7	6	2.93	0	4	2.23	0	8	1.65	1	0	0	0
7901	8	7	2.77	1	9	2.23	0	10	1.87	2	0	0	0
7901	9	5	2.77	1	4	2.23	0	2	1.87	0	0	0	0
7901	10	8	2.77	1	8	2.23	0	8	1.87	0	0	0	0
7901	11	3	2.77	1	7	2.23	0	5	1.87	0	0	0	0
7901	12	11	2.77	3	6	2.23	0	6	1.87	0	0	0	0
7901	13	6	2.77	0	4	2.23	0	16	1.73	3	0	0	0
7901	14	6	2.77	0	4	2.23	0	5	1.73	1	0	0	0
7901	15	5	2.77	0	6	2.23	0	3	1.87	0	0	0	0
7901	16	12	2.77	3	10	2.23	3	4	1.87	0	0	0	0
7901	17	5	2.77	0	2	2.23	0	4	1.87	0	0	0	0
7901	18	10	2.77	0	3	2.23	0	8	1.73	1	0	0	0

Store	Week	Grannies			Golden Prairie			Tastimeal			Private		
		Vol.	Prc.	Pm.	Vol.	Prc.	Pm.	Vol.	Prc.	Pm.	Vol.	Prc.	Pm.
7901	19	11	2.77	0	3	2.23	0	9	1.73	1	0	0	0
7901	20	11	2.77	0	3	2.23	0	9	1.73	1	0	0	0
7901	21	11	2.77	0	3	2.23	0	9	1.73	1	0	0	0
7901	22	2	2.75	0	6	2.23	0	3	1.87	0	0	0	0
7901	23	4	2.97	0	3	2.41	0	6	1.87	0	0	0	0
7901	24	7	2.97	0	1	2.23	1	5	1.87	0	0	0	0
7901	25	4	2.97	0	6	2.23	1	3	1.87	0	0	0	0
7901	26	7	2.97	0	2	2.23	1	2	1.87	0	0	0	0
7901	27	9	2.97	0	7	2.23	1	4	1.87	0	0	0	0
7901	28	3	2.97	0	3	2.23	1	1	2.07	0	0	0	0
7901	29	2	2.97	0	8	2.23	1	3	2.07	0	0	0	0
7901	30	5	2.97	0	3	2.23	1	4	2.07	0	0	0	0
7901	31	7	2.97	0	8	2.23	0	5	2.07	0	0	0	0
7901	32	3	2.97	0	4	2.23	0	4	2.07	0	0	0	0
7901	33	2	2.97	0	5	2.23	0	2	2.07	0	0	0	0
7901	34	5	2.97	0	5	2.23	0	2	2.07	0	0	0	0
7901	35	8	2.97	0	1	2.23	0	0	0.00	0	0	0	0
7901	36	5	2.97	0	2	2.23	0	3	2.07	0	0	0	0
7901	37	2	2.97	0	2	2.23	0	3	2.07	0	0	0	0
7901	38	4	2.97	0	2	2.23	0	2	2.07	0	0	0	0
7901	39	1	2.97	0	1	2.23	0	4	2.07	0	0	0	0
7901	40	6	2.97	0	6	2.23	0	2	2.07	0	0	0	0
7901	41	5	2.97	0	7	2.23	0	1	1.93	1	0	0	0
7901	42	1	2.97	0	2	2.23	0	0	0.00	0	0	0	0
7901	43	4	2.97	0	5	2.23	0	1	1.93	1	0	0	0
7901	44	4	2.97	0	3	2.23	0	4	1.93	1	0	0	0
7901	45	6	2.97	0	3	2.23	0	2	2.07	0	0	0	0
7901	46	6	2.97	0	0	0.00	0	1	2.07	0	0	0	0
7901	47	2	2.97	0	4	2.23	0	3	2.07	0	0	0	0
7901	48	4	2.97	0	4	2.23	0	0	0.00	0	0	0	0
7901	49	3	2.97	0	4	2.23	0	3	2.07	0	0	0	0
7901	50	11	2.97	0	9	2.23	0	3	2.07	0	0	0	0
7901	51	3	2.97	0	10	2.23	0	1	2.07	0	0	0	0
7901	52	11	2.97	0	11	2.23	0	3	2.07	0	0	0	0
7901	53	7	2.97	0	6	2.23	0	4	2.07	0	0	0	0
7901	54	7	2.97	0	12	2.23	0	2	2.07	0	0	0	0
7901	55	17	2.49	1	3	2.23	0	1	1.92	1	0	0	0
7901	56	13	2.97	0	9	2.23	0	5	1.92	1	0	0	0
7901	57	5	2.97	0	6	2.23	0	3	1.92	1	0	0	0
7901	58	4	2.97	0	9	2.23	0	6	2.07	0	0	0	0
7901	59	11	2.97	0	3	2.23	0	3	2.07	0	0	0	0
7901	60	8	2.97	0	7	2.23	0	5	2.07	0	0	0	0
7901	61	9	2.97	0	8	2.23	0	3	2.07	0	0	0	0
7901	62	13	2.97	0	3	2.23	0	1	2.35	0	0	0	0

Store	Week	Grannies			Golden Prairie			Tastimeal			Private		
		Vol.	Prc.	Pm.	Vol.	Prc.	Pm.	Vol.	Prc.	Pm.	Vol.	Prc.	Pm.
7901	63	12	2.97	0	7	2.23	0	1	2.35	0	0	0	0
7901	64	12	2.97	0	5	2.23	0	1	2.35	0	0	0	0
7901	65	12	2.97	0	12	2.23	3	3	2.35	0	0	0	0
7901	66	11	2.97	0	11	2.23	3	3	2.35	0	0	0	0
7901	67	13	2.97	0	1	2.41	0	6	2.35	0	0	0	0
7901	68	3	2.97	0	4	2.41	0	1	2.35	0	0	0	0
7901	69	9	2.97	0	6	2.41	0	2	2.35	0	0	0	0
7901	70	5	3.07	0	7	2.45	0	4	2.35	0	0	0	0
7901	71	4	3.07	0	6	2.45	0	2	2.35	0	0	0	0
7901	72	3	3.27	0	2	2.45	0	3	2.35	0	0	0	0
7901	73	7	3.27	0	10	2.45	3	1	2.35	0	0	0	0
7901	74	6	3.27	0	2	2.45	0	3	2.35	0	0	0	0
7901	75	5	3.27	0	3	2.45	0	2	2.35	0	0	0	0
7901	76	1	3.27	0	4	2.45	0	1	2.35	0	0	0	0
7901	77	4	3.27	0	7	2.45	0	2	2.35	0	0	0	0
7901	78	1	3.25	0	2	2.45	0	2	2.35	0	0	0	0
7901	79	6	3.25	0	4	2.45	0	1	2.35	0	0	0	0
7901	80	3	3.25	0	4	2.45	0	2	2.35	0	0	0	0
7901	81	1	3.25	0	3	2.45	0	3	2.35	0	0	0	0
7901	82	6	3.25	0	4	2.45	0	2	2.35	0	0	0	0
7901	83	2	3.25	0	4	2.45	0	0	0.00	0	0	0	0
7901	84	8	3.25	0	4	2.45	0	1	2.35	0	0	0	0
7901	85	1	3.25	0	0	0.00	0	0	0.00	0	0	0	0
7901	86	3	3.25	0	2	2.45	0	2	2.35	0	0	0	0
7901	87	4	3.25	0	5	2.45	0	0	0.00	0	0	0	0
7901	88	2	3.25	0	3	2.45	0	0	0.00	0	0	0	0
7901	89	8	3.25	0	5	2.45	0	1	2.35	0	0	0	0
7901	90	7	3.25	0	2	2.45	0	1	2.35	0	0	0	0
7901	91	2	3.25	0	2	2.45	0	0	0.00	0	0	0	0
7901	92	3	3.25	0	4	2.45	0	2	2.35	0	0	0	0
7901	93	5	3.25	0	3	2.45	0	1	2.35	0	0	0	0
7901	94	2	3.25	0	0	0.00	0	2	2.35	0	0	0	0
7901	95	1	3.25	0	6	2.45	0	1	2.35	0	0	0	0
7901	96	8	3.25	0	4	2.45	0	3	2.35	0	0	0	0
7901	97	1	3.25	0	1	2.45	0	0	0.00	0	0	0	0
7901	98	8	3.25	0	2	2.45	0	1	2.18	1	0	0	0
7901	99	3	3.25	0	3	2.45	0	1	2.18	1	0	0	0
7901	100	4	3.25	0	2	2.45	0	1	2.18	1	0	0	0
7901	101	0	0.00	0	6	2.45	0	1	2.18	1	0	0	0
7901	102	4	3.25	0	11	2.45	3	4	2.35	0	0	0	0
7901	103	4	3.25	0	3	2.55	0	0	0.00	0	0	0	0
7901	104	5	3.25	0	4	2.55	0	4	2.41	0	0	0	0

Question 1. What do you observe about the seasonal characteristics of the hot cereal category in this market?

Question 2. Discuss the impact of selling price and trade dealing on the trial rate of private label hot cereal.

Question 3. Review the differences in the price and promotion strategies of Grannies, Golden Prairie, and Tastimeal in the five stores. What defensive strategy would you recommend for Grannies?

Question 4. Estimate the response to the introduction of the private label. What is the impact on each of the national brands: Grannies, Golden Prairie, and Tastimeal?

Question 5. Each of the five stores seem to have a different approach to the pricing of hot cereals. What impact does the store pricing policy seem to have on each of the national brands and the private label brand?

Case 6: Regional Promotion

An analyst for the XYZ company is reviewing a market-by-market summary of the promotion results for the company's flagship brand. On a national basis the brand performs very near the average for all products in the top 50 markets as shown in Table 5.9.

Data for the individual markets are given in Table 5.9. The average retail selling price for this product is $1.39, with a manufacturer's list of $0.99. There are two trade promotion periods per year, with a $0.20 off-invoice allowance for product ordered in each promotion period. The deals are accepted by retailers selling 80 percent of all commodity volume (ACV). Of the retailers accepting the deal, about 75 percent (of the 80 percent, or 60 percent of total ACV) give retail performance. The average length of a price reduction deal in a store is two weeks. In constructing the tables, each store week counts as a promotion. The average chain orders enough product at the off-invoice price to cover base and incremental sales for the retail promotion, plus about three weeks worth of extra product (forward buying). Chains not performing a retail promotion typically order three weeks' worth of base sales.

Question 1: Calculate the costs and sales returns to the manufacturer in one promotion period from for each of the following:

a. An account that does not accept the promotion.
b. An account that accepts but does not perform.
c. An account that accepts, performing one week of price reduction only.
d. An account that accepts, performing two weeks of price reduction only.
e. An account that accepts, with one week of display only at average price discount.
f. An account that accepts, with one week feature only at average price discount.

g. An account that accepts, with one week feature and display at average price discount.

Question 2. Based on these results, prepare a charts for a presentation to the sales force illustrating the benefits if any to your company for each of the following:

a. Converting a nonaccepting account into an account with two weeks' price reduction only.
b. Converting a two-week price reduction account into a one-week feature only account.
c. Converting a feature-only account into a feature and display account.

Question 3. Redo question 1 calculating the costs and sales returns from the retailer's point of view. Redo question 2, preparing charts that the sales force can use to present to retailers considering the changes outlined in question 2a, 2b, or 2c.

Question 4. Prepare for your management a summary of the costs and sales returns from the current sales promotion activity. Illustrate the impact on volume sales and manufacturer profit that might be realized by a program that achieves the following objectives:

a. Converts 50 percent of the nonaccepting accounts into two-week price-reduction-only accounts.
b. Converts 50 percent of the current price-reduction-only accounts into feature-only accounts.
c. Converts 50 percent of the current feature-only accounts into feature and display accounts.

Question 5. If the sales force does not call on the nonaccepting accounts, the conversion in question 4a will not occur. How would eliminating their conversion affect the costs and sales returns to trade promotion?

Question 6. Calculate the costs and sales returns called for in questions 1 to 5 on a city-by-city basis using Table 5.9. Assuming that the percentage of nonacceptors in each city mirrors the national average, rank the cities in terms of the current programs result on each of the following:

a. Incremental volume sales and manufacturer trade-promotion spending.
b. Incremental manufacturer profit and manufacturer trade-promotion spending.
c. Incremental retailer profit and manufacturer trade- promotion spending.

Question 7. Classify the markets by high versus low manufacturer profit per dollar of manufacturer trade-promotion spending, and by high versus low retailer profit per dollar of manufacturer trade-promotion spending.

Question 8. For the program proposed in question 4, classify the markets by high versus low change in manufacturer total dollar return from trade promotion and by high versus low change in total promotional expenses. If some sales force effort could be redirected among the markets, which markets should gain and which should lose?

Question 9. What retailer activities should the sales force encourage? What should they discourage?

Question 10 (advanced). Assume that the product has about the same price elasticity in each market. That is, on price reduction only, a 1 percent change in price discount leads to a 2 percent change in sales; and on feature, display, or both, a 1 percent change in price discount leads to a 3.25 percent change in response. Using the average discounts shown in Table 5.9, estimate the additional sales that each market and promotion type with below-national-average discounts would achieve if the discounts were brought up to national average.

Question 11 (advanced). Using the elasticities from question 10 and the national average percentage promotion types, estimate the weighted average increase by market if all promotions were at the national average discount for that promotion type and the relative frequencies for the various promotions were at the national average.

Question 12. Rank the markets by their actual weighted average percentage increase on promotion versus the modeled results from question 11. Where should extra effort be concentrated to improve retailer performance on the trade-promotion program?

Table 5.9

TRADE PROMOTION EFFICIENCY, FREQUENCY, AND IMPACT
by Geographic Market

| | | Market Characteristics | | Sales Increases | | Efficiency |
	Everyday Price	Store Density	Accts (Top 67%)	Unit Sales	Dollar Sales	On Promotion
All 50 Markets	100	1.88	4.5	96.6	67.4	47.6
Albany	100	2.15	3	108.4	76.2	52.0
Atlanta	97	2.23	5	58.6	36.8	37.0
Baltimore	111	1.66	5	113.4	77.6	53.2
Birmingham	87	2.53	5	65.3	50.4	39.5
Boston	102	1.62	7	110.9	75.2	52.6
Buffalo/Rochester	100	1.76	4	219.3	165.1	68.7
Charlotte	84	2.75	4	49.6	36.4	33.2
Chicago	106	2.74	3	121.2	86.6	54.8

| | Everyday Price | Market Characteristics | | Sales Increases | | Efficiency |
		Store Density	Accts (Top 67%)	Unit Sales	Dollar Sales	On Promotion
Cincinnati	108	1.65	3	93.3	61.8	48.3
Cleveland	96	1.60	6	102.9	76.6	50.7
Columbus	103	1.43	5	91.1	60.0	47.7
Dallas	101	1.75	5	83.3	56.2	45.4
Denver	106	1.04	3	80.6	56.1	44.6
Des Moines	99	1.73	3	81.7	54.5	45.0
Detroit	102	1.50	5	105.0	75.2	51.2
Grand Rapids	102	1.54	4	163.4	119.9	62.0
Hartford/New Haven	103	1.73	6	146.8	103.2	59.5
Houston	105	2.01	5	93.4	62.1	48.3
Indianapolis	101	1.39	5	99.2	69.9	49.8
Jacksonville	86	2.47	3	51.8	36.0	34.1
Kansas City	99	1.49	5	150.5	112.5	60.1
Little Rock	95	2.51	5	105.6	74.0	51.4
Los Angeles	112	1.07	5	70.2	43.7	41.2
Louisville	95	2.76	4	93.0	69.1	48.2
Memphis	98	3.43	3	124.4	87.1	55.4
Miami	97	1.50	2	37.1	19.6	27.0
Milwaukee	101	1.19	3	117.1	88.5	53.9
Minneapolis	101	1.34	7	103.5	79.5	50.8
Nashville	99	3.12	4	72.7	49.0	42.1
New Orleans/Mobile	93	2.51	8	72.7	51.4	42.1
New York	109	1.62	7	139.2	90.2	58.2
Oklahoma City/Tulsa	101	2.30	4	121.1	85.6	54.8
Omaha	95	1.44	5	110.7	80.0	52.5
Orlando	93	1.83	3	54.6	37.7	35.3
Philadelphia	106	1.83	5	123.5	83.3	55.3
Phoenix	111	1.42	5	102.8	67.9	50.7
Pittsburgh	100	1.89	5	124.7	89.6	55.5
Portland	109	2.01	4	88.9	59.1	47.0
Raleigh/Durham	88	2.96	5	43.7	30.3	30.4
Richmond	94	2.42	5	80.3	59.8	44.5
Sacramento	111	1.47	4	69.6	45.6	41.0
Salt Lake/Boise	101	1.82	5	56.9	36.0	36.3
San Antonio	99	2.18	6	61.0	35.2	37.9
San Diego	109	1.06	4	73.4	47.9	42.3
San Francisco	119	1.43	3	64.1	40.6	39.0
Seattle	112	1.53	4	93.0	64.5	48.2
St. Louis	104	1.35	4	134.1	94.4	57.3
Syracuse	99	1.76	4	119.6	86.8	54.5
Tampa	96	1.66	3	57.0	37.4	36.3
Washington D.C.	109	1.63	5	124.4	86.1	55.4

| | Price Discount | | | | Frequency |
	Temp Price Cut	Feature Ad	Display	Display and Ad	On Promotion
All 50 Markets	14.9	19.2	10.4	23.6	21.1
Albany	15.3	19.6	8.5	21.1	18.6
Atlanta	15.0	15.8	8.8	20.5	26.6
Baltimore	15.7	21.5	14.6	32.0	20.3
Birmingham	13.1	7.7	5.6	15.0	17.8
Boston	15.9	19.7	13.2	24.4	17.6
Buffalo/Rochester	15.2	22.0	10.1	24.4	15.4
Charlotte	13.5	9.0	4.6	12.2	18.3
Chicago	14.6	22.2	11.8	25.8	22.8
Cincinnati	15.8	23.0	11.8	22.7	22.8
Cleveland	14.8	15.5	7.7	20.7	14.7
Columbus	15.9	21.8	11.5	26.1	28.5
Dallas	15.4	21.4	7.9	23.4	27.7
Denver	14.3	18.4	10.2	23.0	23.4
Des Moines	14.6	19.7	14.6	23.9	21.4
Detroit	15.2	17.8	8.9	24.3	15.8
Grand Rapids	15.7	22.4	13.2	27.4	13.0
Hartford/New Haven	17.7	18.6	12.1	24.6	17.5
Houston	15.8	25.1	11.1	29.1	24.9
Indianapolis	14.3	20.2	11.5	24.3	18.1
Jacksonville	13.7	10.4	2.5	15.0	18.5
Kansas City	15.8	22.9	12.5	27.0	15.8
Little Rock	16.8	19.9	21.1	22.9	21.6
Los Angeles	14.8	20.8	12.2	22.2	24.2
Louisville	14.0	17.3	7.7	21.0	23.9
Memphis	16.5	23.0	13.3	21.8	22.5
Miami	13.2	14.7	8.3	18.4	26.0
Milwaukee	12.2	19.8	11.2	25.9	18.8
Minneapolis	12.7	18.0	9.6	18.5	20.6
Nashville	15.0	16.3	9.1	21.6	24.3
New Orleans/Mobile	14.4	18.5	7.6	17.8	22.2
New York	18.9	25.2	11.9	32.7	21.1
Oklahoma City/Tulsa	16.4	23.0	15.5	24.1	20.8
Omaha	14.8	22.7	11.5	26.9	21.0
Orlando	12.8	12.3	4.9	17.4	17.9
Philadelphia	16.8	25.8	12.6	30.8	21.0
Phoenix	16.0	24.8	11.5	26.9	21.8
Pittsburgh	16.5	19.4	10.9	24.7	15.6
Portland	14.8	19.8	11.4	26.6	24.7
Raleigh/Durham	12.8	9.0	5.3	12.4	19.2
Richmond	14.2	16.3	5.6	25.6	18.7
Sacramento	13.7	18.4	12.8	22.3	24.0
Salt Lake/Boise	13.3	15.6	12.0	22.6	26.8
San Antonio	16.1	21.4	11.9	25.1	28.5

| | Price Discount | | | | Frequency |
	Temp Price Cut	Feature Ad	Display	Display and Ad	On Promotion
San Diego	14.2	19.9	10.5	22.9	24.0
San Francisco	13.8	20.2	10.5	25.5	23.6
Seattle	13.6	20.4	16.1	27.5	24.6
St.Louis	15.9	24.8	13.7	30.0	22.1
Syracuse	15.2	20.4	8.4	23.4	19.5
Tampa	13.8	13.9	8.4	21.5	19.0
Washington D.C.	15.8	22.1	12.7	32.2	16.8

| | Pct of Promotions | | | | Unit Volume |
	Temp Price Cut	Feature Ad	Display	Display and Ad	On Promotion
All 50 Markets	57.5	16.0	22.1	4.4	31.3
Albany	56.5	23.7	15.2	4.7	30.4
Atlanta	61.2	11.6	22.7	4.5	35.0
Baltimore	53.8	17.5	22.2	6.5	33.6
Birmingham	40.7	16.2	37.4	5.7	23.8
Boston	55.6	22.8	14.9	6.7	28.8
Buffalo/Rochester	44.4	31.5	17.5	6.6	32.8
Charlotte	41.6	9.7	45.4	3.2	22.7
Chicago	56.4	14.3	22.2	7.0	37.3
Cincinnati	64.5	14.7	16.6	4.1	33.9
Cleveland	42.4	21.5	30.7	5.4	22.8
Columbus	61.4	17.1	17.2	4.3	40.5
Dallas	61.7	13.8	20.2	4.3	38.8
Denver	67.5	10.4	18.5	3.6	33.5
Des Moines	72.5	13.6	12.1	1.9	29.7
Detroit	44.3	23.5	25.5	6.7	25.8
Grand Rapids	58.4	15.3	20.8	5.5	25.0
Hartford/New Haven	47.3	32.7	12.8	7.1	31.0
Houston	65.2	11.0	20.6	3.2	36.6
Indianapolis	57.8	15.8	21.8	4.6	28.2
Jacksonville	52.0	14.6	31.1	2.3	23.5
Kansas City	54.1	13.0	29.7	3.1	25.2
Little Rock	50.9	9.5	33.7	5.9	33.1
Los Angeles	70.0	16.3	10.4	3.2	34.5
Louisville	56.4	11.5	26.3	5.8	32.3
Memphis	57.8	9.9	26.6	5.6	36.3
Miami	60.5	21.1	14.6	3.7	30.0
Milwaukee	65.0	13.5	17.4	4.1	28.6
Minneapolis	53.4	9.5	32.5	4.5	30.8
Nashville	60.6	8.5	27.5	3.4	32.9
New Orleans/Mobile	44.5	13.7	35.5	6.3	29.9
New York	52.2	26.9	15.3	5.6	37.3
Oklahoma City/Tulsa	50.3	9.6	35.2	4.9	32.2

| | Pct of Promotions | | | | Unit Volume |
	Temp Price Cut	Feature Ad	Display	Display and Ad	On Promotion
Omaha	65.8	10.2	20.6	3.5	33.0
Orlando	56.0	20.4	21.3	2.4	23.8
Philadelphia	59.5	17.8	16.9	5.8	34.8
Phoenix	59.6	19.5	17.6	3.2	32.8
Pittsburgh	50.2	15.2	28.3	6.3	27.2
Portland	61.5	19.7	16.4	2.4	35.3
Raleigh/Durham	45.6	9.5	41.6	3.3	23.7
Richmond	42.7	9.6	43.2	4.5	26.0
Sacramento	74.3	11.2	12.8	1.8	32.8
Salt Lake/Boise	66.3	14.8	16.4	2.5	35.0
San Antonio	71.5	12.8	13.1	2.6	38.7
San Diego	71.9	13.3	11.6	3.2	34.2
San Francisco	73.4	12.0	12.2	2.4	32.2
Seattle	70.9	14.3	12.5	2.3	35.4
St. Louis	64.4	12.7	18.4	4.6	37.1
Syracuse	48.5	29.1	17.0	5.5	30.7
Tampa	57.5	22.0	17.1	3.4	25.0
Washington D.C.	55.2	20.8	18.3	5.6	28.8

| | Percent Promoted Volume | | | |
	Temp Price Cut	Feature Ad	Display	Display and Ad
All 50 Markets	43.4	19.8	25.6	11.2
Albany	38.9	31.0	18.0	12.0
Atlanta	51.1	12.1	27.7	9.0
Baltimore	36.9	21.9	21.8	19.5
Birmingham	33.8	14.9	42.8	8.5
Boston	36.2	25.8	18.4	19.6
Buffalo/Rochester	22.8	42.9	16.2	18.1
Charlotte	37.5	10.4	46.5	5.6
Chicago	41.1	18.1	24.6	16.2
Cincinnati	48.9	20.2	20.0	10.9
Cleveland	30.2	23.6	33.8	12.4
Columbus	46.0	21.7	20.3	12.1
Dallas	47.6	19.4	22.9	10.1
Denver	54.3	11.6	24.6	9.5
Des Moines	57.1	21.2	16.8	4.9
Detroit	29.6	26.0	27.0	17.4
Grand Rapids	35.5	22.6	22.9	18.9
Hartford/New Haven	29.8	36.3	14.5	19.4
Houston	49.3	17.7	23.9	9.0
Indianapolis	44.1	21.1	23.5	11.3
Jacksonville	46.7	14.2	34.5	4.6

	Temp Price Cut	Percent Promoted Volume Feature Ad	Display	Display and Ad
Kansas City	39.5	19.1	33.2	8.2
Little Rock	39.7	11.1	38.5	10.7
Los Angeles	56.3	20.5	14.3	9.0
Louisville	41.6	13.7	33.2	11.5
Memphis	40.9	12.2	32.4	14.5
Miami	52.4	22.4	18.9	6.2
Milwaukee	43.6	17.0	26.1	13.3
Minneapolis	39.1	12.6	38.0	10.3
Nashville	50.1	9.2	33.7	7.0
New Orleans/Mobile	35.9	16.6	35.4	12.1
New York	33.6	34.0	14.5	17.9
Oklahoma City/Tulsa	35.5	12.7	40.4	11.5
Omaha	48.0	15.0	24.6	12.4
Orlando	48.0	21.3	25.8	4.9
Philadelphia	41.5	25.9	17.3	15.2
Phoenix	43.9	27.8	20.9	7.4
Pittsburgh	34.0	19.4	29.6	17.0
Portland	47.6	23.4	22.5	6.5
Raleigh/Durham	39.9	9.8	45.3	5.1
Richmond	33.7	12.0	43.6	10.6
Sacramento	63.1	14.0	18.6	4.3
Salt Lake/Boise	53.9	16.4	23.6	6.1
San Antonio	58.4	14.7	18.7	8.2
San Diego	58.8	16.7	16.0	8.6
San Francisco	62.1	15.0	16.1	6.7
Seattle	54.4	17.8	20.5	7.3
St. Louis	41.5	19.0	21.4	18.1
Syracuse	31.2	36.6	18.6	13.6
Tampa	48.2	24.8	20.6	6.4
Washington D.C.	36.9	25.1	19.2	18.9

	Price Only	Trade Promotion Impact Feature Ad	Display	Display and Ad
Albany	1.39	2.43	2.45	5.44
Atlanta	1.26	1.62	2.00	3.61
Baltimore	1.39	2.48	2.31	7.77
Birmingham	1.18	1.38	2.06	3.79
Boston	1.27	2.24	2.58	5.69
Buffalo/Rochester	1.43	3.71	2.72	8.90
Charlotte	1.20	1.40	1.49	2.47
Chicago	1.50	2.65	2.49	5.45
Cincinnati	1.36	2.68	2.57	5.38
Cleveland	1.28	2.01	2.03	4.29

	Price Only	Trade Promotion Impact Feature Ad	Display	Display and Ad
Columbus	1.38	2.53	2.33	6.10
Dallas	1.36	2.49	2.22	5.19
Denver	1.40	2.04	2.50	5.21
Des Moines	1.32	2.40	2.47	4.98
Detroit	1.23	2.06	2.17	5.60
Grand Rapids	1.41	3.56	2.86	8.46
Hartford/New Haven	1.41	2.41	2.93	6.48
Houston	1.40	2.93	2.30	6.87
Indianapolis	1.36	2.36	2.38	5.43
Jacksonville	1.19	1.35	1.61	2.77
Kansas City	1.37	3.00	2.26	5.08
Little Rock	1.44	2.22	2.44	4.60
Los Angeles	1.37	2.13	2.37	4.65
Louisville	1.30	2.01	2.34	4.81
Memphis	1.49	2.66	2.94	6.91
Miami	1.14	1.47	1.77	2.49
Milwaukee	1.26	2.16	2.98	6.12
Minneapolis	1.26	2.41	2.32	4.56
Nashville	1.34	1.84	2.06	4.66
New Orleans/Mobile	1.23	2.00	1.81	4.80
New York	1.49	2.85	2.35	8.80
Oklahoma City/Tulsa	1.40	2.55	2.55	5.46
Omaha	1.41	3.02	2.59	8.90
Orlando	1.19	1.47	1.77	3.38
Philadelphia	1.50	2.98	2.45	6.31
Phoenix	1.38	2.66	2.38	6.28
Pittsburgh	1.37	2.65	2.39	6.08
Portland	1.34	2.16	2.57	5.44
Raleigh/Durham	1.19	1.32	1.49	2.12
Richmond	1.25	1.87	1.76	5.15
Sacramento	1.33	1.96	2.52	4.01
Salt Lake/Boise	1.23	1.71	2.55	5.75
San Antonio	1.30	1.93	2.56	6.35
San Diego	1.42	2.09	2.39	5.09
San Francisco	1.35	2.04	2.13	4.32
Seattle	1.43	2.26	3.19	6.38
St. Louis	1.45	3.17	3.07	8.93
Syracuse	1.26	2.42	2.23	4.98
Tampa	1.20	1.64	2.04	3.16
Washington D.C.	1.43	2.39	2.42	8.19

CHAPTER 6

RETAILER STRATEGIES

R etailers can effectively use sales promotion themselves, apart from any strategies employed by manufacturers. In fact, almost any of the same techniques can be applied with similar results. The retailers should, however, analyze their sales promotion programs in much the same way: from a financial perspective.

HEADQUARTERS' STRATEGY. The retailer headquarters faces a number of basic decisions about the methods that the chain will use in persuading consumers to shop in the stores of the chain. Many of these decisions relate to pricing practices, use of retailer promotions, and methods to be used in selecting and performing on promotional offers from the manufacturer. The net profit per dollar of sales is very low, usually in the 0 to 2 percent range. With such margins, acceptable returns on investment (ROI) are obtained only if the ratio of annual sales per average dollar invested to average investment is high. The cases in this book illustrate the kinds of short-term sales gains that can be made with retail promotional activity, but they also illustrate that those sales gains can easily lower profitability if the wrong price level is chosen.

Pricing Strategies. The predominant pricing strategy, regular pricing sets a general margin or markup level by department that is somewhat cost related. Produce, meat, and frozen foods, for example, carry somewhat higher margins than dry groceries to cover spoilage and date expiration problems. On the highest velocity products in a product category, the margins may be lower, reflecting price competition with other stores and sales pressure from the manufacturer. Trade promotion generally reflects a pass-through of manufacturer discounts, and the chain purchases additional product on manufacturer promotions for resale later at regular prices (forward buying). The chain may carry a private label brand as well as generic items.

An alternate strategy is the *everyday low price* store. In this case, the store seeks to maintain a low price relative to the rest of the market for most frequently purchased high-penetration products. Many slow-moving items will be priced nearly the same as in regular price stores. Instead of being concentrated in a few retail events, manufacturer promotion dollars will be used to lower the average shelf price of the products. Ad features will emphasize the everyday low price and will often carry little if any discount. Where price reductions are required as a condition of receiving manufacturer promotional allowances, they are usually the minimum possible.

An infrequently used pricing strategy is referred to as *premium products-premium price.* In this strategy, a store offers an assortment of unusual and often premium grade products with only the best moving regular items. Retail promotion may be minimal, unless the items qualify as exceptional. Markups are high and are usually coupled with higher than average service levels.

Store Format. In surveys of consumers on the important factors influencing the choice of store, low prices typically rank about fifth in importance. Such factors as cleanliness of the store, quality of products carried, location convenience, and customer service often rank higher than price. The physical layout of the store and the organization of the employees can strongly influence store image on such items. On the price dimension, a format that is associated with everyday low price is the *box store* format, where product is stored in its shipping cases, there is a minimum of customer service, and prices are generally low.

A store at the low price end of regular price format may ask customers to bag their own groceries, offer an aisle of specials that are sold out of the shipping cases, and have relatively few employees per 1,000 square feet of floor space. Moving up the price scale on regular pricers, consumers will find the addition of high markup auxiliary departments such as deli, seafood, salad bar, soup and sandwich snack bar, and plants. Depending upon the range of neighborhoods in a chain's market, its stores may span the whole range of regular price services, and they may have associated price zones that reflect the affluence of the neighborhood and the strength of the competition.

One extreme is the *hypermarket.* In this format, a large grocery operation is coupled with a mass-merchandiser operation and, perhaps, other operations such as a drugstore. Purchases from all sections may be combined in a single checkout, and acceptance of credit cards is more common than in other formats.

Seasonal Promotional Surcharges. One of headquarter's important decisions revolves around the management of manufacturers' requests for ad features or in-store displays on specific holidays such as the Fourth of July or Christmas. Such requests usually arise from an industrywide supposition that promotion is more effective on the dates requested. At these times, more than one manufacturer will probably be requesting such performance. In this event, retailers may demand a premium allowance for exclusivity, or they may accept offers from multiple manufacturers. In extreme cases, major retailers covering a significant portion of the market may require a holiday premium surcharge or allowance for performance on specific dates. As scanner data become broadly available, such surcharges will probably be under strong review by both manufacturer and retailer.

Allocation Rules for Category Promotions. Another important decision usually made by the retailer headquarters concerns allocation of the relatively fixed amount of in-store display space available. Even when the retailer headquarters offers the store manager a great deal of flexibility in choosing which items to display, it makes the category decision. The policy may suggest featuring only one major item from a category in a given ad. Alternatively, multiple-category products that include direct competitors may be allowed in the ad. Some features are constrained by the store's desire to stay within fixed ad space requirements, such as one, two, or four pages.

Acceptance of Promotional Terms. Manufacturers usually offer choices of promotional activity that will qualify for a trade-promotion offer. The chain headquarters decides which alternative to choose. The headquarters may aggressively negotiate trade terms. One chain recently adopted a rule in dealing with manufacturers that any promotional offer had to be valid for all stores in the chain. Such a policy severely restricts the ability of the manufacturer to use retail-sales promotion as part of a local or regional marketing strategy.

On the other hand, the manufacturer is required by law to make equivalent, but not identical, offers to all retailers in a marketing area. This may lead to behavioral quirks in the system. For example, there are a few retailers who do not use store ad features. In extreme cases, these retailers have qualified for a manufacturer's unyielding requirement for newspaper ad performance by announcing the product's availability among a newspaper's personal ads. At least one retailer is experimenting with a policy of guaranteed sales performance in order to qualify for a manufacturer's allowance. During the 1990s, we may expect to see moves toward manufacturer's performance requirements based on profitability to the manufacturer, and retailer acceptance based on profitability to the retailer.

Category-Management Strategies. In the past, simple pricing rules within a category were based upon sheer volume of an item sold, that is, percentage markup with some adjustment for high- and low-velocity items. Items or brands that were higher velocity—items that tended to generate greater sales volume—were the logical candidates for more promotion within a product category. Little attention was paid to the impact that promotion of the one item had on the remainder of the category.

Today's data collection and analysis make possible considerable refinement in terms of optimizing prices within a category to maximize retailer profit in the entire product category. *Cannibalization effects*—the impact a promotion of one brand or item within a category has on other items—can be quickly determined within a category. The other non-promoted items might have been more profitable for the retailer than the promoted items. The concern of the retailer ought to be promoting profitability within the category across all items and brands rather than for a single item or brand within the category.

STORE MANAGER'S STRATEGY. The degree of authority of the store manager in making promotional decisions varies greatly from retailer to retailer. In some chains, nearly all the product stocking, pricing, and promotional decisions are made by market or regional headquarters. In other chains, store or store cluster managers may be given a great deal of discretion in product stocking, pricing, and promotional decisions.

Allocation of Discretionary Display Space. The store manager is most commonly delegated the authority to allocate in-store display space. In such cases, managers may be restricted to only those products appearing in the feature ads, or they may have the ability to place on display any item in the store. The amount of discretionary space may vary from 2 percent to over 75 percent of total display space. The manager who correctly assesses the category products that are most responsive to display promotion in a particular store can significantly stimulate overall store sales.

Store-Specific Specials. Store-specific specials may be used for a variety of purposes. They may involve display-only activity, or they may be announced in local papers and fliers with notes of store restrictions. The specials may reflect the demographic composition of the neighborhood, such as a giant sale on baby supplies or on products for dentures and silver hair, or they may reflect a local event such as a town festival or sports championship. If slow-moving items are periodically pruned from the store, a significant number of items may be promoted as store closeouts. The data-processing task of evaluating store-specific specials has been beyond the capacity of most retailers prior to 1990, but this can be expected to change as microcomputers gain sufficient capacity to process a store's complete data.

Shelf Allocation and Delisting. Shelf space in a retail outlet is usually inflexible and cannot be easily modified from week to week. Overall allocations of shelf units to product categories may be made at the chain headquarters, but it may fall to the store manager to shift some allocations to account for specific products stocked and their shelf requirements. Analysis of sales rates on an item-by-item basis is a key requirement in assigning a product to a shelf placement. Both IRI and Nielsen have computer products designed to assist the retailer in shelf-space decision making. One of the striking outputs of these products is an analysis of the relative profitability of current brand space allocations. Measured in gross margin per linear foot, per square foot, or per cubic foot, most stores will find differences by over a factor of ten times between the best and worst items in the category.

Improved data-processing capabilities will allow the store manager greater responsibilities in the allocation and delisting process in the future. The availability of evaluation software will lay out explicit sales targets that a new item will have to promise in order to gain a position on the shelf and that the new item will then have to achieve in order to remain on the shelves. As data-handling improves, we would expect to see the shelf space allocation and product-delisting process delegated more and more to the store manager.

PRICING, MARGIN, AND PROFITS. The retailer, like the manufacturer, must always consider the impact a sales promotion program will have on the profitability of the firm. A retailer must also be aware that there is a fundamental relationship between the selling price of products and the sales volume of those products. The retailer has the advantage over the manufacturer in being able to directly estimate this relationship without having to rely on intervening organizations. In other words, the retailer doesn't need to go through other retailers as the manufacturer does to reach the final customer.

The retailer, like the manufacturer, should also obtain the individual purchase data and estimate the appropriate demand curve. A retailer who already collects scanner data and has the necessary computing power could certainly perform all the analysis internally. The retailer could also use an external research service organization just as the manufacturer could.

The retailer should analyze a product in terms of its contributions to margin, to selling expenses, and to profit. Ideally, the retailer could perform such an analysis for every product sold in the store. The problem, of course, is that this would require thousands of analyses, making it somewhat impractical for most retailers. A partial solution would be to select either high volume products or products that are deemed especially important to the retail outlet for whatever reason. A product may have a history of building store traffic, having special seasonal significance, or being especially attractive because of special allowances and offers made by the manufacturer. Despite the difficulties, the retailer should carefully examine the profitability of a given promotion in the same way as should the manufacturer.

Trade Promotion. A major consideration to any retailer should be trade promotions from manufacturers. Trade promotions come in several forms, including the familiar trade allowance or trade deal and even interest promotions, such as contests and sweepstakes for the trade. Normally a manufacturer supports trade promotion with advertising, in-store displays and related material, and sometimes additional consumer promotion. Cooperative advertising programs may be part of the package offered by the manufacturer as well.

All offers made by the manufacturer can potentially stretch the retailer's promotional budget and increase this profit. The trade allowance usually means a short-term reduction in price from the manufacturer, which immediately translates to reduced cost of goods for the retailer. Other advertising and promotional support from the manufacturer can substantially reduce the retailer's promotional expenses. The cost to the retailer is giving that manufacturer special advantage within the store with the potential of shifting sales volume from higher- retail-profit items to lower-profit items.

The retailer must carefully weigh the decision to take advantage of any manufacturer's offers, especially since there are likely to be many such offers. The retailer must consider each offer, in light of alternative promotion offers, in terms of the customer that the retailer currently serves or wishes to attract, the likely profit directly generated by the promotion, and the possible cannibalization effects.

COMPETITIVE STORES.   A retail store must view competitive stores in almost the same way that a manufacturer must view competing product brands. The retailer gives very special attention to the kind of customers it currently enjoys and considers what kind of customer a sales promotion program is likely to attract.

Source of Store Business.   The same ways of describing purchasers of a particular brand can be used to describe shoppers at a particular store. The same basic variables, including brand loyalty, deal proneness, and product usage can all be adapted to the individual store. Instead of brand loyalty, the concept becomes store loyalty toward a type of store within a geographical location. Product usage can be easily translated into store category usage.

Store switching by consumers is a fact of life for retailers. A Nielsen study covering this found that in a year the average household shops about 4.8 grocery retailers. Only about 10 percent of households limit themselves to one or two retailers in a year. However, a report from the FMI (Food Marketing Institute) "Trends - Consumer Attitudes and the Supermarket - 1991" indicates that supermarket switching based on advertised specials is only of modest importance, and may have declined during the 1980s. Consumers do compare prices among retailers from time to time, but as long as prices are competitive, tend to use a primary retailer based on convenience. While at that retailer, they economize by using price-off coupons, stocking up on bargain priced items, buying store brands or lower priced brands, particularly those on special.

An important tool for the retailer in understanding store switching behavior is the analysis of customer profiles. Using Nielsen Electronic Household Panel information, consumers may be profiled into four major groups based on household income and size: "Poor," "Just-Getting-By," "Living-Comfortably," and "Affluent." The importance of product categories, product pricing, and the use of specials to save money varies considerably among these groups. Using information available from the Donnally Marketing Information service, retailers can assess the consumer demographic profile of each individual store in their chain. Store shelf prices, and product display choices, can be managed against the specific consumer profile for a store.

Cherry Picking.   As the volume of promotion has increased, consumers can more frequently take advantage of some type of promotion to buy products. This has created a relatively new shopping behavior described by the term cherry picking, discussed in chapter 4. This phenomenon is an important side effect of the growing volume of sales promotion.

Store Switching.   Shoppers might tend to be loyal to a particular store, just as to a particular brand, or they may tend to switch stores frequently. In the first case, the shopper might be categorized as *store loyal* and in the latter case as a *store switcher*. The store can use this consumer characteristic in the same way as a manufacturer can use brand switching. The physical proximity of competing stores is an important determinant of store loyalty.

STORE COUPONS AND DOUBLE COUPONING.
Coupons are a common form of sales promotion, making them a very competitive form. Coupon clutter has become a major concern today because of the tremendous number of coupons distributed to consumers. As the popularity of coupons increases, there is more opportunity for stores to take advantage.

The store has very little control over the coupons that the manufacturer issues. The manufacturer may place the coupons on and in the package, or distribute them through the media. The only work left for the store is to redeem them.

In order for the store itself to take advantage of opportunities that coupons represent, it must offer its own coupons or take special advantage of the manufacturer coupons. A retail or store coupon—a coupon offered by a store and redeemable by that store—may or may not be offered in response to a trade allowance or other special incentive provided to the retailer by a manufacturer. The store, interested in generating store traffic, might pick any single product or combination of products that would provide the greatest advantage. Retail or store coupons are then entirely the responsibility of the store management.

Because manufacturers' coupons are available to consumers in abundant supply and because they may be redeemed at virtually any supermarket in the area, some stores offer special additional incentives to coupon holders. The additional incentive may be a *double coupon*—a coupon that gives the consumer twice the face value of the manufacturer's coupon. If a coupon offers ten cents off, then the store would offer twenty cents off. The store, of course, would need to absorb the additional ten cents.

Some stores offer other versions of double couponing and, perhaps, even triple couponing. Some stores may even offer to redeem competing store or trade coupons. The important consideration, regardless of the offer, is the profit that the promotional program provides the store. The store should be guided by the same underlying principles as the manufacturer. One particularly effective usage is the practice of giving double or triple coupon value only during selected hours of operation, such as Tuesday only or 11:00 P.M. to 6:00 A.M. only. Such practices can balance labor requirements or checkout and restocking considerations.

PRIVATE BRANDS AND GENERIC BRANDS.
Larger store chains or members of wholesale groups often are able to offer private brands and generic brands. The term *private brands* refers to brands that are owned by the retailer or wholesaler rather

than the manufacturer. The term *generic brands* refers to products offered with no brand identification at all. Both private brands and generic brands are usually offered to consumers at normal prices lower than the manufacturer brands.

Part of the reason the private and generic brands have lower prices is that they do not require the same margin from the manufacturer as do the manufacturer's own brands with their substantial selling, advertising, and promotion expenses. This means, however, that the retailer does not have the same advertising and sales promotion support for the private and generic brands that is available for the manufacturer's brand. The store itself must bear all the selling expense associated with the private brand in addition to any sales promotion program.

Manufacturers who supply private and generic brands to the trade may also be packaging a lower quality product, keeping the highest quality product for their own brand. This is especially convenient for food packagers that are always faced with a differing quality in the raw material they are able to obtain. Products that have a less desirable color, for example, would more likely be packaged as a private or generic brand.

Private and generic brands shift all the advertising and promotional responsibility to the retailer. Presumably the private and generic brands generate a greater margin for the store, but thus may also incur greater selling expenses.

CONTINUITY PROMOTIONS. Not only are retailers interested in generating store traffic with promotional programs, but they are also interested in promoting store loyalty. One method of providing an incentive for store loyalty is the *continuity promotion.* Continuity promotions are typified by trading-stamp programs and store-premium programs. Store-premium programs are normally designed so that one piece of a set, such as a set of books or dishes, can be purchased each week.

There are several problems with continuity programs. First, they normally take a long time to run. A trading-stamp program, for example, is difficult to change or stop, and it must run for several years. Another problem with continuity programs is that the offer may not appeal to all consumers, or even to a very large proportion of consumers. Books, for example, might appeal only to a very small segment. Also, consumers usually want immediate gratification, and may not want to wait an extended period of time to complete the set. Moreover, continuity promotions do not always tie in well with other promotions and displays. Continuity promotions represent a relatively small proportion of the promotional programs, but they do represent a viable alternative.

RETAILER DECISIONS. Retailers receive many promotional offers from manufacturers as part of the normal course of doing business. Such offers cause the retailer to face several decisions. First, the promotional program a manufacturer offers probably includes a trade allowance and assorted consumer promotions such as coupons, consumer advertising support, and in-store display material. Second, promotional programs would be offered by competing manufacturers in the same product category. Third, the typical retailer could probably not possibly use all the promotional material provided by all the manufacturers. The retailer must, therefore, be somewhat selective in choosing promotional programs.

Use of Display. Probably one of the resources that is in shortest supply for most retailers is display space. Space on shelves, at the end of aisles, and in other locations in the store is usually very limited. In-store point-of-purchase displays are very frequently supplied by manufacturers to support both consumer advertising and promotional programs. The problem for the retailer is deciding which displays to choose.

Retailers may also want to use displays that they themselves have developed, or they may not want to use any display at all. To make the best decision, the retailer must understand the impact of the display on the sales of the product.

Change of Regular Price. When a product is sold to the retailer with a trade allowance, the retailer must decide whether to pass along the price reduction to the consumer. The argument for not lowering the regular price would be that the margin would increase, thereby increasing the profitability. The argument for lowering the price might be that the volume would increase, thereby increasing the profitability. Another consideration must also be the competitive environment of the store—would lowering the price have an impact on store traffic?

Additional Price Reduction. Knowing that the competing retailers in the market area may be receiving the same trade allowance or other special price promotion from the manufacturer, a retailer may want to increase the incentive by providing an additional price reduction. An additional price reduction not only provides the retailer with a competitive edge over other retailers, but it also takes advantages of the advertising and promotion that the manufacturer already has in place. Rather than trying to overcome or to compete with the manufacturer's efforts in the very crowded and cluttered media and promotional environment, the retailer can reinforce the manufacturer's program and probably reap substantially greater benefit.

Additional Promotions. In the same way that a retailer can take advantage of a special price by increasing the offer, the retailer can provide additional promotion to support the manufacturer's effort. The retailer can also feature the promotion in its own advertising, emphasizing the special price or other aspects of a promotion. Not only does using additional promotion provide the opportunity to increase the impact of the program, but it may also provide the retailer with the opportunity to take advantage of cooperative advertising programs the manufacturer may have.

The criterion the retailer should use for these decisions should be the same as does the manufacturer: profit. The retailer must be able to perform the same type of analysis as the manufacturer.

RETAILER BUYING DECISIONS.

When a manufacturer makes a trade allowance or other special price offer, the retailer must make the decision whether or not to buy. Some of the considerations here involve much more than promotion, and for more discussion, a book dealing with retail inventory management should be consulted.

Promotion Buying. Anytime a manufacturer makes a special price offer, the retailer is tempted to buy because the cost of goods is reduced. The question is how much, if any, of the product should be purchased at the promotional price?

A major consideration for the retailer should be what volume can be sold to the consumer at what price. Certainly, if the retailer can sell additional volume of the product at a special price and make additional profit, the retailer should purchase the appropriate volume of the product. However, the retailer must be able to estimate the volume it can sell at various price levels. Otherwise the decision becomes guesswork.

A store that overbuys a product at a special promotional price is in a position of having to lower the price beyond the point of generating profit and, in fact, may actually incur loss. A store that has too much inventory must pay carrying costs for that inventory. However, a store that has too little inventory loses the opportunity to make a sale and may substantially reduce its long-term image. Being out of stock on a promotional item may anger customers and cause loss of goodwill.

Diverting. When manufacturers offer different promotional terms to retailers in different regions in the country, they create the opportunity for the retailer to engage in the practice known as diverting. When a retailer has the opportunity to purchase a large quantity of merchandise at an especially favorable price it may buy considerably more than it believes it can sell through its own stores. The additional merchandise is resold, or diverted, to other retailers in other regions. The practice can include international as well as domestic merchandise.

Diverting can be quite profitable for the retailer, especially when the retailer is selling the merchandise to other retailers at a slightly higher price. It is also profitable for the buying retailer that acquires the merchandise at a lower price from the diverting retailer who directly from the manufacturer, broker, or wholesaler. The practice of diverting might defeat some manufacturer's regional marketing strategies and could create sales force morale problems. Manufacturers generally downplay the significance of diverting in the implementation of their promotional strategies. Estimates generally are that 10 percent to 20 percent of the merchandise sold to retailers is diverted. On the positive side, a manufacturer could view the practice of diverting as a way of building volume and providing retailers with an additional incentive.

Forward Buying. The term forward buying refers to promotional programs offered by manufacturers that provide the retailer an opportunity to buy a product at a special price with a delivery date some time in the future different from normal delivery. This provides the manufacturer with more stability in the business and may provide operating cash. From the point of view of the retailer the product is available at a lower price, with a longer period during which to prepare promotional and advertising programs. The same requirement to analyze and understand the data apply to this situation as they do to all of the other promotional decisions faced by the retailer.

Goodwill and Carryover. The long-term image of the store is a very important consideration for the retailer. Special promotional offers from manufacturers should be seriously considered. The retailer must carefully evaluate its source of business and make sure that the promotional programs it takes advantage of enhance rather than damage the store's image. For example, a store can easily acquire a reputation for having a poor selection or only selling items that no one really wants. The long-term impact of selling heavily promoted items might be damaging to the image of the store and to the goodwill that store may have established.

Manufacturer and Retailer Interactive Strategies. This book has provided many examples of manufacturer's sales promotion programs that have been successful in generating profit. There have also been examples of sales promotion programs that have been successful for retailers. However, the most effective strategies are those in which the efforts of the manufacturer and the retailer work together.

When the manufacturer's and the retailer's strategies supplement and reinforce each other, the effect is almost always considerably better than the two strategies would have been if they had not been carefully coordinated. The advertising and sales promotion done by the manufacturer is always considerably more effective when it is reinforced by the advertising and sales promotion done by the retailer, and vice versa. Strategies that interact always do a much better job of breaking through the clutter and reaching the consumer.

A retailer must carefully weigh the advantages of supporting a manufacturer's program against the competitive pressures of other retailers. A retailer may not participate in a program that would be more effective overall in order to weaken the relative competitive position among other retailers.

Case 7: Colas II

Colas are sold through a variety of retail outlets, but this case considers only sales through grocery outlets. Around 90 percent of all households purchase a cola carbonated beverage at least once per year. This figure is based upon a sample of 10,000 households. The average time between purchases is 37 days.

The cola segment of carbonated beverages sold through grocery outlets is dominated by two brands. On an overall basis, including all diet and related products, each company holds about a 45 percent market share of total grocery sales. The business, however, is conducted through the operations of individual bottlers, both corporately operated and franchised. Market shares, prices, dominant package sizes, and levels of promotional activity vary widely from market to market.

Cola sales through grocery stores are one of the heaviest areas of trade promotion activity. About 67 percent of all cola sales are made with some form of trade promotion. About 40 percent of all cola sales are made with a feature price in an advertisement, 40 percent with an in-store display, and 40 percent with a shelf-price reduction.

This case is based on cola sales for the two leading brands, labeled Brands A and B. In a chain of grocery outlets in a single market, sales data are collected by scanners. The chain uses only one type of trade promotion on all carbonated beverages, including colas. Nearly 80 percent of total cola sales are concentrated in a single dominant package size. This chain uses only two types of promotional support for Brand A and Brand B dominant packages—price reduction only and price reduction in conjunction with one additional element of trade support. Tables 6.1 and 6.2 provide the data for this case. An adjusted volume is given that removes fluctuations due to week-to-week variations in total store sales (volume per $1,000 ACV normalization).

The promotion column in Tables 6.1 and 6.2 indicate whether additional support beyond price reduction was given. Prices are given for a standardized unit, and while proportional to shelf prices per package, they are not the actual prices to which shoppers were exposed.

Question 1. Plot the Brand A share by week. Use different symbols to indicate the following conditions:

a. No additional promotion support on either Brand A or Brand B.
b. Support on Brand A; no support on Brand B.
c. No support on Brand A; support on Brand B.
d. Support on Brand A, and support on Brand B.

What conclusions does this plot suggest about the relation of trade support to share of weekly sales?

Question 2. Plot Brand A's adjusted volume by week, again using four symbols to differentiate among the promotional support possibilities. What conclusions does this plot suggest about the relation of trade support to volume sales?

Question 3. Plot the total of Brand A's and Brand B's adjusted volumes by week, again using four symbols to differentiate among the promotional support possibilities. What conclusions does this plot suggest about the relation of trade support to total store movement?

Question 4. Weeks 36 through 44 were all nonpromoted periods for Brand A, but there were some Brand B promotions. Make separate bar charts of the adjusted volume for Brand A and Brand B during these weeks. Indicate which weeks had Brand B promotions. What do these charts indicate in terms of the sources of Brand B promotion volume, and of the direct impact of Brand B promotions on Brand A sales?

Question 5. Plot Brand A adjusted volume versus its price difference to Brand B. What conclusions would you draw from this chart about the importance to Brand A sales of price differentials to Brand B?

Question 6. Plot Brand A adjusted volume versus Brand A price. Calculate the average adjusted volume for Brand A at each different level of observed Brand A price. Plot these averages. What conclusions would you draw from these charts about the importance to Brand A sales of Brand A's absolute price?

Question 7. Plot Brand A share versus its price difference to Brand B. What conclusions would you draw from this chart about the impact of price differentials to Brand B on Brand A's share?

Question 8. Plot Brand A share versus Brand A price. Comparing this chart to the chart from question 7, which relation is strongest?

Question 9. Discuss the importance of price reductions and additional promotional activity to Brand A's annual volume and share in this chain.

Table 6.1

CHAIN SALES OF DOMINANT COLA PACKS BY WEEK

Share is Dominant Brand A and Brand B Packs Only

Week	Brand A Volume	Brand A Price	Brand A Promotion	Brand A Share	Price Difference
DEC 08	713	4.91	1	27.6	–0.01
DEC 15	6010	2.65	1	73.4	–1.34
DEC 22	1900	3.99	1	16.4	1.34
DEC 29	1351	3.98	1	23.2	–0.01
JAN 05	1297	4.31	1	38.4	–0.30
JAN 12	4357	3.32	1	72.5	–1.86
JAN 19	1284	5.13	1	46.5	–0.04
JAN 26	741	4.92	0	33.4	–0.24
FEB 02	628	5.31	0	30.6	0.27
FEB 09	494	5.31	0	22.1	0.49
FEB 16	6096	3.05	1	76.6	–1.77
FEB 23	1501	5.32	0	45.9	0.61
MAR 02	5534	3.32	1	76.6	–1.09
MAR 09	180	4.59	1	9.2	0.15
MAR 16	1345	4.70	1	42.0	0.25
MAR 23	783	4.63	1	29.3	0.16
MAR 30	780	4.32	1	32.1	0.03
APR 06	1013	3.83	1	36.7	–0.53

Week	Brand A Volume	Brand A Price	Brand A Promotion	Brand A Share	Price Difference
APR 13	1981	3.84	1	53.4	–0.37
APR 20	1336	3.84	1	14.3	1.19
APR 27	2012	3.84	1	41.6	–0.47
MAY 04	1089	4.72	0	40.3	0.42
MAY 11	1019	4.48	0	10.4	1.83
MAY 18	7276	2.83	1	72.8	–2.01
MAY 25	1985	4.70	1	15.4	2.19
JUN 01	736	4.65	1	18.2	–0.03
JUN 08	6610	2.61	1	79.2	–2.19
JUN 15	1745	4.58	1	48.9	0.66
JUN 22	6146	2.65	1	78.7	–1.59
JUN 29	1797	4.56	1	66.8	–0.05
JUL 06	1019	3.84	1	51.9	–0.95
JUL 13	2620	3.84	1	78.4	–0.94
JUL 20	1308	3.84	1	61.5	–0.94
JUL 27	3679	3.84	1	73.3	0.00
AUG 03	1652	3.84	1	21.2	0.00
AUG 10	3923	3.84	1	61.1	–0.28
AUG 17	1724	4.79	1	49.6	0.80
AUG 24	1108	4.78	1	22.7	0.79
AUG 31	670	4.79	0	25.9	0.95
SEP 07	698	3.84	1	11.3	0.00
SEP 14	2397	3.84	1	51.2	–0.87
SEP 21	1219	4.67	1	45.6	–0.12
SEP 28	1051	4.86	1	39.1	–0.01
OCT 05	990	5.06	0	32.6	0.06
OCT 12	877	5.06	0	33.0	0.26
OCT 19	899	5.05	0	30.1	0.05
OCT 26	870	5.06	0	34.6	0.01
NOV 02	794	5.05	0	35.6	0.00
NOV 09	805	5.05	0	36.9	0.00
NOV 16	825	5.05	0	32.4	0.00
NOV 23	5485	2.65	1	80.2	–2.40
NOV 30	2725	4.70	1	30.0	2.05

Table 6.2

CHAIN SALES OF DOMINANT COLA PACKS BY WEEK

Share Is Dominant Brand A and Brand B Packs Only

Week	Brand B Volume	Brand B Price	Brand B Promotion	Brand B Share	Price Difference
DEC 08	1871	4.92	0	72.4	−0.01
DEC 15	2181	3.99	1	26.6	−1.34
DEC 22	9698	2.65	1	83.6	1.34
DEC 29	4463	3.99	1	76.8	−0.01
JAN 05	2082	4.61	0	61.6	−0.30
JAN 12	1656	5.18	0	27.5	−1.86
JAN 19	1477	5.17	1	53.5	−0.04
JAN 26	1477	5.16	0	66.6	−0.24
FEB 02	1421	5.04	1	69.4	0.27
FEB 09	1737	4.82	1	77.9	0.49
FEB 16	1861	4.82	1	23.4	−1.77
FEB 23	1768	4.71	1	54.1	0.61
MAR 02	1692	4.41	1	23.4	−1.09
MAR 09	1784	4.44	1	90.8	0.15
MAR 16	1855	4.45	1	58.0	0.25
MAR 23	1886	4.47	1	70.7	0.16
MAR 30	1647	4.29	1	67.9	0.03
APR 06	1746	4.36	1	63.3	−0.53
APR 13	1728	4.21	1	46.6	−0.37
APR 20	7981	2.65	1	85.7	1.19
APR 27	2820	4.31	1	58.4	−0.47
MAY 04	1611	4.30	1	59.7	0.42
MAY 11	8780	2.65	1	89.6	1.83
MAY 18	2714	4.84	1	27.2	−2.01
MAY 25	10882	2.51	1	84.6	2.19
JUN 01	3312	4.68	1	81.8	−0.03
JUN 08	1731	4.80	1	20.8	−2.19
JUN 15	1822	3.92	1	51.1	0.66
JUN 22	1668	4.24	1	21.3	−1.59
JUN 29	892	4.61	1	33.2	−0.05
JUL 06	945	4.79	1	48.1	−0.95
JUL 13	723	4.78	1	21.6	−0.94
JUL 20	819	4.78	1	38.5	−0.94
JUL 27	1340	3.84	1	26.7	0.00
AUG 03	6150	3.84	1	78.8	0.00
AUG 10	2495	4.12	1	38.9	−0.28
AUG 17	1752	3.99	1	50.4	0.80
AUG 24	3782	3.99	1	77.3	0.79
AUG 31	1915	3.84	1	74.1	0.95

Week	Brand B Volume	Brand B Price	Brand B Promotion	Brand B Share	Price Difference
SEP 07	5489	3.84	1	88.7	0.00
SEP 14	2289	4.71	1	48.8	–0.87
SEP 21	1452	4.79	1	54.4	–0.12
SEP 28	1638	4.87	1	60.9	–0.01
OCT 05	2048	5.00	1	67.4	0.06
OCT 12	1781	4.80	1	67.0	0.26
OCT 19	2083	5.00	1	69.9	0.05
OCT 26	1643	5.05	1	65.4	0.01
NOV 02	1439	5.05	1	64.4	0.00
NOV 09	1378	5.05	1	63.1	0.00
NOV 16	1724	5.05	1	67.6	0.00
NOV 23	1358	5.05	0	19.8	–2.40
NOV 30	6370	2.65	1	70.0	2.05

Case 8: Category Management

The XYZ Grocery Company has just received a copy of "Trade Promotion Evaluation," a publication from the SCAN*PRO Promotion Evaluation Service of Nielsen Marketing Research. This report gives the results from a number of categories on the average impact of a 10 percent price reduction both alone and in connection with ad feature only and in-store display (Table 6.3). The XYZ Grocery Company has additional information about the average percent discount which is given in their stores and the relative frequency of promotion types within these categories. After reviewing the stores' margins, the following guidelines were established:

1. The chain's average margin is about 20 percent. That is, the cost of purchase from manufacturer (including deal allowances) = 80 percent of average retail selling price. This estimate will be used except as noted.
2. Exceptions to the 20 percent rule are Chocolate Candy, Gourmet Cat Food, and Frozen Potatoes at 25 percent; and Peanut Butter and Shortening at 15 percent.

Management wants to use this information to make a first-cut comparison of the relative profitability of merchandising various categories. In particular, the store from time to time runs loss leaders, which are price reductions not supported by manufacturer trade allowances. Infrequently, the store may also support a loss-leader with ad-feature or in-store displays. Since these promotions are not supported by the manufacturer, forward buying is not a consideration in evaluating the impact of the promotion, but bottom-line results are important.

Question 1. Using the percent volume increase with 10 percent price reduction column, estimate the change in total dollar sales per 100 dollars of base sales, and the change in gross margin dollars per 100 dollars of base sales for:

a. One week of 10 percent price reduction only.

b. One week of 10 percent reduction with ad feature.

c. One week of 10 percent reduction with display only.

d. One week of 10 percent reduction with ad and display.

e. Four weeks of 10 percent price reduction.

Question 2. Management asks that a table similar to the one in question 1 be prepared. However, the results are to be estimated at the average percent discount for promotion in the chain. After some reflection, the analyst decides on the following procedure for adjusting for depth of discount: An average percent increase per percent of price reduction will be estimated for price reduction only (pro) by dividing the estimated impact of a 10 percent price reduction only(pro) by 10 percent. For ad feature, store display, or both, the analyst will use 3.5 times this number.

For example, the price reduction only number for laundry detergents is 50 percent divided by 10, or 5.0 percent per percent of price decrease. Taking 3.5 times 5 percent yields 17.5 percentage points increase per percent of price decrease for feature or display on laundry detergent. We would estimate a price reduction only number at 12.1 percent price decrease this way:

$$50\% - (10.0 - 12.1)*5.0\% = 60.5\% \text{ increase.}$$

For display only at 6.3 percent reduction, we would estimate as:

$$431 - (10.0 - 6.3)*17.5\% = 266.3\% \text{ increase.}$$

Comment on the results, comparing the various promotion types within categories, and across the categories.

Question 3. Pick the most profitable category for each of the four promotion types. Look at each category in terms of total gross margin per $100 of base sales for the alternatives of price reductions of 0, 5, 10, 15, and 20 percent. Generalize your results into a few simple rules. (For example, "Discounts should be about one-third of total gross margin" or " We are currently about optimum on discounts.")

Question 4. Assuming that the current average percent price reductions reflect roughly the same level of pass-through of manufacturer allowances for all categories, where would you recommend giving additional retailer funding (that would result in deeper discounts to the consumer)? Where would you recommend reducing the pass-through of manufacturer discounts.

Table 6.3

SCAN*PRO PROMOTION EVALUATION SERVICE

Category	volume sales index with 10% price reduce				average % price reduction			
	tpr only	fea only	dis only	f&d comb	tpr only	fea only	dis only	f&d comb
Laundry Det	150	308	431	615	12.1	11.7	6.3	14.3
Dishwashr Det	135	278	358	524	13.3	12.6	6.7	13.9
Toothpaste	134	199	211	316	12.7	12.3	5.9	15.4
Cookies	131	205	238	305	9.8	10.2	2.2	13.8
Nuts	131	186	270	286	8.6	11.1	3.4	12.2
Bath Tissue	130	221	321	452	14.4	13.9	8.9	16.8
Peanut Butter	128	207	249	379	15.2	14.4	7.9	18.5
Canned Vegs	128	235	284	420	11.2	10.9	8.8	12.3
Dry Cat Food	128	164	228	294	6.4	7.6	3.6	7.1
Catsup	127	207	262	343	10.1	9.4	5.9	14.5
Dry Dog Food	127	177	265	334	8.4	8.1	4.0	9.3
Chocolate Candy	125	186	248	416	9.3	8.9	4.9	11.4
Deodorant	125	161	163	223	7.6	7.0	3.9	9.2
Gourmet Cat Food	125	164	203	248	4.3	5.7	2.2	5.5
Potato Chips	120	181	218	310	12.5	13.8	7.9	15.6
Mayonnaise	120	184	188	392	17.2	16.4	10.2	18.0
Shortening	120	192	185	258	15.2	17.1	8.6	17.9
Canned Soup	119	184	254	381	7.3	8.7	4.1	9.2
RTE Pudding	118	147	197	247	8.1	7.8	5.3	10.9
Dry Soup Mix	117	164	216	268	11.8	12.0	7.4	13.1
Frozen Potatoes	114	159	190	262	13.1	9.8	8.2	16.4
Salad Dressing	107	145	161	227	12.4	10.4	6.3	14.9

Table 6.3 (continued)

SCAN*PRO PROMOTION EVALUATION SERVICE

Category	Percentage			
	tpr only	fea only	display only	feat & display
Laundry Det	36.2	33.5	21.4	9.0
Dishwashr Det	36.9	36.1	19.5	7.5
Toothpaste	51.9	19.8	21.3	7.1
Cookies	63.0	13.4	17.3	6.3
Nuts	80.8	9.3	7.4	2.5
Bath Tissue	26.8	29.9	34.8	8.5
Peanut Butter	52.9	23.2	15.9	8.0
Canned Vegs	62.7	16.5	14.7	6.2
Dry Cat Food	80.5	4.2	12.4	2.8
Catsup	49.0	17.6	27.2	6.3
Dry Dog Food	83.0	8.4	6.9	1.7
Chocolate Candy	81.4	2.3	13.5	2.8
Deodorant	50.2	17.9	23.5	8.4
Gourmet Cat Food	77.2	19.2	1.3	2.2
Potato Chips	30.1	22.5	36.3	11.1
Mayonnaise	49.0	27.4	17.4	6.2
Shortening	63.4	26.4	7.5	2.8
Canned Soup	57.1	18.9	18.8	5.3
RTE Pudding	61.8	10.3	23.1	4.8
Dry Soup Mix	84.0	8.0	5.8	2.2
Frozen Potatoes	81.8	8.7	7.4	2.1
Salad Dressing	41.1	19.7	32.8	6.4

CHAPTER 7

ANALYSIS TECHNIQUES
FOR DISAGGREGATE DATA

This chapter reviews some of the methods for analyzing the impact of short-term promotional activity on retail sales of a product. The chapter is quite technical and may not be appropriate for all readers. Unless otherwise noted, the discussion applies to sales data collected weekly on an outlet-by-outlet basis. The objective is to measure the short term increase in sales as a result of short-term price reductions that will later be rescinded, in-store promotion such as special display location, and local advertising (feature) of the type that is typically delivered each week in newspaper ads or advertising fliers.

The collection of scanner data provides timely and accurate information about sales of items at the very low level of brands, size, and flavor, on an outlet-by-outlet basis. Typically information is available on many different competitive brands. This wealth of information can lead to "analysis paralysis" in determining the structure of the analysis. Academic research suggests that promotion responses may vary across markets, across retail chains within a market, and across individual outlets within a chain. Responses may vary across subcategories within a main category (e.g., regular versus diet product variations), by relative price level (e.g., premium, regular, or generic), and by size and flavor. This richness can lead to significant decision problems in defining the analysis. Should flavor data be added to give total brand size? Should size data be added to give total brand? Should data be added across stores to give total chain? Should data be added across chains to give total market? Should markets be added to give regions or total U.S. figures? Should data be added across weeks to give four-weekly, eight-weekly, or quarterly data observations? In this chapter, very detailed disaggregate data will be examined. In the next chapter, some of the methods that can be used to provide analyses of data at higher levels of aggregation will be examined.

DATA PREPARATION. Some of the most common data preparation procedures used for analysis of sales promotion data are discussed in this section. For some more advanced discussions, see Blattberg and Neslin (1990) and Hanssens, Parsons, and Schultz (1990).

A critical first step in planning any analysis is outlining the objectives of the study: What questions are to be answered, and at what level of detail? As an example, consider the question What is likely to happen if I take a 5 percent price hike on Brand

X? In this case, although responses to the 5 percent price hike might vary significantly from market to market, there may be many reasons why price hikes cannot be set differently on a market-by-market basis. However, because the answer is required on a national basis, this does not mean that the data should be summarized to a national level in order to perform the analysis. Typically, the data would be prepared at the store, chain, or market level, and these individual observations would be used in the analysis, even though only one average response number is to be calculated. This inclusion of observations from different collection points is called *pooling of data.* Similarly, if the price hike is contemplated on several related brands, the data might be prepared individually by brand and pooled for the analysis to give a single point estimate of the impact of the price increase. The general rule is to aggregate within a store week all individual items that will have identical promotional treatment and to analyze these data pooled to the appropriate level of chain, market, region, brand, and size to answer management questions. To avoid distortion of the results when pooling, some preprocessing of the data is required beyond aggregating to the appropriate level.

Time Series Analysis. Scanner data are obviously time series data. As such they exhibit change over time due to trend and seasonality, and they may have overlays of irregular or semiregular effects such as those caused by holiday and pay weeks (such as weeks in which government transfer payments like Social Security are delivered). Although the data are generally collected on the same weekly cycle across markets, the start of the advertising cycle for retailers (best-food day) may vary from market to market. When attempting precise analysis of subtle effects, this may cause problems. Techniques based on time series analysis may be used to simplify the analysis. A common technique is to express the data as a ratio or index to a moving average of nearby data. The baselining methodology discussed in the following section is an example of an analysis based on time series methods. The branch of time series analysis known as intervention analysis may be useful in studying promotions that occur infrequently and that may have carryover effects. Time series analysis of the residuals from regression estimation can be extremely useful in detecting problems associated with trend and seasonal specifications in the model.

For many product categories, sales promotion can stimulate category sales within the channel and can even stimulate overall category consumption. There are many product categories considered to be in peak demand around holidays such as Christmas or Fourth of July. In such categories, the special holiday weeks will typically have heavy promotional activity. It becomes extremely difficult to separate increases in sales due to promotional activity from seasonal increases in sales. In later sections this problem will be reviewed in more detail.

Univariate time series analysis of the residuals from a regression model should identify problems with specification of trend or seasonality. If carryover effects from sales promotion, trend, or seasonality are not properly handled, then time series diagnostics should assist in locating the problems.

Indexing. The most common transformation used in data preparation is to convert the time series of sales data (volume and prices) to time series of indexes. Since stores vary in sizes, unless all stores in the analysis have identical promotional conditions, some combinations of promotional conditions will be unbalanced on store size and will represent the results of stores with higher- or lower-than-average sales. Although sales of an item within a store across time can be indexed to its average weekly sales over time in that store, a preferred procedure is to index over conditions with roughly equal promotional conditions. Indexing to average sales in nonpromoted weeks is most common, with indexing to average sales during which there was neither feature nor display as an alternative. For price data, prices may be indexed to the average nonpromoted price, recent non-promoted prices, the average price across all stores in the city, or other price series, such as the price of a major competitor.

Indexing also aids in the interpretation of analysis results. Regression coefficients become more directly interpretable as the index point change in sales per point change in the independent variable. Analyses run across different chains or different cities using the same analysis procedure become directly comparable. Instead of generating results that report "Memphis feature adds 437 cases to city sales while a Los Angeles feature adds 14,885 cases," results can report that "Memphis feature increases sales by 87 percent of the average sales in a nonpromoted week in Memphis, while a Los Angeles feature increases sales by 54 percent of the average sales in a nonpromoted week in Los Angeles." The latter conveys information in a more suitable form for making comparisons.

Price Representation. One of the striking findings from the study of scanner data was the diversity of prices and price environments that exist. Prices vary within a store across time. Within a chain in one city, there may be several price zones across which prices vary as a reflection of very local competitive conditions. In one market some chains may have prices that reflect a policy of everyday low pricing, while other chains may have significantly higher prices. Promotional policies with respect to price may range from frequent promotions with small price reductions to infrequent promotions with deep price discounts. The amount of pass-through of manufacturers' incentives may vary widely from chain to chain.

As a result of this diversity, the actual price charged for a product is generally not usable directly in an analysis of pricing and promotion, unless the objective is to study per capita consumption as related to price charged. Even then, it is probable that transformations will have to be made to reflect market-to-market differences in economic factors such as household income. As a result, most price-promotion analyses focus on the impact of changes in price over time within a store (time series response), and transform the data to minimize the impact of price differences across stores (cross-sectional response).

The most common transformations are to consider price differences relative to competitive prices in the store or to index prices to some base or average condition for the product in a store. Differencing versus a competitor is seldom used unless there is one and only one major competitor per store. If there is more than one competitor, constructing an adequate price difference function becomes quite difficult. Even if the difference series can be constructed, price differences may be quite wrapped up with promotional activity. In the previous section, several alternatives were mentioned for constructing price index series. The exact choice will depend very specifically upon the objective of the analysis. If one of the goals is to assess the impact on sales of long-run price changes, then both price and sales variables for a store should be indexed to bases that change only slowly over time. For analyses covering a relatively short period of time (18 months or less), prices might be indexed to the average nonpromoted price over the time period. For longer periods of time, it might be necessary to construct a price series that accounts for price inflation over the analysis period. See the next section.

When the focus of the study is to analyze the impact of short-run price reductions on sales, the prices may be indexed versus an average of recent prices charged by the store. A problem arises when the recent past contains other promotional prices. This may complicate the meaning of a particular price index versus base. A preferred transformation is to remove previous promotional prices and index versus recent regular price, or base price. This choice of transformation may still cause problems when pooling across a everyday-low-pricer set of stores and a set of regular-price stores in a market. In this case, the same advertised price might represent little if any discount in the everyday-low-price store, but might represent significant price reduction in the higher-priced store. Thus, a highly composite price series might be in order where the base is constructed from recent history within a store if unadvertised but constructed from market average advertised prices when advertised.

Deflating Series. When a study is conducted that covers a long period of time, pricing variables may have to be adjusted to account for the pattern of general inflation of consumer prices that has prevailed in the United States since the early 1960s. The typical procedure for grocery store prices entails first indexing a monthly consumer price index to its average over the analysis period and then dividing store prices by this index. After completing this price deflation, the analysis can proceed in the same manner as an analysis using undeflated prices. Similarly, sales volumes for a long-run analysis might have to be placed on a per capita basis or otherwise adjusted for changes over time in the population being served by the store.

For shorter-run analyses, the most common type of series deflation is a seasonality adjustment. If a product has significant changes in sales level within a year on a regular and predictable basis, promotion usually occurs during periods of high seasonality rather than during low seasonality periods. In this case, a comparison of average weekly sales during non-promoted weeks versus average sales during promoted weeks could be significantly biased by seasonality effects.

Another problem that can cause the need for series adjustment is the presence of a time-trend component that the impact of pricing and promotional activity by the brand and its competitors cannot explain. If the category sales are relatively stable and smooth across time, then many of the problems associated with seasonal changes and category growth or decline trends can be eliminated by analyzing share instead of volume. However, a more robust and generally applicable procedure is to construct a moving average of total category sales by store, convert each such series to an index series, and use that index series as a deflator that removes category trend and seasonality from a brand-sales series.

Problems may arise if the specific brand (or size) set being modeled has a trend component or seasonality pattern that is different from that of the overall category. For example, diet products often are not as strongly seasonal as other products in the category. Where possible, the category definition should be based on the notion of similarity of seasonal pattern as well as strength of competition. In the extreme, analysis methods should be used that allow construction of a seasonal series based on data for a single brand (and size). In chapter 8, examples of such a method based on aggregate data will be discussed.

BASELINING. The need to separate promotional impacts from normal sales when analyzing manufacturer shipments, and later, scanner data led to the development of time-series-based analysis methods modified to cope with the special problems associated with sales promotion. These methods are variations on the ratio-to-average methods of time series and attempt to separate weekly sales into two components: (1) base sales, which refer to the level of sales expected, including trend and seasonality but excluding the impact of sales promotion (including short-term carryover or loss) and (2) incremental volume, that extra amount of sales attributable to retail sales promotion activity. Variations of this methodology are used by SPAR, IRI, and Nielsen Marketing Research in the analysis of promotional activity.

Once the separation has been made into base and incremental volumes, analysis of many questions relating to volume sales is also simplified. Short-term promotional effects of price reduction, ad featuring, and in-store display can be analyzed using only promoted observations, and studying the relation of total sales to base sales. Long-run effects such as the impact of changes in the base price, the introduction of new competitors, the impact of TV or print advertising, and the general pattern of trend and seasonality can be studied using the base volume, without confounding by short-term promotional activities.

Algorithm. The baselining method described here is the SCAN*PRO model developed for Nielsen Marketing Research. Its general flow is illustrated in Figure 7.1. The separation of total sales into base and incremental volume is the basis of NMR'S SCAN*PRO Monitor promotion analysis and evaluation system. It is generally applied on a retail-outlet-by-retail outlet basis so that the base volumes are adjusted for any trends in sales due to changes in overall store size over time. The basis of the method is a time series analysis that uses non-promoted store-week observations.

The steps in estimating SCAN*PRO baselines are the following:

1. For each store-week-item, identify the "regular or base" price. Identify observations with significant price reductions as "temporary price reduction weeks (TPR)".

2. Identify observations that have promotions (feature, display, or TPR), and flag them as "excluded."

3. Form a preliminary forward estimate of the baseline by setting the initial baseline, b(o), equal to the average of the first deseasonalized observations not flagged as excluded for all observations prior to and including the first non-promoted week.

4. For each week i (i = 2, 3, . . . n), after the first non-promoted week, update the forward baseline estimate by the formula:

B(i) = baseline estimate in week i (i = 2,3, . .)

= B(i - 1) if week i is flagged as excluded,

or

= a times deseasonalized volume in week i plus (1 - a) times B(i - 1) if week i is not excluded. (This method of updating estimates is known as an exponentially weighted moving average. A typical value for a is 1/3.)

5. Repeat step 4 in reverse time, to obtain a backward baseline.

6. Calculate the preliminary baseline for week i as the average of the forward baseline for week i - 1 and the backward baseline for week i + 1.

7. Using only the unflagged observations for the brand and its close competitors during week i, compute the average ratio of actual sales to baseline sales. Assuming that there are at least some minimum observations, such as six to ten, then adjust all baselines, whether flagged as excluded or not, by the average ratio. This covariate adjustment process adjusts for single period peaks or valleys in seasonality.

8. The baseline is the expected sales in the absence of promotion. Incremental sales due to promotion are then determined as follows for promoted items:

Incremental Sales = Total Sales - Base Sales.

Assumptions and Problems. Baselining is a heuristic procedure and depends upon many assumptions. One of the first assumptions occurs in the flagging of observations as promoted or not. In the generally inflationary environment that has existed in the United States since the mid-1960s, most consumers have been conditioned to accept upward changes in price as permanent and to view downward changes in price as temporary. With this in mind, weeks with price increases are generally not flagged and removed from the baselining procedure. Weeks of reduced price are flagged as promotion weeks (temporary price reduction). Occasionally, examination of the time series of prices will reveal that a price reduction was permanent.

Due to the general consumer conditioning, it seems likely that the initial weeks of the reduced price will be responded to as if they were temporary, but as time passes, the reduced price will become accepted as the new base price. The length of time for this to occur probably varies from product category to product category (and is probably related to the length of the average purchase cycle). Analysis methods such as SCAN*PRO require that each week be marked as promoted or not prior to calculating the baseline, so the length of time that a reduced price is considered to be a promoted price as opposed to a base price often becomes an input assumption rather than an analytically derived output.

Blattberg and Neslin (1990) note that when promotions are frequent, baselines may be biased downward by deal-to-deal buying, and be unrealistically low. They further note that baseline estimation typically does not include adjustment for competitive effects. Since competitors are more likely to promote when the analysis brand is not being promoted, the net effect is to give the baselines a downward bias. The setting of such factors as the length of price-reduction series that are tagged as promoted, the amount of price change that qualifies as a price reduction (typically 5 percent or more) as opposed to a nonpromotion, the choice of the smoothing constant, and the treatment of extreme values (outliers) is all highly judgmental. Different analysts given the same data might respond with somewhat different conclusions. The statistical properties of the baseline estimates have had little study and are not yet well known.

A significant problem encountered in baselining scanner data occurs when several different UPC codes are logically related. For example, bath soap may be sold routinely as single bars and two-bar packs. From time to time, a four-bar pack might appear with the label "Buy three get one free" (bonus pack), or a specially printed two-bar pack may have the legend "Ten cents off" (price pack). The presence of the temporary special packs will obviously affect the sales of the regular packs, and there is no special requirement that the trade maintain consistent per-volume pricing on different packs of the bar soap. In this case, an aggregate data series and an aggregate price series may have to be prepared, and the presence of the special packs in sufficient quantity may in itself constitute a type of promotion.

The strongest competitors to a brand size are often other sizes of the same brand, as loyal brand buyers may shift sizes to obtain promotional discounts. This may make the combining of individual brand baselines and base volumes up to the brand level a nontrivial task. Finally, in extreme cases such as the heavily promoted carbonated beverage categories, virtually all the observations may be marked as promoted, leaving few, if any, observations on which to establish a baseline value.

Despite the problems noted above, the positive attributes of baselining methods for use in evaluating short-term promotion impacts have led it to be the basis for promotion analysis on scanner-based sales-tracking data. Significant research is being conducted to address the issues noted, and the properties of baselining should become more and more well-known as this research progresses.

REGRESSION. Most statistical analysis and spread-sheet analysis programs have the ability to use linear regression in order to relate changes in a set of independent variables to changes in a variable of interest, the dependent variable. In this discussion, the variable of interest is some measure of sales, and we assume that it has been converted to an index series (refer to the subsection on indexing). Market share is a possible alternative choice, but modeling share poses a number of problems. Some choices of model specification for market share can lead to estimates of market share for a brand that are logically impossible—to negative shares or shares greater than one. This becomes more of a problem if several brands are being modeled simultaneously. In this case, the total estimated brand shares seldom add up to 100 percent. It is possible to construct models that yield logically consistent market shares, but these models have a fairly high degree of complexity in the solution procedure. See Cooper and Nakanishi (1988) for an example of such a model.

This discussion will be restricted to linear models and multiplicative models that can be transformed into linear models. The primary output of a regression analysis is the expression of a predicted value for the dependent variable as a weighted sum of the values of the independent variables. Given a particular set of data for the dependent variable and the values of the associated independent variables, nearly all regression packages will deliver the same weights for each variable. These variable weights indicate the expected change in the dependent variable per unit change in the independent variable. For a detailed discussion, see an econometrics textbook such as Mansfield (1983), or Wonnacott and Wonnacott (1979).

The independent variables may have continuously varying values, such as the ratio of actual price to base price, or the independent variable may be restricted to only two values, zero and one. In this case, the variable is known as a dummy variable, and it represents the presence or absence of some condition.

Choice of Space. It is assumed that a linear regression solution package will be used for the regression analysis. The dependent variable may be entered directly as coded (*linear dependent*), or we may take the natural log of the dependent (*log dependent*). The usual case in analyzing volume series or volume index series of data is to take the log of the dependent variable. This implies that the relation of the independent variables is a multiplicative relation and closes off one side of the logical consistency problem. With the log dependent expressed as a linear combination of the independent variables, we in effect state that the dependent is expressible as the fully multiplicative product of the result of exponentiating the product of each variable value times its weight. In equation form, the two expressions are as follows:

(A) Multiplicative: dependent = b0 × exp(b1*variable1) × exp(b2*variable2)

and

(B) Log: log(dependent) = b0 + b1*variable1 + b2*variable2.

These equations might be contrasted with the linear form,

(C) Linear: dependent = A0 + A1*variable1 + A2*variable2.

In examining scanner data, it is frequently found that the residuals from the linear equation (C above) are larger as the predicted values increase. When residuals are plotted versus the predicted value, one finds a pattern that is megaphone or fan shaped, indicating that the error standard deviation is proportional to the mean predicted value. In this case, the transformation to log dependent is usually mandated (see Winer 1971), as the linear formulation leads to a violation of the regression assumption that forecast errors have about the same mean and standard deviation across all observations.

It is usually only at levels of aggregation higher than the chain level (market, region, or national) that scanner data stabilizes to the point that the linear form of the dependent variable can be used for UPC-, size-, or brand-level analyses. If the data at store or category level are aggregated across many brands (manufacturer or subcategory level for example), the linear form of the dependent variable might be possible to use.

Secondary Issues. It is assumed that the products to be modeled have on the average some amount of sales in each retail outlet in each week. For infrequently purchased or low-household-penetration products, this assumption may not be correct. Low-purchase-frequency items may be carried by the outlet but have no sales in a week. Products of this type usually tend to have a distribution of weekly sales that follows the Poisson type of distribution. The presence of zeros in the observation set for the dependent variable can cause problems in attempting a transformation to the log of a dependent variable. One method of overcoming this problem is to aggregate across stores with similar pricing and promotion policies and model the aggregated data with log transformation. Less frequently, the modeler may aggregate over time periods with similar promotional conditions and replace the sales variable in a set of time periods by its average. Still another possibility is to eliminate all periods of zero sales from the data set and analyze sales relative to those periods in which a purchase was made.

Another consideration is the interaction effects that are expected. A dummy variable that is typically used for coding the presence of feature or display has slightly differing interpretation in log versus linear space. In a linear model, the feature 0-1 variable measures the expected extra sales when a feature is present, while in a multiplicative model, the feature 0-1 coefficient determines a multiplier $K = \exp$ (feature coefficient) that multiplies sales when a feature is present. If we assume that the sales data have been coded so that the average level of sales without promotion is 1.0, then the linear model coefficient (AF) shows the proportionate increase in sales when a feature is present. The multiplicative version of the model should return an estimate for the feature coefficient of approximately $\log (1 + AF)$. Thus, in both cases, the estimated change in sales would be AF.

A linear model with terms for feature and display suggests that a feature or display combination has an impact estimated by adding the feature effect and the display effect (Sales $= 1 + AF + DF$). In the multiplicative formulation, the feature or display impact is estimated by the product of the terms $(1 + AF)$ and $(1 + DF)$. Thus, the multiplicative formulation would suggest that a feature display combination always has an incremental impact greater than the sum of the incremental impact of a feature only and the incremental impact of a display only. To allow more flexibility, we either code three separate events (feature only, display only, and feature or display combination), or we code a feature or display interaction term as the product of the feature dummy and the display dummy. This additional term compensates for the structural differences generated by the log model versus the linear model.

Price Terms. There are a number of methods of expressing the price series. Price is seldom entered directly, even in linear models, but is converted into an index series of some sort. Most common is transformation to a ratio by dividing by a base price or average price, and transformation to a percentage difference from base price. Further transformation may be made for the regression analysis. The most common variations for entering price into the regression equation are as follows:

1. Log (price/base price).
2. Price/base price.
3. Discount as defined by (base price - price)/base price.
4. Reciprocal discount as defined by $1/(1 + \text{discount})$, where discount is calculated in (3) above.

Competitive prices are typically transformed in the same manner as the brand price.

The choice of a log dependent with log price (1) is known as the log-log model and is the classic model used in economic analysis. The coefficients of the price terms are directly interpretable as price elasticities, the percentage change in volume per percentage change is price. When log dependent is combined with the price ratio (2) or price discount (3), the resulting model is known as log-lin modeling. The combination of linear dependent with price ratio (2) or price discount (3) is known as lin-lin modeling. The possibility exists of combining a linear dependent with the log price (1) in a lin-log formulation, but little research has been reported on this form. The reciprocal discount (4) variation is usually paired with log dependent, and is used to allow the price response function to assume an S-shape. Comparing the models for log-log and log-lin, significant differences occur only at deep discounts (35 percent or more), so if most discounts fall in the 0 to 35 percent price range, there will be little difference in the predicted results from the model.

Results from Log Model. Few studies compare one single model fitted across a wide number of categories. Totten (1986) reports on one log-log model fitted across 116 product categories. In that study, scanner data were summarized to the brand level for 780 major national and regional branded products. Private label and generic items were excluded. The data were collected from 79 grocery stores in 8 markets. Brand-size data were summarized to give total brand volume, and a volume-weighted average price was calculated. Individual observations were at the brand-store-week level. All brands in a category were pooled to obtain "average brand" results. Model coefficients were not reported.

Wisniewski and Blattberg (1988) report on a more-detailed semi-log model. Using 48 weeks of data from a single chain, they analyzed 28 brands in 4 product categories. The model structure estimated both the brands own response to price and promotion, and its cross impact on other category brands. Its detail specification is:

Unit sales of brand i in period t
    = Exp(constant for brand i
      + A1* Regular price of brand i in period t
      + A2/(1 + discount for brand i in period t)
      + sum for competitors k of (Gk/Price of comp k)
      + B1*discount for brand i, period t and first deal week + B2*discount fo
        brand i, period t, when ad occurred in other than first deal week
      + B3*discount for brand i, period t, last deal week
      + B4*number of full weeks after deal start
      + Trend/(Seasonal terms).

This study found evidence of a very distinct pattern of asymmetry in the competitive cross-impacts among the brands. Brands were classified into premium priced, moderate priced, and generic. In 14 of 15 comparisons, premium priced brands showed significant deal cross-impact on other premium priced brands. In seven of eight cases, premium priced brands on deal were found to draw sales away from brands in the moderate priced or private label classification. In only one of four cases did a premium priced brands dealing affect a generic brands sales. In four of six cases, moderate priced or private label brands dealing affected the sales of other moderate/private label brands, and in two of four cases, the dealing of moderate priced brands significantly affected sales of generic brands. In only three of 32 comparisons did dealing by lower price tier brands show statistically significant unit sales impact on higher price tier brands. The conclusion was that when higher-price, higher-quality brands price deal, they steal sales from their own price tier and the price tier below.

For two additional categories, the analysis was extended to the brand-size level. Significant own-brand size cannibalization was found. There was evidence of price-tier competition within a size. Particularly for dog food, deals on the smaller size affected sales of larger size other brands, but the reverse direction interaction did not take place.

The complexity of these reported findings suggest first that extreme care should be taken in formulating regression models on store scanner data. A variety of complex interactions are possible among the various brand-sizes in a product category, and differences in the mix of brands and sizes available, possibly coupled with different pricing policies from chain to chain and market to market make it difficult to draw general conclusions about the strength and nature of cross-competitive deal impacts.

SPECIAL ANALYSES. Once the basic analysis model has been specified, one often desires to examine some special issues. Most manufacturers and retailers have long-held beliefs about the way particular products and categories respond to pricing and promotional activities. Using a model similar to the one described in the preceding subsection, it is easy to add additional variables to the regression equation in order to test some of these beliefs. This model uses the B4 term to test the hypothesis that pricing and promotional responses vary as a function of the time the deal has been offered in sequential weeks. Examination of sales data where deals are offered for an extended period of time typically show a response decay over time similar to that shown in Figure 7.1.

Similar terms can be used based on depth of discount to test explicitly to see if the model has constant price elasticity over various levels of price cut, or whether the price elasticity changes as a function of the level of discount.

Representing Causal Factors. The log model accounts for regular price, competitive pricing, and deal activity all in one model. Often, we wish to study only the short term impacts of deal without regard to competition, and without the complexities of assessing the impact of base price both in absolute and relative to competition. In

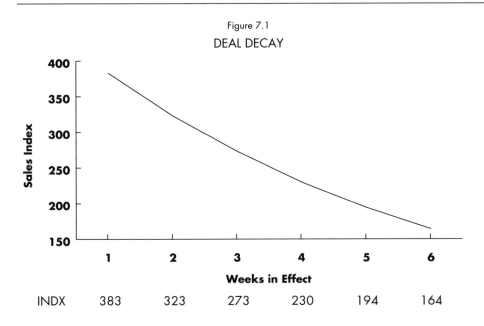

Figure 7.1
DEAL DECAY

	1	2	3	4	5	6
INDX	383	323	273	230	194	164

Weeks in Effect

this case, a simple and robust model can be developed by using the baseline model from the baselining section as a starting point for data transformation. The baseline summarizes the long run average impact of brand price, competitive prices, store trends, and the short term week to week variations expected due to seasonality.

After the data has baselined, we can study short term promotional effects using only the data flagged as promoted (ad-feature, in-store display, or TPR).

Model definitions are:

PEI = Promotion Effectiveness Index
   = 100* Promoted Week Sales/Baseline sales
PCT = Percent Price Discount
   = 100*(regular price - actual price)/regular price
FEA = Ad Feature indicator variable
   = 1 if an ad feature in week, 0 otherwise
DIS = In-store Display indicator variable
   = 1 if an in-store display in week, 0 otherwise
PM = Store feature or display promotion
   = 1 if either ad-feature or in-store display, 0 otherwise.

The model specification is:

PEI in promoted week i

$$= \text{EXP}(\text{constant} + A_1 {}^* PCT + A_2 {}^* PCT {}^* PM + B_1 {}^* FEA + B_2 {}^* DIS + B_3 {}^* FEA {}^* DIS).$$

The model is actually estimated by linear regression of the form:

$$\log(PEI) = \text{constant} + A_1 {}^* PCT + A_2 {}^* PCT {}^* PM + B_1 {}^* FEA + B_2 {}^* DIS + B_3 {}^* FEA {}^* DIS).$$

This model illustrates a number of points concerning model construction and data preparation for that model. The construction of the discount variable as a proportion of regular price allows one to run the model estimation across a large number of products and cities and still have the A1 and A2 model coefficients directly comparable. The B3 term, where the variable is derived as the product of the feature variable and the display variable, is a typical interaction term. In its absence, the main effects of the B1 (feature) and B2 (display) terms would be added to estimate the combined effect of a feature and display combination. When it is present, it adjusts for a combined effect that is on average either higher or lower than the sum of the individual effects.

An alternative method of representing this possibility is to redefine the variables. The three coded variables would be feature only, display only, and a feature and display combination. If this regression were to be done, the feature-only coefficient would be the same as B1, the display-only coefficient would be the same as B2, and the feature and display coefficient would equal B1 + B2 + B3. The major difference in the output of most regression packages is that in interaction, as shown in the model, the t-test for the B3 feature and display term represents a test as to whether the combined effect is significantly different from the sum of the individual effects. The A2 Price*Promo term tests to see if price elasticity changes for feature or display observations versus ordinary price changes. This term is usually significant and negative, indicating that price elasticities are higher on feature or display weeks than in other weeks. The terms multiplied by Shrindx represent tests to see if pricing or promotional response changes predictably versus share.

Many tests of category or brand-specific hypotheses can be made by creating simple 0-1 dummy variables and incorporating them into the model. The exact construction of the variables, and the meaning attached to their coefficient will vary across model specification types (i.e., the interpretation of a variable in a log-log model is usually different from that given the same variable in a lin-lin model). In this section, we assume a base model of the log-lin form described above. Some hypothesized effects that might be handled by a single 0-1 dummy variable for each question are as follows: Do sales of my product increase significantly on a holiday week? on the week before a holiday? on the week after a holiday? on the week containing the first of the month? Did the introduction of competitor X cause a significant decrease in sales? How are my promotion increases on brand-size A affected if there is another size of my brand on promotion at the same time? How have my sales been affected since the freeze in Florida?

Sometimes, a series of dummy variables is used to capture an effect that might be handled by a continuous variable. The results of such an analysis might indicate the proper type of continuous variable to construct in order to measure the effect. For example, instead of constructing seasonal or trend variables for the model, we might put in a separate 0-1 variable for each week. The resulting weekly estimates might suggest a method of constructing a seasonality series that captures much of the week-to-week fluctuations that might be attributable to trend and seasonality.

Another example might be in testing for wear-out effects if displays are up for a product in a retail store for several weeks in a row. If variables are constructed for "this week is the second week of a display," "this week is the third week of a display," and so on, plotting the estimates by week might indicate the types of mathematical representation required. Estimating the time path of sales in response to a price change is another type of question we might explore by using sets of dummy variables (first week of new price, second week of new price, third week, and so on). After the exploration, it would probably be best to substitute a single variable template rather than retain the dummy variables. The dropping of a manufacturer's coupon is another activity where we might wish to estimate the impact of an event lasting over several periods of time.

Some typical effects that might be tested via dummy variables are listed below. An interpretation of each variable is given for the case where dependent variable is logged. (The interpretation is for exp(variable coefficient). The variables are as follows:

1. *Holiday Week.* This 0-1 variable would test whether sales are significantly higher or lower during the weeks coded as "1." The interpretation is the average multiplier during weeks coded as "1" versus sales in weeks coded as "0."

2. *Promotion on Holiday.* This 0-1 variable would be coded "1" on observations on a holiday week which were also coded as promotion weeks. The interpretation is the average multiplier for promotion sales on weeks coded as "1" versus promotion sales on weeks coded as "0."

3. *Introduction of Competitor X.* All weeks on or after the introduction of competitor X into a store would be coded as "1." The interpretation is the average multiplier for sales in the post-introduction period versus sales in the pre-introduction period. The *t*-test for significance versus 0 would indicate whether the introduction of the competitor significantly altered brand sales.

4. *Impact of Other Size Promotion.* This variable would be coded as "1" if another size of the same brand was promoting in the same store during the period of observation. This variable would measure the average cross-impact of brand-size promotions.

5. *Promotion Exclusivity.* This variable would be coded as "1" if a competitor had a promotion in the same store during the observation period in which the analysis brand also had a promotion. This variable would measure the average impact on total weekly sales when the promotion is nonexclusive versus weeks in which the analysis brand has exclusive promotion.

6. *Advertising Plan Change.* This variable would be coded as "1" after a signifi-
    cant change in the brand's advertising plan—a copy change or major
    change in spending level, for example—and coded as "0" before the change.
    This variable would measure the average change in brand sales after the
    advertising plan change versus sales prior to the change.

Multiperiod Effects. A second class of variables arises when an activity has
an impact over several time periods. In this case, we might use a continuous variable to
model the impact over time. As mentioned above, we might first run a number of analyses using dummy variables to model the effect and then establish a "template" variable
that captures the average time relationship. Examples of such activity might be the dropping of a manufacturer's coupon. The impact might be greatest in the first week of the
drop, and decline thereafter at a rate related to such factors as the coupon value and the
repurchase cycle for the category. One choice of simple representation might be a continuous variable that is weeks since the last coupon drop. If there is a template that shows
the average percentage of a total coupon effect that is realized in each week, then this
template could be used. There are several typical time-path effects that can be studied.

Weekly change in response to price reduction is a typical time-path effect. It
seems reasonable to assume that response to price reduction would be greatest in the
first week of the reduction and would gradually decay as people become accustomed to
the new price. If we were attempting to determine the optimum length of time to maintain a temporary price reduction, the time path of response could become an important
subject of study.

Time path of response to continued in-store display is another typical effect to be
studied. Often, in-store displays may be left in place for several weeks. Studies often show
little falloff in display response from the first week to the second, and even from the second week to the third, but response may show rapid falloff after the third successive week.

Seasonal effects are another typical path. The log model estimates the average
promotional response as a function of the price discount and promotional condition,
and it estimates this response as a ratio to non-promoted sales. This ratio might, however, vary from peak season to sales trough. Constructing a variable that is equal to the
seasonality index, or the log of the seasonality index when the brand is on promotion,
and zero otherwise will allow testing to determine if the effects vary as a function of
the season of the year.

Effects that vary by brand share are yet another typical path to study. The construction of a share index variable by dividing a brand's long run share in a store by its
long run share in the market or total U.S. could be used to test the hypothesis that the
brand's response to its own pricing and promotion activities, and its response to the
pricing and promotional activities of competitors, is related to its share level. A similar

set of variables could be constructed to test the hypothesis that a brand's pricing and promotional response will vary as a function of its brand or category development level (sales per million category buyers, or category sales per million households in a marketing area).

The resulting models can represent quite varied and complex behavior. The log model, for example, allows for sales response to deal that varies depending upon the presence of promotion (features or displays) and whether the ad appeared in the first week or a deal, or later weeks. The incorporation of a time wear-out function (with coefficient B4) allows the model to fit a wide range of response functions beyond the simple constant log-elasticity form allowed in its absence.

Forecasting Versus Statistical Analysis Models. One distinction should be clearly made as part of the initial specification of the model. Is the model analysis to serve as a basis for management decision making, or is the model to be used as a basis for preparing a forecast of future brand performance? The answer will usually materially alter the form of the analysis in the rich environment of scanner data. When the purpose of the analysis is to prepare a forecast of future sales, one must forecast all the independent variables. If the model were to contain a term like feature exclusivity, then one of the inputs required in preparing a forecast of future sales would be an assessment of the probable split of future features into exclusive features and nonexclusive features. If no effort is going to be made in the future to control feature exclusivity, the base model should not include a feature-exclusivity term. Without this term, the feature impact estimated is the average feature impact based on the historical relative frequencies of exclusive and nonexclusive features.

In contrast, if the model is not to be used for forecasting, then ANOVA (ANalysis Of VAriance) methods may offer some powerful shortcuts in the construction of models designed to compare the relative impact on sales of alternative actions. For example, if the focus of our investigation is to determine the relative impacts of feature exclusivity versus nonexclusivity, we might use the principles of analysis of covariance to include variables that are powerful adjusters for changes in marketing conditions not explicitly included in the model. For example, provided that the focus of the study does not include questions about trend, seasonality, and major competitive effects, one might include category volume in a store as a covariate. This would summarize all the effects of trend, seasonality, and competitive marketing actions, considerably simplifying the model. To use the resulting model for forecasting brand sales, however, would require first preparing a forecast of category sales (including the sales of the analysis brand), in order to forecast sales of the analysis brand.

In the course of a total analysis, both types of models might be used. The first phase of the analysis might be based on variables appropriate for statistical analysis. As a result of this analysis, one might make decisions to alter marketing actions in the future, or to continue current practices. The result of the feature-exclusivity analysis might show, for example, that 40 percent of all features are nonexclusive, and that total sales on nonexclusive features are reduced by 10 percent. In the second phase of the analysis, a base-case forecast might be prepared using the "average effect" simple model, with alternative scenarios based on the degree of success in eliminating nonexclusive features. The most common cases occur with the use of precise disaggregate models to estimate response curves for various factors in the statistical analysis phase and with the use of simple robust models on aggregate data to prepare base-case forecasts of the expected levels of next year's sales under the assumption of "business next year much the same as this year."

Case 9: Frozen Orange Juice II

Frozen concentrated orange juice (FCOJ) provides an interesting case history to examine the impact of sales promotion. Frozen orange juices are sold primarily through food stores and are frequently promoted by both the manufacturer and the retailer. This case is based upon 104 weeks of scanner sales history in one city. Please answer all the questions at the end of the case.

Background. Sales promotion, including features, displays, and price reductions, is extremely important in this category, with around 60 percent of annual category sales moving with some sort of sales promotion. Shelf-price reductions, when they are used, average about 30 percent of the regular shelf price.

The major competitors in this category and their market share are as follows in Table 7.1:

Table 7.1

FCOJ MAJOR COMPETITORS BY MARKET SHARE

Brands	Share
Sunshine Valley 12 oz	18.6
Sunshine Valley 6 oz	1.0
Florida Morning 12 oz	8.7
Florida Morning 16 oz	0.2
Golden Ridge 12 oz	27.5
Golden Ridge 6 oz	0.1
All Other Brands	43.9

The data for this case were collected from grocery store scanner installations in one market area and consist of the following:

1. Weekly store sales by brand;
2. Weighted average price charged by brand by store (on a equivalent unit basis);
3. Baseline sales per store; and
4. Occurrence of promotional activity by brand by store.

The use of equivalent units (such as quarts or pounds) allows direct comparison of prices and volumes across brand sizes. In the market chosen, the 12 ounce size is dominant. There are 6 ounce and 16 ounce sizes, but their distribution is spotty, and they receive little promotional activity. There is little if any interaction of the 6 ounce size with other sizes.

The data have been summarized across stores in the market on a weekly basis for a total of 104 weeks. Table 7.2 contains information at the market level on sales of Sunshine Hidden Valley 12 ounce (SSHV12) and on the total category, and Table 7.3 contains information summarized across all stores in one chain for SSHV12 and the category.

During the time of data collection, some extremely "hot" promotional activity had recently occurred as the result of strong promotional program by both Sunshine Valley and Golden Ridge. Some retailers decided to use Golden Ridge 12 ounce and Sunshine Valley 12 ounce as loss leaders in addition to manufacturer promotions and combinations of both.

These activities resulted in substantial variations in price, volume, and share of Sunshine Valley. Management is interested in the possible volume impact that would occur if they raised their wholesale list price to cover the increased cost of dealing. Currently, the wholesale price translates into a retail price of about 37 per equivalent unit for the 12 ounce size. The proposed price increase should translate to a price of 42 per equivalent unit. You have been asked to assess the probable impact on volume sales of this action. As a first step, you have prepared the data found in Tables 7.2 and 7.3. These tables summarize SSHV12 sales in the city, and in one major account, showing volume, price, and baseline volume for both SSHV12 and the category.

Questions Based on Tables 7.2 and 7.3.

Question 1. Hoping for a quick solution to the question, you prepare two regressions. The first uses SSHV12 equivalized volume at market level as dependent variable, and the actual price of SSHV12 at market level as independent. The second regression uses SSHV12 share as dependent variable, and the actual price of SSHV12 as independent. What are the predicted values at a price of 37? What are the predicted values at a price of 42? Plot equivalized volume vs price and share vs price. What do these regressions suggest will be the impact of the proposed change?

Question 2. After some reflection, you feel that the base price series more accurately reflects the translation of wholesale prices to list prices, and that the actual prices reflect the list price plus the impact of the promotional program. You decide to repeat the regressions from question 1, but using base price instead of actual price. Review the results of these regressions. How confident would you feel about your ability to project the impact of the price change from 37 to 42?

Question 3. Repeat Questions 1 and 2, using data from the retail chain (Table 7.3).

Question 4. You decide to review some plots of the data, and notice that your price, the category price, and overall levels of category volume have been changing over time. You decide that if your brand does not change the level of category volume very much, then you can use market category volume as a substitute for seasonal and trend factors. Using Table 7.2, plot SSHV12 volume vs category volume. Perform a correlation analysis between these two variables. How strong is the relation between SSHV12 sales and Category sales?

Question 5. Since the overall category has had some significant changes in price over time, you decide that you cannot study your own price without also studying category price. Using Table 7.2 data, run a regression with SSHV12 volume as the dependent variable, and dependent variables of SSHV12 price, category price, and category volume. Interpret the results. Rerun using category volume from Table 7.2, but all other variables from Table 7.3. How do the results at the chain level compare with the results at the market level?

Question 6. Given the commodity nature of the category, and the results from question 5, you decide to construct a new variable, price relative to the category RELPR, which is your price divided by the category price. Using the SSHV12 volume from Table 7.2, RELPR calculated from Table 7.2, and category volume from Table 7.2, regress volume (dependent) vs RELPR and Category volume. Repeat using category volume from Table 7.2, but other variables from Table 7.3.

Question 7. Have you answered management's question yet? How would you forecast category volume in the future? category price in the future? Using Table 7.2, plot category price vs SSHV12 base price. Are there any outlier weeks that you should remove from the analysis of relation between SSHV12 price and category price? Consider how you might model changes in the relation between SSHV12 price and category price over time. Fit your model.

Question 8. Using the knowledge gained from the prior questions, prepare two scenario's for management consideration: (1) the price increase is unique to Sunshine Valley, and other brands hold present price values, and (2) other FCOJ manufacturers are feeling the same cost pressures felt by Sunshine Valley, and it is likely that if SSHV raises price, most other manufacturers will also raise price a similar amount. Assume that promotional practices continue unchanged into the future.

Questions Based on Tables 7.4 and 7.5.

Question 9. Using the chain data from Tables 7.4 and 7.5, you wish to explore the issues of pricing and promotion. Divide the data into the first 52 weeks, and second 52 weeks. For each brand, summarize actual sales and base sales in the period by each value of the PM code for the brand (0= no promotion, 1 = temporary price reduction only, 2 = feature only, 3 = display only, and 4 = feature and display). Count the total number of weeks in each cell. Estimate the incremental volume due to promotion in promotion cells by: Incremental = Total sales in cell - base sales in cell. Estimate the average percentage increase in sales in the cell as 100* Incremental/Base sales. What fraction of each brands total annual sales is incremental due to promotion? What fraction is base? Prepare charts indicating the promotion frequencies and relative impacts of each promotion type.

Question 10. Week 88 was an important sales week for Golden Ridge 12's. During this week, the retailer advertised "free Golden Ridge 12 ounce frozen orange juice with each $10.00 purchase." There were also significant sales of additional units, leading to a weighted average price of 7.7 per equivalent unit. Redo the second year table for Golden Ridge prepared in question 8 but omit the week 88 data. How much did this one promotional event affect the brands annual sales in the chain? In weeks 77, 93, and 103, SSHV12's achieved high sales rates. How did these weeks affect total category sales for the chain? How about sales of other brands in the same week? What about sales borrowed from future weeks?

Question 10. For SSHV12's, plot only the nonpromoted sales versus the non-promoted price. Discuss the probable percentage impact on SSHV12 sales on a change in base price from 37 to 42. How does this change compare with the impact of trade dealing? (Hint: Use table from question 9, and apply the estimated change to base volume, holding incremental volume constant).

Question 11. For SSHV12's, plot the featured only sales vs the featured only price. Discuss the probable impact on SSHV12 sales in feature only condition of a change in average discounted price to price $1.00 lower, keeping all other things equal.

Question 12. Repeat question 11, but for for price discounts which are 5 percent lower.

Advanced Questions. Omit data for week 88 from the following questions:

Question 13. Using Table 7.3, regress volume vs price for SSHV12's non-promoted observations. Regress share versus price for the same set of data. Perform residual analyses on both models, and compare and contrast the results. Estimate the impact on non-promoted volume of a change in price from 37.00 to 42.00.

Question 14. Use Table 7.3. Run the following model:

SSHV12 Volume (from Table 7.3) = Intercept
    + B1*SSHV12 Average Price (from Table 7.3)
    + B2*(0-1 dummy for Feature Only)
    + B3*(0-1 dummy for Display Only)
    + B4*(0-1 dummy for Feature and Display).

Interpret the results and compare them to those from question 13. Estimate the impact on SSHV12 volume of a change in price from $0.99 to $1.09.

Question 15. Repeat question 14 using percent price discount instead of Average Price. Contrast the results with the results obtained from question 14.

Question 16. (Difficult). Repeat questions 14 and 15 using the natural log of SSHV12 volume as the dependent variable. Contrast the results obtained with the results from questions 14 and 15. Pick one form of the models (volume or log (volume), and absolute price or percent price discount). Adjust for category trend and seasonality as appropriate. Investigate SSHV12's and the other brands. Contrast the similarities and differences among the brands in their response to pricing and promotion.

Question 17. Summarize your findings in this case based on the questions assigned. The summary should include: (A) your answer to managements initial question, (B) your assessment of the relative impacts of changes in regular price vs changes in the type and frequence of promotion, and (C) the importance of the pricing and promotion of competitive brands.

Table 7.2

SUNSHINE HIDDEN VALLEY 12 OZ.

Total Market—Chicago

Week	Volume	Base Volume	Actual Price	Base Price	Category Base Volume	Category Actual Volume	Category Average Price
1	1877	1777	44.4	45.7	10424	18443	36.6
2	2082	1761	43.7	45.5	10523	16939	35.8
3	3316	1811	40.0	45.4	10589	17639	37.0
4	3791	1960	36.1	44.4	10669	19164	34.8
5	2839	2004	38.1	44.0	10806	36207	26.3
6	3138	1882	35.9	44.3	10614	24919	29.2
7	3340	1902	36.9	44.1	10671	15485	36.1
8	2356	1884	39.2	44.3	10596	16873	34.9
9	2014	1791	38.0	45.5	10597	18287	34.2

Week	Volume	Base Volume	Actual Price	Base Price	Category Base Volume	Category Actual Volume	Category Average Price
10	3175	1778	35.6	43.2	10295	18440	34.9
11	2806	1688	35.5	43.0	10195	17653	30.9
12	2565	1719	37.3	42.6	10402	23645	28.3
13	3463	1722	33.7	42.3	10476	28402	25.1
14	2267	1720	35.0	42.2	10475	23793	26.1
15	2123	1667	37.4	41.1	10422	22020	27.7
16	5053	1681	31.4	39.8	10381	22531	27.8
17	3545	1637	33.6	39.4	10322	30738	27.4
18	6720	1635	22.6	38.8	10300	27852	25.6
19	4371	1579	23.5	38.6	10153	43465	20.1
20	2928	1649	33.5	38.5	10050	26425	23.1
21	2426	1596	35.9	38.5	9822	18123	29.3
22	1760	1637	36.3	38.2	9918	21816	25.9
23	1777	1621	36.1	38.2	9786	26241	24.4
24	2392	1581	35.1	38.3	9671	19270	28.7
25	4158	1586	30.4	38.1	9597	27283	24.5
26	1895	1592	35.0	38.3	9648	23806	24.7
27	2533	1583	31.1	38.2	9474	19338	27.2
28	2303	1592	30.3	38.2	9454	16711	28.6
29	3205	1609	29.3	38.1	9657	20234	27.8
30	2961	1566	32.3	37.6	9536	16965	28.7
31	1813	1562	32.6	37.3	9301	23916	25.9
32	3076	1550	29.7	36.7	9256	18241	27.8
33	2661	1530	30.4	35.6	9261	21938	26.2
34	1746	1552	34.3	35.2	9280	22314	26.7
35	4202	1564	23.1	34.3	9439	17583	28.9
36	2345	1552	29.4	34.1	9366	17118	27.8
37	3279	1548	27.0	34.1	9421	25330	24.0
38	3733	1546	28.0	33.9	9337	21011	27.8
39	5629	1567	26.2	34.0	9190	19503	27.3
40	2347	1524	31.5	33.9	9038	20548	24.8
41	1875	1534	31.7	33.9	9086	21116	26.3
42	2401	1488	29.9	33.7	8966	20278	27.3
43	1749	1548	31.4	33.4	9114	19591	27.3
44	1685	1494	32.8	33.5	9035	21811	24.5
45	1933	1490	31.6	33.7	9053	20195	25.7
46	6049	1487	23.4	33.8	9205	25347	21.6
47	8209	1460	22.5	34.0	9050	20941	25.4

Week	Volume	Base Volume	Actual Price	Base Price	Category Base Volume	Category Actual Volume	Category Average Price
48	8851	1491	22.6	34.2	9123	20702	25.3
49	7979	1447	23.9	34.1	9050	22220	25.2
50	4551	1435	26.4	34.1	9074	20675	25.9
51	1964	1488	31.2	34.1	9195	18811	27.4
52	4587	1515	26.9	34.0	9313	20545	25.9
53	2529	1518	29.6	33.9	9368	21799	25.9
54	2252	1503	32.7	33.9	9322	22412	25.5
55	1589	1557	31.9	33.9	9520	26585	22.8
56	2048	1543	29.9	33.8	9556	24611	26.0
57	4462	1621	25.5	33.8	9695	19255	26.1
58	5443	1591	25.6	33.7	9468	19506	26.9
59	3832	1650	28.0	33.7	9574	20945	26.2
60	9182	1677	22.4	33.4	9427	21814	24.6
61	4759	1704	23.0	33.3	9464	25910	23.6
62	2735	1713	31.1	33.2	9552	22209	26.6
63	2346	1734	31.1	33.5	9520	20834	26.6
64	4591	1841	29.8	33.3	9778	17810	27.9
65	3233	1826	28.3	33.6	9574	23727	26.8
66	4632	1859	27.0	33.7	9862	21643	26.7
67	6424	1897	25.9	33.6	10209	24958	26.2
68	4474	1877	27.7	33.7	10162	21963	26.6
69	2825	1814	33.1	33.9	9903	21440	28.2
70	2454	1811	34.9	36.9	10242	24772	27.3
71	5121	1747	31.0	37.6	9861	24733	27.6
72	9425	1762	25.5	37.8	10082	25387	27.9
73	4618	1721	29.1	38.4	9868	21375	28.2
74	2091	1690	36.9	40.0	9705	26694	27.2
75	3118	1646	33.6	40.0	9451	26489	26.6
76	2094	1617	36.4	40.1	9343	17956	30.3
77	8931	1582	24.9	40.1	9266	24508	27.4
78	1855	1572	37.6	40.1	9144	15670	32.0
79	2224	1546	36.2	40.1	9087	18359	30.6
80	2600	1527	33.1	40.3	8994	18599	31.0
81	2991	1554	34.2	40.5	8954	22266	30.3
82	1651	1542	39.2	40.4	8954	20594	28.7
83	1990	1546	37.7	40.2	8931	19032	29.6
84	2411	1554	36.2	40.3	8724	17417	32.6
85	2732	1551	35.7	40.5	9019	30264	25.7

Week	Volume	Base Volume	Actual Price	Base Price	Category Base Volume	Category Actual Volume	Category Average Price
86	2398	1553	34.7	40.5	8934	22690	27.7
87	1957	1512	36.3	40.5	8851	16204	30.3
88	1973	1526	35.8	40.5	8843	25925	21.2
89	4672	1508	30.7	40.4	8799	14175	32.1
90	2670	1526	33.5	40.2	8662	14062	32.7
91	5725	1518	25.0	39.1	8732	20376	28.4
92	4127	1543	26.0	38.7	8642	20146	27.1
93	7037	1564	24.5	38.5	8554	21055	27.5
94	6319	1582	20.3	38.1	8545	17651	26.4
95	1910	1619	33.6	37.7	8571	20777	26.8
96	3643	1581	26.4	37.3	8306	17343	27.5
97	3421	1605	29.5	37.3	8495	15992	29.5
98	3715	1584	28.8	37.3	8472	18572	27.3
99	3127	1594	32.1	37.3	8557	15655	29.4
100	7078	1615	28.1	36.6	8278	16593	29.0
101	6038	1601	28.7	36.5	8190	18886	27.2
102	1956	1631	33.7	36.5	8572	14636	29.7
103	6029	1623	26.4	36.3	8616	17052	28.9
104	1946	1615	34.7	36.2	8507	14343	29.5

Table 7.3

SUNSHINE HIDDEN VALLEY 12 OZ.

Chicago—Chain A

Week	Volume	Base Volume	Actual Price	Base Price	Category Base Volume	Category Actual Volume	Category Average Price
1	297	432	49.6	49.7	1964	3532	38.3
2	468	378	49.7	49.8	1925	3036	38.0
3	1755	399	38.2	49.8	1912	3525	39.7
4	550	398	38.1	49.7	1945	3274	37.0
5	418	462	38.7	46.8	2015	5636	28.4
6	281	411	42.3	48.6	1968	3119	35.7
7	365	414	43.6	49.0	1967	3692	33.9
8	843	406	35.8	49.4	1983	3370	36.5
9	461	404	36.0	49.5	1995	2807	36.4
10	465	398	39.8	44.4	1893	4042	35.6

Week	Volume	Base Volume	Actual Price	Base Price	Category Base Volume	Category Actual Volume	Category Average Price
11	282	395	39.9	44.4	1980	4321	29.0
12	637	401	39.9	44.3	1926	4427	29.8
13	1638	401	31.0	44.2	1972	3996	28.0
14	520	392	31.0	44.4	1946	3816	30.2
15	500	355	39.9	40.4	1894	3622	31.8
16	1940	373	31.0	40.4	1915	4145	31.4
17	350	362	39.7	40.3	1901	6919	26.7
18	303	326	39.9	40.3	1826	5228	26.4
19	250	295	40.3	40.2	1791	5633	25.4
20	1443	298	31.0	40.1	1746	3092	30.2
21	331	286	39.9	40.0	1679	3061	33.2
22	280	293	40.0	40.1	1696	2791	31.1
23	284	284	40.0	40.0	1635	5813	24.4
24	277	275	40.1	40.0	1643	6187	26.0
25	1490	274	31.0	40.0	1534	3073	32.3
26	245	274	39.9	40.0	1590	3463	28.3
27	291	259	39.8	40.0	1510	5317	24.8
28	312	267	35.8	39.9	1534	2467	32.8
29	339	268	35.6	39.9	1626	3574	30.5
30	745	268	33.2	39.9	1534	2480	32.8
31	304	268	35.7	39.9	1570	5569	24.2
32	246	267	35.6	39.9	1550	2608	29.7
33	243	267	35.7	39.8	1549	5588	25.3
34	469	268	35.6	39.9	1536	3851	27.5
35	2963	268	19.0	36.0	1510	4350	23.8
36	305	266	34.6	35.5	1523	4151	26.8
37	246	276	35.5	35.6	1543	4657	25.9
38	322	266	35.2	35.4	1516	2851	29.5
39	333	270	35.2	35.6	1526	3828	27.4
40	1041	273	31.0	35.4	1539	2445	31.4
41	284	280	35.7	35.5	1554	4633	25.1
42	316	256	35.3	35.5	1501	2673	31.5
43	245	275	35.4	35.5	1552	3472	26.8
44	272	261	35.5	35.4	1461	2342	31.0
45	261	265	35.6	35.4	1432	4548	27.9
46	272	261	35.4	35.5	1400	8800	15.6
47	4516	262	17.8	35.4	1368	5759	20.5
48	215	265	35.5	35.6	1332	3152	27.0

Week	Volume	Base Volume	Actual Price	Base Price	Category Base Volume	Category Actual Volume	Category Average Price
49	645	258	34.3	35.5	1306	4004	27.3
50	3109	269	23.8	35.5	1352	4161	25.7
51	247	270	35.3	35.5	1369	3463	26.7
52	1369	272	28.6	35.5	1434	2609	30.0
53	267	269	35.5	35.5	1522	2869	30.4
54	289	268	35.3	35.6	1523	2498	31.5
55	256	276	35.6	35.5	1544	3189	28.2
56	270	275	35.5	35.6	1596	4822	24.0
57	273	282	35.6	35.5	1526	2419	30.9
58	304	271	35.5	35.5	1493	4129	26.7
59	268	286	35.5	35.7	1415	5066	25.9
60	3235	276	23.8	35.7	1386	4366	25.7
61	252	294	35.9	35.5	1437	4833	26.0
62	295	307	35.7	35.5	1481	3795	27.6
63	366	302	35.6	35.6	1459	4508	27.0
64	1740	324	32.1	35.6	1574	3015	31.2
65	321	325	35.6	35.6	1518	3296	29.3
66	312	324	35.6	35.5	1564	4642	26.6
67	325	356	35.4	35.5	1659	5486	26.1
68	1226	354	28.6	35.5	1683	4438	26.8
69	490	326	35.6	35.4	1541	3214	30.0
70	349	337	35.4	35.6	1647	5560	25.9
71	2265	323	30.7	35.6	1550	3702	31.9
72	917	323	22.1	35.6	1549	4100	27.3
73	337	322	41.3	35.6	1519	3211	32.2
74	277	318	41.1	41.3	1508	3085	33.3
75	303	297	41.9	41.2	1461	7972	23.5
76	289	292	42.0	41.3	1489	2781	30.9
77	5237	301	23.4	41.5	1593	6743	25.6
78	269	301	41.7	41.6	1594	2380	35.4
79	309	300	41.6	41.8	1673	2792	33.1
80	310	300	41.6	41.8	1637	2441	35.6
81	1250	303	32.0	41.8	1672	2669	33.7
82	288	311	41.8	41.7	1645	2338	35.0
83	323	299	41.8	41.8	1602	4903	27.6
84	298	312	41.8	41.7	1611	2620	34.8
85	320	302	41.7	41.7	1621	2221	35.0
86	1167	306	32.0	41.7	1616	2757	33.4

Week	Volume	Base Volume	Actual Price	Base Price	Category Base Volume	Category Actual Volume	Category Average Price
87	312	303	41.7	41.6	1615	2469	34.9
88	221	291	41.7	41.7	1576	13506	11.9
89	1446	291	30.9	41.7	1629	2906	32.4
90	284	297	41.9	41.6	1528	2743	34.4
91	279	294	41.5	41.7	1581	4093	27.7
92	292	299	41.8	41.6	1574	3134	30.9
93	4854	302	21.4	41.7	1587	6627	23.8
94	355	299	38.4	41.7	1590	2122	33.2
95	346	302	37.6	41.7	1586	2067	34.5
96	311	300	37.2	41.8	1398	1998	34.3
97	316	303	37.0	41.6	1571	2624	32.9
98	354	300	37.1	41.5	1499	2154	32.9
99	299	312	37.2	41.4	1540	2694	31.8
100	917	305	32.6	38.4	1189	1880	34.0
101	727	311	35.3	38.0	1182	1679	35.1
102	311	322	37.0	37.5	1429	2359	33.6
103	4268	313	23.8	37.3	1439	5606	26.0
104	336	304	37.4	37.1	1373	2763	27.4

Table 7.4

FROZEN ORANGE JUICE

Week	Florida Morning				Golden Ridge			
	Price	Volume	Base V.	Promo.	Price	Volume	Base V.	Promo.
1	45.85	94	167	0	46.68	184	187	0
2	45.54	142	162	0	30.97	1351	186	2
3	45.77	262	149	0	46.55	181	190	0
4	33.35	1372	171	2	46.92	157	208	0
5	45.65	143	171	0	46.71	324	190	0
6	46.04	154	172	0	31.99	1778	214	2
7	45.90	301	161	0	32.03	439	214	1
8	33.35	1153	179	2	40.92	183	214	1
9	33.93	359	163	1	42.59	173	212	1
10	45.71	169	169	0	30.97	1570	212	2
11	44.58	257	140	0	41.49	210	212	0
12	33.36	1259	142	2	42.44	278	212	0
13	44.44	90	137	0	35.97	286	214	1

Week	Florida Morning				Golden Ridge			
	Price	Volume	Base V.	Promo.	Price	Volume	Base V.	Promo.
14	42.66	105	114	0	28.56	1948	216	2
15	39.91	117	104	1	36.01	296	214	1
16	39.62	128	103	1	35.71	283	218	1
17	39.31	118	103	1	35.76	314	216	1
18	40.00	110	103	0	35.58	228	217	1
19	39.82	90	103	0	23.76	4204	217	3
20	39.84	83	102	0	35.50	195	224	0
21	30.97	1159	119	2	35.58	243	211	0
22	38.82	92	108	0	35.50	206	226	0
23	39.35	84	93	0	35.63	206	229	0
24	39.61	74	92	0	23.76	5055	230	3
25	39.85	68	90	0	35.21	276	217	0
26	40.08	89	84	0	35.53	199	237	0
27	39.85	94	75	0	35.24	263	215	0
28	30.96	857	87	2	35.21	229	220	0
29	40.45	94	88	0	28.55	2166	217	2
30	40.22	110	81	0	34.93	255	209	0
31	35.68	90	85	1	35.38	198	202	0
32	35.76	72	82	1	35.34	177	194	0
33	36.02	55	81	1	23.76	4015	185	3
34	35.55	65	84	1	35.42	199	179	0
35	35.52	66	83	1	35.39	165	185	0
36	35.87	71	83	1	35.52	177	177	0
37	34.15	99	83	1	23.76	3421	179	3
38	26.16	1203	92	4	35.78	176	180	0
39	34.16	136	83	0	35.74	183	176	0
40	33.03	79	84	0	35.66	167	190	0
41	33.76	87	89	0	35.54	269	178	0
42	33.43	90	88	0	30.95	1066	186	2
43	33.48	85	84	0	31.06	283	186	1
44	33.27	101	83	0	35.40	163	184	0
45	23.76	2106	89	4	35.33	157	169	0
46	33.47	88	79	0	35.29	150	157	0
47	32.90	86	82	0	35.38	141	147	0
48	33.57	74	81	0	35.34	142	136	0
49	33.56	77	84	0	23.76	2545	134	3
50	33.01	82	85	0	35.89	106	139	0
51	33.24	100	87	0	35.43	140	126	0
52	33.17	94	96	0	35.40	112	134	0

Week	Florida Morning				Golden Ridge			
	Price	Volume	Base V.	Promo.	Price	Volume	Base V.	Promo.
53	33.68	88	104	0	35.31	133	131	0
54	30.93	666	105	2	35.16	177	128	0
55	33.13	112	106	0	24.51	1594	134	2
56	33.17	113	121	0	35.53	123	136	0
57	33.21	125	121	0	35.35	133	129	0
58	23.76	2812	125	4	35.49	136	129	0
59	32.56	121	118	0	23.76	3802	128	3
60	32.47	116	118	0	35.57	110	132	0
61	32.78	134	120	0	23.76	3666	132	2
62	23.76	2304	128	4	36.89	294	140	0
63	33.30	158	118	0	35.58	189	133	0
64	33.34	101	127	0	35.27	118	157	0
65	33.52	114	126	0	35.17	144	158	0
66	23.76	3207	114	4	35.64	165	174	0
67	33.21	115	113	0	23.76	4011	194	2
68	23.76	1608	115	2	23.96	639	194	1
69	23.76	945	116	1	35.25	265	181	0
70	33.45	94	107	0	23.76	4322	200	2
71	37.58	85	102	0	35.55	193	201	0
72	37.76	108	106	0	35.64	188	194	0
73	37.79	103	100	0	41.66	144	197	0
74	28.57	1284	108	2	38.39	631	189	1
75	28.60	252	107	1	23.76	3052	192	2
76	39.11	142	105	0	23.86	971	192	1
77	37.93	112	107	1	41.89	131	207	0
78	37.34	116	115	1	35.75	882	200	2
79	37.61	153	112	1	41.57	225	196	0
80	35.55	581	120	2	41.90	240	197	0
81	37.74	109	122	0	41.41	201	193	0
82	37.64	132	124	0	41.66	184	190	0
83	37.58	159	123	0	41.56	195	174	0
84	36.66	182	126	1	33.37	1121	175	2
85	31.98	799	129	2	41.48	147	180	0
86	31.95	305	129	2	41.89	159	186	0
87	32.19	270	129	2	41.08	290	172	0
88	35.31	86	121	2	7.68	11433	185	4
89	37.56	84	125	0	35.74	367	179	1
90	35.81	545	121	0	35.99	412	185	2
91	37.78	134	116	0	41.57	181	192	0

		Florida Morning				**Golden Ridge**		
Week	**Price**	**Volume**	**Base V.**	**Promo.**	**Price**	**Volume**	**Base V.**	**Promo.**
92	37.49	108	124	0	35.97	786	186	2
93	37.50	102	127	0	42.02	248	184	0
94	35.83	123	134	0	37.33	203	185	1
95	33.39	438	135	4	36.80	196	183	1
96	34.83	168	134	1	36.72	178	183	1
97	35.40	151	139	1	30.76	1185	180	2
98	35.46	176	147	1	31.36	363	177	1
99	28.68	1377	148	2	36.55	169	179	0
100	34.19	201	142	1	36.47	171	175	0
101	34.06	211	138	1	35.81	167	172	0
102	36.00	160	139	0	31.81	1011	175	2
103	36.45	120	130	0	32.21	293	177	1
104	35.63	115	124	0	36.49	171	178	0

Table 7.5

FROZEN ORANGE JUICE

		Sunshine Valley 12 oz.				**Sunshine Valley 6 oz.**		
Week	**Price**	**Volume**	**Base V.**	**Promo.**	**Price**	**Volume**	**Base V.**	**Promo.**
1	49.56	297	432	0	50.71	56	61	0
2	49.72	468	378	0	50.33	60	61	0
3	38.15	1755	399	2	46.87	61	62	1
4	38.15	550	398	1	47.48	61	62	1
5	38.68	418	462	1	47.00	62	61	1
6	42.30	281	411	1	46.85	59	62	1
7	43.61	365	414	1	46.83	60	61	1
8	35.76	843	406	2	47.20	60	61	0
9	36.00	461	404	1	47.43	61	61	0
10	39.78	465	398	0	42.55	84	61	1
11	39.86	282	395	0	42.49	51	61	1
12	39.94	637	401	0	42.22	68	61	1
13	30.95	1638	401	2	42.38	65	61	1
14	30.98	520	392	1	42.23	64	61	1
15	39.92	500	355	0	42.32	62	61	0
16	30.96	1940	373	2	43.74	72	60	0
17	39.65	350	362	0	43.28	65	56	0
18	39.89	303	326	0	43.64	53	57	0
19	40.29	250	295	0	42.67	48	55	0

	Sunshine Valley 12 oz.				Sunshine Valley 6 oz.			
Week	Price	Volume	Base V.	Promo.	Price	Volume	Base V.	Promo.
20	30.96	1443	298	2	42.17	54	52	0
21	39.89	331	286	0	42.16	55	51	0
22	39.97	280	293	0	43.07	46	53	0
23	40.01	284	284	0	42.13	53	50	0
24	40.07	277	275	0	42.61	44	51	0
25	30.97	1490	274	2	42.53	60	50	0
26	39.90	245	274	0	42.86	44	50	0
27	39.79	291	259	0	43.10	51	47	0
28	35.82	312	267	1	42.80	46	50	0
29	35.57	339	268	1	42.24	50	47	0
30	33.25	745	268	2	42.28	47	50	0
31	35.65	304	268	1	42.92	51	47	0
32	35.61	246	267	1	42.07	46	49	0
33	35.74	243	267	0	42.77	47	48	0
34	35.65	469	268	0	42.04	50	48	0
35	18.96	2963	268	4	42.21	48	49	0
36	34.57	305	266	0	42.16	50	48	0
37	35.46	246	276	0	42.56	48	48	0
38	35.21	322	266	0	42.64	47	48	0
39	35.15	333	270	0	42.25	48	47	0
40	30.97	1041	273	2	42.98	45	48	0
41	35.68	284	280	0	42.00	48	47	0
42	35.31	316	256	0	42.20	51	47	0
43	35.38	245	275	0	42.87	45	48	0
44	35.45	272	261	0	42.20	49	44	0
45	35.56	261	265	0	42.43	46	43	0
46	35.44	272	261	0	42.00	39	42	0
47	17.77	4516	262	2	42.95	41	39	0
48	35.48	215	265	0	42.46	35	40	0
49	34.30	645	258	0	42.12	41	39	0
50	23.76	3109	269	2	43.15	41	40	0
51	35.34	247	270	0	42.56	41	41	0
52	28.56	1369	272	2	42.65	43	43	0
53	35.54	267	269	0	42.06	48	42	0
54	35.30	289	268	0	42.48	44	45	0
55	35.60	256	276	0	42.47	47	42	0
56	35.45	270	275	0	42.48	42	44	0
57	35.62	273	282	0	42.31	42	43	0
58	35.54	304	271	0	42.25	44	43	0

	Sunshine Valley 12 oz.				Sunshine Valley 6 oz.			
Week	Price	Volume	Base V.	Promo.	Price	Volume	Base V.	Promo.
59	35.54	268	286	0	42.24	49	42	0
60	23.76	3235	276	2	42.02	41	44	0
61	35.93	252	294	0	42.59	41	44	0
62	35.74	295	307	0	42.39	44	45	0
63	35.56	366	302	0	42.09	55	42	0
64	32.12	1740	324	2	43.09	33	49	0
65	35.59	321	325	0	41.83	48	46	0
66	35.60	312	324	0	41.86	51	49	0
67	35.43	325	356	0	41.83	64	51	0
68	28.57	1226	354	2	42.08	51	56	0
69	35.60	490	326	0	42.44	59	48	0
70	35.37	349	337	0	42.86	42	50	0
71	30.70	2265	323	2	50.17	47	45	0
72	22.07	917	323	1	49.78	41	46	0
73	41.33	337	322	0	49.91	47	43	0
74	41.11	277	318	0	49.34	41	43	0
75	41.89	303	297	0	49.73	40	42	0
76	41.97	289	292	0	49.14	43	40	0
77	23.41	5237	301	2	48.98	42	42	0
78	41.69	269	301	0	49.74	39	42	0
79	41.62	309	300	0	49.19	42	42	0
80	41.61	310	300	0	49.93	43	42	0
81	32.05	1250	303	2	49.93	46	42	0
82	41.76	288	311	0	49.98	40	45	0
83	41.85	323	299	0	50.00	47	42	0
84	41.75	298	312	0	49.40	42	45	0
85	41.65	320	302	0	49.09	45	45	0
86	31.99	1167	306	2	49.49	47	44	0
87	41.66	312	303	0	48.84	44	45	0
88	41.65	221	291	0	49.17	44	43	0
89	30.88	1446	291	2	43.61	51	44	2
90	41.86	284	297	0	44.19	53	44	1
91	41.54	279	294	0	43.96	46	44	1
92	41.76	292	299	0	44.09	46	44	1
93	21.36	4854	302	2	44.07	43	43	1
94	38.37	355	299	1	45.07	46	44	1
95	37.63	346	302	1	44.96	50	43	0
96	37.25	311	300	1	45.95	38	44	0
97	36.99	316	303	1	44.93	45	43	0

	Sunshine Valley 12 oz.				Sunshine Valley 6 oz.			
Week	Price	Volume	Base V.	Promo.	Price	Volume	Base V.	Promo.
98	37.12	354	300	1	45.02	44	42	0
99	37.18	299	312	0	45.21	47	40	0
100	32.61	917	305	2	45.34	38	42	0
101	35.29	727	311	1	43.35	34	37	0
102	36.99	311	322	0	45.41	41	40	0
103	23.76	4268	313	2	44.68	44	40	0
104	37.45	336	304	0	45.29	38	41	0

Case 10: Hot Cereal II

Data for this case is hot cereal major brand sizes drawn from Case 5. Use only the data for stores 155, 550, and 7901. The category is somewhat seasonal. Promotional support is primarily price reduction only, with occasional in-store displays. This case will demonstrate some of the problems which can occur with disaggregate data.

Background. Throughout this text, we have emphasized the need for disaggregate data where possible. However, having those data does not guarantee a successful analysis. When we have the individual series from different stores and brands, they must be combined in the analysis. As mentioned previously in this chapter, this is known as pooling the observations. If done carelessly, the resulting analysis can be worse than the results of an aggregate analysis. The major source of this problem lies in differences in the average sales of each brand-store combination. In this case, we will illustrate some typical problems.

Prepare a data set from the hot cereal case with data for Grannies, Golden Prairie, and Tastymeal. First, construct a total sales variable for each store which is the sum of all four brands volume. Build for each store a 5 week centered moving average of the total volume variable. If TV(i) is the total volume for week i, then the centered moving average CVi = (TV(i-2) +TV(i-1) + TV(i) + TV(i+1) + TV(i+2))/5. For the first two weeks, use the CV value from week 3. For the last two weeks, use the CV value from the third from last week.

Use a 0-1 dummy variable to indicate the presence or absence of display. Build a dummy variable GRAN which is 1 if the observation is for Grannies sales, 0 otherwise, and a similar dummy variable GOLD which is 1 if the observation is for Golden Prairie and 0 otherwise. Similarly, include a dummy variable STR155 which is 1 if the observation is from store 155 and 0 otherwise, and a dummy variable STR550 which is 1 if the observation is from store 550 and 0 otherwise. Eliminate any store-week-brand combinations where volume sales = 0. Build a display price variable by multiplying the display dummy variable by the price variable. The final data set will have as variables brand volume sales (VOL), brand price (PRICE), display dummy (DISP), store dummies (ST155 and

STR550), two brand dummies (GRAN and GOLD), the week number (WEEK), the promoted price variable (PRCPM), and the category moving average sales (CV) for that store. There will be one observation for each brand-store-week with non-zero volume, excluding all private label observations.

Question 1. Run the following regression pooling data for Grannies, Golden Prairie, and Tastymeal:

Dependent = VOL, Independents = PRICE, DISP.

Prepare plots showing actual and predicted values by week for the three brands in store 550 and in store 7901. Discuss the results.

Question 2. Run the following regression pooling data for Grannies, Golden Prairie, and Tastymeal:

Dependent = VOL, Independents = PRICE, DISP, CV.

Compare the model R-squared with those from question 1. Prepare plots showing actual and predicted values by week for the three brands in store 550 and in store 7901. Discuss the results.

Question 3. Run the following regression pooling data for Grannies, Golden Prairie, and Tastymeal:

Dependent = VOL, Independents = PRICE, DISP, CV, GRAN, GOLD.

Compare the model R-squared with those from question 1 and 2. Prepare plots showing actual and predicted values by week for the three brands in store 550 and in store 7901. Discuss the results.

Question 4. Part I. Run the following regression pooling data for Grannies, Golden Prairie, and Tastymeal:

Dependent = VOL, Independents
= PRICE, STR155, STR550, DISP, CV,GRAN, GOLD, and PRCPM.

If there are any variables that are not statistically significant, remove them.

Part II. Create 4 additional dummies by multiplying existing dummy variables:

SB1 = GRAN*STR155, SB2 = GOLD*STR155, SB3 = GRAN*STR550, and
SB4 = GOLD*STR550.

Run the following regression pooling data for Grannies, Golden Prairie, and Tastymeal:

Dependent = VOL, Independents = PRICE, STR155, STR550, DISP,
CV,GRAN, GOLD, PRCPM , SB1, SB2, SB3, and SB4.

If there are any variables that are not statistically significant, remove them. How did the R-Squared change with the addition of the new variables? Make a final comparison of model R-Squares across the 4 questions. Select a final model, and prepare plots showing actual and predicted values by store and week for each of the 3 brands. Discuss the results.

Questions 5 to 8. The STR, SB, GOLD and GRAN dummy variables account for cross-sectional differences in the average sales levels of the brands within a store, and across stores. The CAT variable also accounted for some difference in store sizes. Indexing the variables within a store removes a significant amount of this cross-sectional variation. Convert the volume measure to an index series by dividing each brand-store series by its average within the store. Similarly, convert the price series by dividing by its average taken only during weeks without display. Recalculate the PRCPM variable by multiplying the indexed price by the DISP dummy. Convert the store category volume series by dividing by its 104 week average. Repeat questions 1 to 4 replacing volume with the brands volume index, price with its price index series, and category volume with its index series.

Repeat the regression runs specified in questions 1 through 4 with the new indexed data series, but include an additional step in the comparison of actual and predicted values. In addition to comparing the actual index to the predicted index and discussing the results, multiply the predicted index for a store-brand combination by the average sales volume used as a divisor in cheating the volume index, and compare this predicted series with the actual volume before indexing. Contrast the results obtained with the predictions of actual versus predicted volume from steps 1-4.

Question 9. Using the full variable index series model from question 8, plot the residual series (predicted - actual) for Golden Prairie from all 3 stores versus week. Compare the residual series with the plots of Grannies sales by time, and with plots of Tastymeal sales by time. How might information on these competitors be incorporated into a model to estimate Golden Prairie sales?

Suggested Readings

Blattberg, Robert C. and Scott A. Neslin.
Sales Promotion: Concepts, Methods, and Strategies.
Englewood Cliffs, New Jersey, Prentice Hall, 1990.

Blattberg, Robert C. and Kennneth J. Wisniewski.
"Price-Induced Patterns of Competition,"
Marketing Science, Vol. 8, No. 4 pp. 291-309.

Cooper, Lee G. and Masao Nakanishi.
Market Share Analysis.
Boston: Kluwer Academic Publishers, 1988.

Hanssens, Dominique M., Leonard J. Parsons, and Randall L. Schultz.
Market Response Models: Econometric and Time Series Analysis.
Boston: Kluwer Academic Publishers, 1990.

Mansfield, Edwin.
Statistics for Business and Economics: Methods and Applications.
New York: W. W. Norton, 1983.

Mosteller, Frederick and John W. Tukey.
Data Analysis and Regression: A Second Course in Statistics.
New York: Addison-Wesley Publishing, 1977.

O'Muircheartaigh, C. A. and C. Payne.
Model Fitting.
London: John Wiley & Sons, 1977.

Ortega, J. M. and W. C. Rheinbolt.
Iterative Solution of Nonlinear Equations in Several Variables.
London: Academic Press, 1970.

Totten, John C.
"Measuring Retail Sales Response to Retail Sales Promotion,"
Paper presented at ORSA/TIMMS Marketing Science Conference.
1986. Unpublished Paper.

Tukey, John W.
Exploratory Data Analysis.
Reading, Massachusetts: Addison-Wesley Publishing Company, 1977.

Winer, B. J.
Statistical Principles in Experimental Design.
New York: McGraw-Hill, 1971.

Wittink, Dick R., Micheal J. Addona, William J. Hawkes, and John C. Porter.
**"SCAN*PRO(R): The Estimation, Validation, and Use of Promotional
Efforts Based on Scanner Data,"**
Paper presented at ORSA/TIMS Marketing Science Conference
1988. Unpublished Paper.

Wonnacott, Ronald J. and Thomas H. Wonnacott.
Econometrics.
New York: John Wiley & Sons, 1979.

Wisniewski, Kenneth J, and Blattberg, Robert C.
"Analysis of Consumer Response to Retail Price Dealing Strategies,"
University of Chicago, April 1988, Final Report under NSF Grant SES8421165

CHAPTER 8

ANALYSIS TECHNIQUES FOR AGGREGATE DATA

In chapters 3 and 7 we noted that precise explanatory analysis cannot be conducted once data are summarized beyond the level of retail outlet by week. However, often we don't desire a highly precise, time consuming and expensive analysis—only a ballpark estimate of an effect. For example, management might make the following exploratory request: "Last year we ran two trade deals. What was the average increase in our business for each deal?" A simple tabulation of average U.S. weekly sales during the deal periods versus average U.S. sales during nondeal periods might suffice to answer management's question. Alternatively, the question, "Should we revise our discount structure for this year's two trade deals?" might require extensive and precise analysis of promotional responses versus price. When significant questions have been identified that occur repetitively, an aggregate data analysis can be defined that highlights the answers to the core questions identified while averaging over all other effects.

CROSS-TABULATION. One of the simple analysis methods used with scanner data is based on cross-tabulation. One or more variables of interest are chosen, and the observations are classified into mutually exclusive groups based on the selected variables. The tabulation results may be expressed in tabular or graphic form. Simple tabs and plots of the data may suggest relations among the variables that can be further explored using more complex analysis techniques. Much of the case data in this book is presented in tabulation form.

Statistical Tests. One of the most commonly used statistical techniques applied to cross-tabulation data is the chi-square test for association. In this test, one typically compares two rows or columns of a tabulation of frequencies of occurrence for some variable such as sales and tests whether the relative proportions are significantly different. As an example, one might tabulate market shares of several brands for two different periods. A chi-square test can be applied to determine whether the distribution of market shares is significantly different between the two periods. If the shares are not significantly different, then further analysis attempting to relate other variables to changes in brand share might not be productive.

Demonstrating Relationships. Cross-tabulations are frequently used to demonstrate that a relationship exists between two variables. One variable is selected and its total range broken into several sub-ranges, each of which defines a cell. For all variables to be related to the initial variable, descriptive statistics are calculated. A typical analysis might examine the relation between sales volume and price. We might break price into ranges of ten-cent increments and compute the average weekly sales for the observations in each range. If it is suspected that the presence of features or in-store displays is also important, then one can tabulate two averages for each price range—the average when the feature or displays were absent and the average when they were present. Graphing the resulting averages versus the midpoint of each price range might assist in determining the shape of the response function required to model the relation between price and sales in a regression analysis. It might also assist in determining if the split into two groups based on feature or display activity is required.

The problem with stopping after the cross-tabulation is that if observation counts are small in some of the cells, the assessment of the relation might be distorted. A cure of sorts might be achieved by insisting upon a certain minimum number of observations in a cell before considering that cell in the analysis. More than likely, other factors which should also be considered in assessing the relationships and the application of more detailed techniques such as multiple regression is required. Some methods (primarily related to smoothing and removal of outlier observations) can be applied to cross-tabulation data to demonstrate more clearly the relations among the variables involved. These methods are discussed in detail in Tukey (1977) and Mosteller and Tukey (1977).

SEASONALITY.   As noted in the section on Deflating Series in chapter 7, proper calculation of seasonal indexes is difficult. Weekly seasonality indexes are generally not provided as measures, as proper generation might require a different seasonality index series for each major brand (size) included in the database. For analyses at an aggregate level, seasonality estimates are usually provided from external sources, particularly at the regional and total U.S. levels. For simple analyses at the aggregate level, moving averages of the total sales of a brand or group of related brands are usually used in constructing seasonality series. Where more precise measures of seasonality are required, an analysis of aggregated data may be used to provide a more precise series for weekly seasonal effects.

Many retail products exhibit short-term changes in sales level that are repetitive and predictable from year to year. Often these changes are related to the weather, but there are many other factors, such as social custom and traditions, that lead to cyclic fluctuations in product sales over the months of the year. Until the advent of large quantities of scanner data in the mid 1980s, most seasonality analyses for consumer products were conducted on highly aggregated data series such as Nielsen bimonthly sales audit data, monthly SAMI estimates of warehouse withdrawal, or monthly shipment data by plant, sales region, or nation. The typical analysis method was based on univariate time series methods and generated a seasonality index by month.

Problems with Traditional Methods. The emergence of weekly scanner data available on a city-by-city basis stretched the usefulness of monthly seasonal indexes to the breaking point. Initial methods of converting monthly seasonality indexes to weekly indexes involved the construction of weekly data series from the historical monthly series that, when adjusted for the number of trading days in a month, recovered the original monthly data series. An alternative method emerged that was based on smoothing category sales on a market-by-market basis. As research on the impact of sales promotion on retail sales progressed, both methods showed shortcomings. Univariate time series analyses of the errors of sales forecast models that used seasonality indexes developed from monthly indices typically showed patterns of systematic errors which differed on a city-by-city basis, indicating the need for market specific seasonality factors. The method of developing weekly seasonality indexes by smoothing category sales by market overcame those problems but led to recognition of some new problems. For example, the seasonalities based on aggregate total data were confounded with sales fluctuations caused by marketing factors. In addition, some significant seasonality events occur irregularly from year to year, which caused problems for time series-based methods of estimating seasonality.

Lag Structure Requirements. The year is not evenly divisible into 52 seven-day weeks. In order to accommodate this, every four years a year must contain 53 weeks. Over this cycle, a holiday such as Christmas week will cycle from the beginning of the week to the end of the week. This shift in position also impacts the manner in which Christmas-associated products are purchased. If Christmas is near the beginning of the week, much of the holiday-related purchasing will take place in the week before Christmas; if Christmas is at the end of the week, much of the holiday-related purchasing will take place during Christmas week. Even more vexing is that holidays such as Easter can shift as much as six weeks from year to year. Such factors disrupt the 52-week lag factor that most univariate methods rely on to establish annual relationships.

For those products whose sales might be related to key pay weeks (weeks containing the first or 15th of the month), a similar problem arises. Since the number of days in most months is not divisible by seven, the weeks containing the first of the month generally cycle in a 4-4-5 pattern, again disrupting the regular lag pattern upon which simple univariate time series analyses depend. Analysis of seasonality must then be conducted by intervention analysis time series methods, where holidays and pay week effects are viewed as short-term effects intervening with normal levels of sales. Even with this level of detail, exceptional factors still remain that affect sales across all product categories. A major blizzard in the winter, for example, or a heat wave or air quality-weather alert in the summer may significantly disrupt sales for all consumer products on selected markets.

Sensitivity to Marketing Factors. When sales promotion (both trade and consumer) activity is relatively low, category sales are probably a good reflection of seasonal demand. For products that are somewhat seasonal, the growth in sales promotion has caused a measurement problem. For many products, particularly food products, sales promotion can stimulate primary demand and consumption for a category at the expense of other food and drink categories. Extremely low promotional prices may also generate stockpiling by consumers.

When the marketing program for a seasonal product is examined, one usually finds that promotional activity is not balanced over the year. It is most logical to advertise more, drop more coupons, offer more promotions to the retail trade, and to offer hotter promotional prices during periods of peak seasonality. In extreme cases, during peak holiday periods, nearly every brand may be on promotion, often with very special prices. This multicollinearity of sales demand and promotional activity over time can make proper allocation of total sales into primary seasonality demand levels and incremental volume due to promotional activity very difficult.

In extreme examples, the analyst may find examples of industry-induced seasonality. For example, a one- or two-week period has become known throughout the industry as a peak week, primarily due to seasonality analyses based on total sales. As time passes, more and more promotional activity is aimed at that period, with deeper and deeper consumer discounts offered. Heavy category buyers and price-conscious buyers notice this activity, and they delay purchasing prior to the special period, running their in-home inventories to low levels. During the special period, a significant amount of purchasing may go into inventory for later consumption. The end result is that sales during the special period are once again significantly higher than sales levels during preceding or following weeks, reinforcing the perception that this period is special. Because of the manufacturer's demand for retail performance during the special period, retailers may demand higher allowances for merchandising activity such as feature or display. In analyzing the profitability of such activity, proper allocation of sales between base demand and incremental demand due to promotion becomes critical.

Iterative Solution. Construction of weekly seasonal series from scanner data is still evolving at the time of this writing, but some directions have begun to emerge. The newest approaches are based on iterative solution methods, in which an initial estimate of seasonality based on traditional methods is made, and through univariate time series analysis, a seasonality correction is developed from the prediction errors of the analysis. This process is repeated until the resulting revised seasonal series stabilizes and generates errors with no time series or cross-sectional cross-correlations. An example of such a procedure follows. The example is based on the following typical data, aggregated to the market level:

1. Total category sales volume by week, for at least one complete year.
2. Percentage of category sales volume sold with feature or display.
3. Average price per volume sold.

Prices are indexed to the average during periods of low promotional activity, such as the average during the five to ten weeks with the lowest percentage of sales on promotion. An initial estimate of seasonality is generated by constructing a five-week centered moving average of category sales. For week i, an average sales value is generated for weeks i - 2, i - 1, i, i + 1, and i + 2. The resulting series is indexed to its mean over the 52 or 53 weeks of the first year. This initial estimate might contain some trend component. This can be roughly eliminated by using the difference in the average of the first n weeks of the index series versus the average of the weeks 53 through 52 + n as an estimate of the annual change in sales due to trend, removing this on a week-by-week basis, and reindexing.

An initial regression model is run where the model is as follows:

Weekly Category Sales = B0 (Intercept)
+ B1*week   (Trend)
+ B2*Price Index   (Price factor)
+ B3*Pct Vol on FD   (Trade factor)
+ B4*Seasonality   (Seasonal)

Using the resulting model, each week is adjusted for trend, price, and promotion by subtracting from total sales the total of B1*Week, B2*Price Index, and B3*Percentage Volume on Feature or Display. (Note: if promotional levels are high, it may be desirable to center the price index series and the percentage volume on FD—Feature or Display—by subtracting its mean value from each series.) The resulting series is then detrended and adjusted to a constant level of price discount and promotional activity across all weeks. This new volume series can then be used to develop a revised trial seasonality, and the process repeated until the B4 coefficient in the regression stabilizes. For further notes on this type of iterative process, see Ortega and Rheinbolt (1970).

The seasonality time series developed by this procedure will retain the impact of all the year-to-year exceptional factors such as local weather. To determine that portion that is truly seasonal in nature, cross-sectional analysis may be used to study the similarity of seasonal patterns from market to market. This allows identification of patterns that repeat across regions versus those sales variations that are local in nature.

AGGREGATE DATA SOURCES. Traditional methods of data reporting and analysis have been primarily based on aggregate data with simple models. Comparison of the results of a time period and the same period a year ago is commonly used for bimonthly, quarterly, or annual data. Causal data have been limited to measures of average price and to gross promotional measures, such as the number of feature ads run per account or the percentage of volume sold with promotion.

The advent of weekly scanner-based tracking data makes weekly data available at the key-account level for many accounts, as well as on the market, regional, and national levels on a week-by-week basis. The need to support many types of analyses for product brand management, product sales management, retail category promotional management, retailer stocking, shelf management, pricing decisions, and broker accounting has led to a proliferation of data measures that prepare the data precisely to support both traditional and emerging types of analyses. From 20 to 50 specific data series on a weekly basis might be required to support commonly performed analyses. The growing capacity of personal computers allows an analyst to keep such weekly aggregate series on a large variety of levels of geographical levels. Because the data are available, it becomes tempting to perform an analysis with data series that are close to the desired series, often with puzzling results.

Typical measures available at the aggregate level include the following:

1. Volume measures such as total sales volume, base sales volume, incremental sales volume, and sales volume per million dollars of retail sales (ACV). Transformations of volume might be brand share, base share, and incremental share. Volumes are typically equalivalized across items.

2. Pricing measures, such as average price per volume, average base price per volume, average promoted price per volume, average non-promoted price per volume, average penny price reduction per volume when on price reduction, average percentage price reduction per volume when on price reduction. These measures are usually available on either a price per sale unit or a price per equalized volume basis. These measures are generally available for each of the most common retail promotion types—feature/display combination, feature without display (feature only), display without feature (display only), and price reduction only (price reduction without feature or display). Depending on the predominant forms of promotion, composite measures might also be provided based on the following conditions—any feature, any display, or any promotion.

3. Compositional measures show the level of volume activity by promotional type. Examples include the percentage of volume sold with feature and display, with feature only, with display only, with price reduction only, with any feature, with any display, or with any promotion. Another class of compositional measures shows the brand performance based on the ACV of stores performing some activity. Examples are percentage ACV of stores carrying the product (ACV distribution), percentage ACV of stores with feature and display, feature only, and so on.

4. Performance measures show the estimated response to promotional activity. Usually based on a model (like PromotionScan), examples are include the average percentage increase on feature and display, on feature only, and so on. An alternative is to report performance measures in terms of incremental weeks. For example, promotion that generates 1.5 incremental weeks in the store in which it is run generates a 150 percent increase in weekly sales. If the stores which carried the promotion accounted for 15 percent of the brand sales, the promotion would generate .225 incremental weeks for the market.

AGGREGATE REGRESSION.   In planning and designing an analysis that will be used to forecast future business levels, it is often tempting to try and directly assess the impact of various marketing actions from aggregated data—data where the relative levels of various actions vary from observation. In general, the results of such an analysis will contain a number of confounding effects that can easily lead to misinterpretation of the results.

Interpretation of Coefficients.   Interpretation of the coefficients of an aggregate-level regression model analysis is seldom straightforward. For example, consider an analysis in which the dependent variable is volume, and the only independent variable in the regression analysis is average price per volume. Suppose we run the regression model Volume = Bo + Br*Average Price per Volume. It is tempting to interpret the resulting Br coefficient as the change in volume per unit change in price. More correctly, the coefficient Br is the average change in volume associated with changes in the marketing mix sufficient to generate a unit change in weighted average price. This problem is illustrated by the following example:

Consider a product that has a linear response to price such that a price cut of 1 index point in price generates a 3-index-point rise in sales in stores cutting price. Suppose all stores in the market charge $10.00 per volume and generate total market volume of 100,000 units per week. Consider a week in which a chain with 25 percent of the base volume runs a temporary price reduction of 20 index points in price (a cut to an $8.00 price). For the market, the average price is reduced by 7.442 index points ($0.744). Volume for the promoting store increases by 15,000 units (the store's base volume was 25,000, so a 3-point-sales increase per point of price decrease times 20-index-points price decrease times 250 units per point of sales = 15,000 units). Suppose however, that due to cross-store cannibalization, the total market sales only increased by 7,500. Then volume at the total market would equal 107,500 units, dollars spent in the market would equal $995,000, and the average price per unit would equal $9.26, a 7.442-index-point decrease. Sales changes per index-point change in price are then 7.5/7.442, or about 1.008 point changes in sales per point change in price, considerably different from the 3-points-sales increase per point of price reduction at the store level. In this instance, the relation between price and volume determined at the aggregate level is significantly different from the relation that holds for an individual store.

This difficulty in interpreting the coefficients at an aggregate level (aggregation bias) causes problems if the coefficients are used for action beyond a "business as usual" aggregate forecast of future business. If measures of base volume are available, the problem can be reduced. If we define the price weighted by base volume rather than by actual sales volume, the above example has a 7.5-point change in total volume per 5 points of change in base volume weighted price. Alternative weightings for constructing the "price" series can lead to a variety of estimates for the effect of price on sales. Even though the 1.5 points of net increase per point of price change calculated just above is correct for the manufacturer in net, it is incorrect for use in assessing the impact of price on the sales for a specific retailer. Similar sorts of cannibalization problems can arise across different brands within one retailer as well as for the same brand across several retailers.

Using ACV weighting as opposed to base-volume weighting is an alternative specification for promotion for constructing aggregate promotional variables. If base volumes are proportional to store size (ACV), then both methods give the same results. An alternative weighting method is to assign each store a weighting based on its long-run category or brand sales and construct pricing and promotional variables based on those weights. When the volume response to a promotional activity is incorporated into time-varying weights, such as happens with measures such as percentage of volume on a given promotional type, then measurements of the relation between that variable and the dependent variable will be biased. This can lead to apparent instability in the responses to marketing activity measured at different times, due to changes from one period to the next in the relative weighting of promotional activity.

Constructing Explanatory Series. The most common method of constructing series of explanatory variables for use in aggregate regressions is to weight stores by their total dollar sales across all categories (ACV). Sales can then be reported by each type of promotional condition an a sales per million ACV basis. While taking a volume-weighted average price within a promotional condition still introduces some bias in the estimation of price relations, this bias is usually small compared to the bias introduced when averaging across promotional types with different response. Sales per million ACV at a market level may be calculated based on total market ACV, or based on only those stores carrying an item. Most common is to report based on total market ACV and to account for incomplete market coverage by reporting percentage ACV distribution, the ACV of stores carrying an item divided by total market ACV.

To report promotional activity, the typical measure is an ACV-weighted week. This measure also easily allows time aggregation. In a four-week period, assessment of promotional activity in one ACV-weighted week might be accomplished in a variety of ways. Suppose chains A, B, C, and D each have 25 percent of the market ACV. If chain A puts up a display for an item and leaves it up for four weeks, the result is four weeks times .25 ACV = 1 ACV-weighted week. If all chains display during only week one, the result is one week times 1.00 ACV = 1 ACV-weighted week. If chain A displays in week one only, chain B displays in week two only, chain C displays in week three only, and chain D displays in week four only, the result is still one ACV-weighted week at the market level during the four-week period. Similarly, an ACV-weighted price discount variable can be constructed by noting that a price reduction of size times on 25 percent of the ACV is (on the average) equivalent to a reduction of x/4 on 100 percent of the ACV.

The Scan*Pro model described previously (chapter 7: Algorithms) is fit at a disaggregate level. For business analysis purposes, the model results may be aggregated in many ways such as by brands, sizes, time periods, key accounts, and markets. The model provides information on average price discounts, average volume increase, and promotion frequency. For an example, refer again to the case 8 at the end of chapter 6. This highly summarized and compact set of data can be reviewed to identify key problem areas and to suggest methods for improving promotion effectiveness.

In summary, analysis on disaggregate data is preferable where possible, to understand the response at the point where the marketing action is applied. However, confounding effects such as cross-store or cross-size cannibalization which may require analysis of aggregate data in order to fully capture the net effect of a retail marketing action on manufacturer sales. Disaggregate data may not be available, or it may represent an amount of data too large to accommodate in the analysis. In addition, analysts can construct data series that minimize aggregation bias by avoiding the volume weighting of results of marketing actions that have clearly different sales responses.

Case 11: Mouthwash I

The data for this case is drawn from a report on annual sales in grocery stores for some of the highest volume items in a market. In this case, we will be using the summarized data to compare marketing mix effects, and to estimate the impact of changing the marketing mix. The reports shown in the 8.1 Tables are typical of the level of aggregation that an analyst might receive in a personal computer database. Similar tables would be available for over 50 markets and over one hundred key accounts across the country. The report contains sufficient information to review the state of the business for a number of key brands and sizes, and will support analyses and conclusions about the potential impact of changes in the marketing mix.

Table 8.1

MOUTHWASH VOLUME SALES—52 WEEKS

Brand	Product Name	Volume	Base Volume	Incremental Volume	Weeks
1	Lmnt Mw&G/F Mt Gn Oa 18 Oz	70712	63435	7277	5.7
1	Lmnt Mw&G/F Mt Gn Oa 24 Oz	100100	91215	8885	4.9
1	Listerine Antsp Yl Oa 32 Oz	624644	537181	87463	8.1
1	Listerine Antsp Yl–.50 Oa 32 Oz	11920	10567	1353	6.4
1	Listerine Antsp Yl Oa 48 Oz	401588	356320	45268	6.4
2	Scope Mw&G Gn –.15 Oa 12 Oz	57932	55441	2491	2.2
2	Scope Mw&G Yl Oa 18 Oz	43956	42611	1345	1.6
2	Scope Ms&G Gn Oa 24 Oz	257888	246354	11534	2.3
2	Scope Mw&G Pm Bl Oa 24 Oz	93224	89703	3521	2.0
2	Scope Mw&G Gn Oa 32 Oz	281352	270720	10632	2.0
2	Scope Mw&G Pm Bl Oa 32 Oz	85316	81479	3837	2.4
2	Scope Mw&G Pm Bl –.60 Oa 40 Oz	5120	4876	244	2.5
2	Scope Mw&G Pm Bl Oa 40 Oz	74292	70576	3716	2.6
3	Plax Lq Rd Or 8 Oz	120880	119974	906	0.4
3	Plax Lq S–M Gr Or 24 Oz	86652	84183	2469	1.5
3	Plax Lq Rd Or 24 Oz	65524	61818	3706	3.0
4	Chlr Sr Thrt Sp C–M Bl Oa 6 Oz	39216	37754	1462	1.9
4	Close–Up Lq Cn Rd Or 6 Oz	15068	14554	514	1.8
4	Act F Trt Lq Cn Rd Or 12 Oz	100108	96220	3888	2.0
4	Close–Up Lq Cn Rd Or 12 Oz	9260	8897	363	2.0
4	Dr Tichenors Ms&Antsp Yl Oa 16	67076	63724	3352	2.6
4	Act F Trt Lq Cn Rd Or 18 Oz	50624	49411	1213	1.2
5	Ctl Br Mw Mt Gn Oa 24 Oz	236808	227802	9006	2.0
5	Ctl Br Lq Rd Or 24 Oz	4768	4723	45	0.5
5	Ctl Br Lq Mt Gn Or 24 Oz	7432	7420	12	0.1
5	Ctl Br Mw Mt Gn 32 Oz	15068	14926	142	0.5
5	Ctl Br Mw Pm Bl Oa 32 Oz	4648	4540	108	1.2
5	Ctl Br Mw Gn Oa 32 Oz	1560	1534	26	0.8
5	Ctl Br Gn Oa 32 Oz	5476	5351	125	1.2

Table 8.1 (continued)

WEIGHTED WEEKS OF PROMOTIONAL ACTIVITY

Brand	Product Name	Total	P Red Only	Feat Only	Disp Only	Feat & Disp
1	Lmnt Mw&G/F Mt Gn Oa 18 Oz	11.4	4.5	2.8	2.6	1.2
1	Lmnt Mw&G/F Mt Gn Oa 24 Oz	8.7	3.5	1.9	3.0	0.7
1	Listerine Antsp Yl Oa 32 Oz	13.1	4.8	2.8	3.4	1.5
1	Listerine Antsp Yl–.50 Oa 32 Oz	8.5	3.3	2.4	2.1	0.7
1	Listerine Antsp Yl Oa 48 Oz	10.5	3.7	2.3	3.5	1.1
2	Scope Mw&G Gn –.15 Oa 12 Oz	7.8	4.3	1.6	1.7	0.5
2	Scope Mw&G Yl Oa 18 Oz	6.1	3.5	0.6	1.7	0.4
2	Scope Ms&G Gn Oa 24 Oz	7.5	4.0	1.5	1.5	0.7
2	Scope Mw&G Pm Bl Oa 24 Oz	7.4	4.1	1.3	1.7	0.6
2	Scope Mw&G Gn Oa 32 Oz	6.5	3.9	1.3	1.0	0.4
2	Scope Mw&G Pm Bl Oa 32 Oz	8.7	4.7	1.6	1.8	0.7
2	Scope Mw&G Pm Bl –.60 Oa 40 Oz	8.5	5.5	1.4	1.2	0.4
2	Scope Mw&G Pm Bl Oa 40 Oz	5.1	1.5	1.5	1.3	0.6
3	Plax Lq Rd Or 8 Oz	2.1	1.6	0.3	0.3	0.1
3	Plax Lq S–M Gr Or 24 Oz	3.9	1.7	0.6	0.9	0.7
3	Plax Lq Rd Or 24 Oz	4.5	1.7	1.3	0.9	0.4
4	Chlr Sr Thrt Sp C–M Bl Oa 6 Oz	4.4	2.1	0.6	1.6	0.4
4	Close–Up Lq Cn Rd Or 6 Oz	3.3	1.1	1.2	0.7	0.3
4	Act F Trt Lq Cn Rd Or 12 Oz	2.9	1.1	0.7	0.9	0.2
4	Close–Up Lq Cn Rd Or 12 Oz	3.0	1.0	1.0	0.7	0.3
4	Dr Tichenors Ms&Antsp Yl Oa 16	0.4	0.4	0.0	0.0	0.0
4	Act F Trt Lq Cn Rd Or 18 Oz	2.7	1.6	0.6	0.5	0.2
5	Ctl Br Mw Mt Gn Oa 24 Oz	5.8	4.9	0.5	0.2	0.2
5	Ctl Br Lq Rd Or 24 Oz	4.1	3.6	0.4	0.0	0.0
5	Ctl Br Lq Mt Gn Or 24 Oz	1.2	1.1	0.0	0.1	0.0
5	Ctl Br Mw Mt Gn 32 Oz	2.5	1.9	0.2	0.2	0.1
5	Ctl Br Mw Pm Bl Oa 32 Oz	3.3	3.0	0.0	0.3	0.0
5	Ctl Br Mw Gn Oa 32 Oz	2.9	2.5	0.4	0.0	0.0
5	Ctl Br Gn Oa 32 Oz	1.8	0.9	0.2	0.6	0.1

Table 8.1 (continued)

PROMOTIONAL EFFICIENCY INDICES

Brand	Product Name	P Red Only	Feat Only	Disp Only	Feat & Disp
1	Lmnt Mw&G/F Mt Gn Oa 18 Oz	151	313	231	386
1	Lmnt Mw&G/F Mt Gn Oa 24 Oz	165	352	237	397
1	Listerine Antsp Yl Oa 32 Oz	205	375	261	546
1	Listerine Antsp Yl–.50 Oa 32 Oz	128	389	197	373
1	Listerine Antsp Yl Oa 48 Oz	173	363	246	465
2	Scope Mw&G Gn –.15 Oa 12 Oz	138	170	188	321
2	Scope Mw&G Yl Oa 18 Oz	132	164	207	236
2	Scope Ms&G Gn Oa 24 Oz	131	184	209	353
2	Scope Mw&G Pm Bl Oa 24 Oz	119	187	180	341
2	Scope Mw&G Gn Oa 32 Oz	125	192	225	338
2	Scope Mw&G Pm Bl Oa 32 Oz	115	197	186	298
2	Scope Mw&G Pm Bl –.60 Oa 40 Oz	121	174	230	460
2	Scope Mw&G Pm Bl Oa 40 Oz	102	182	167	304
3	Plax Lq Rd Or 8 Oz	103	232	140	283
3	Plax Lq S–M Gr Or 24 Oz	119	196	180	275
3	Plax Lq Rd Or 24 Oz	180	215	341	400
4	ChlrSr Thrt Sp C–M Bl Oa 6 Oz	145	223	223	323
4	Close–Up Lq Cn Rd Or 6 Oz	127	185	291	403
4	ActF Trt Lq Cn Rd Or 12 Oz	145	174	431	501
4	Close–Up Lq Cn Rd Or 12 Oz	188	182	292	526
4	Dr Tichenors Ms&Antsp Yl Oa 16	199	100	100	100
4	Act F Trt Lq Cn Rd Or 18 Oz	144	241	177	445
5	CtlBr Mw Mt Gn Oa 24 Oz	142	195	202	405
5	Ctl Br Lq Rd Or 24 Oz	100	147	119	100
5	Ctl Br Lq Mt Gn Or 24 Oz	100	100	152	100
5	Ctl Br Mw Mt Gn 32 Oz	112	214	131	292
5	Ctl Br Mw Pm Bl Oa 32 Oz	105	100	255	100
5	Ctl Br Mw Gn Oa 32 Oz	108	186	100	100
5	Ctl Br Gn Oa 32 Oz	143	193	154	190

Table 8.1 (continued)

WEIGHTED AVERAGE PERCENT PRICE REDUCTIONS

Brand	Product Name	Total	P Red Only	Feat Only	Disp Only	Feat & Disp
1	Lmnt Mw&G/F Mt Gn Oa 18 Oz	27.3	21.2	29.5	19.7	28.8
1	Lmnt Mw&G/F Mt Gn Oa 24 Oz	28.7	23.9	32.1	18.7	31.3
1	Listerine Antsp Yl Oa 32 Oz	29.2	24.6	31.3	20.1	29.9
1	Listerine Antsp Yl–.50 Oa 32 Oz	22.5	7.3	26.0	17.1	23.6
1	Listerine Antsp Yl Oa 48 Oz	28.6	23.1	32.1	18.7	29.9
2	Scope Mw&G Gn –.15 Oa 12 Oz	15.5	13.5	14.1	8.1	13.5
2	Scope Mw&G Yl Oa 18 Oz	11.5	5.5	7.3	9.5	8.2
2	Scope Ms&G Gn Oa 24 Oz	15.7	13.4	14.0	9.7	14.0
2	Scope Mw&G Pm Bl Oa 24 Oz	15.8	18.9	13.0	8.6	14.1
2	Scope Mw&G Gn Oa 32 Oz	16.7	19.4	15.1	14.0	14.5
2	Scope Mw&G Pm Bl Oa 32 Oz	16.0	13.5	14.1	8.6	13.5
2	Scope Mw&G Pm Bl –.60 Oa 40 Oz	15.5	13.0	12.0	10.3	13.6
2	Scope Mw&G Pm Bl Oa 40 Oz	14.8	10.1	15.3	6.9	15.3
3	Plax Lq Rd Or 8 Oz	13.1	11.9	16.1	–0.8	17.4
3	Plax Lq S–M Gr Or 24 Oz	11.9	6.9	6.9	5.5	9.6
3	Plax Lq Rd Or 24 Oz	19.9	11.8	14.8	19.7	27.1
4	Chlr Sr Thrt Sp C–M Bl Oa 6 Oz	12.3	9.5	9.0	9.9	8.6
4	Close–Up Lq Cn Rd Or 6 Oz	22.6	7.8	16.1	18.0	28.8
4	Act F Trt Lq Cn Rd Or 12 Oz	17.8	9.9	12.8	20.2	31.5
4	Close–Up Lq Cn Rd Or 12 Oz	25.1	15.9	17.9	20.8	29.5
4	Dr Tichenors Ms&Antsp Yl Oa 16	55.8	46.2	0.0	0.0	0.0
4	Act F Trt Lq Cn Rd Or 18 Oz	11.4	10.1	6.4	2.8	8.3
5	Ctl Br Mw Mt Gn Oa 24 Oz	15.3	11.7	16.2	8.9	16.8
5	Ctl Br Lq Rd Or 24 Oz	12.3	7.3	13.6	7.3	0.0
5	Ctl Br Lq Mt Gn Or 24 Oz	9.2	12.6	5.5	–0.8	0.0
5	Ctl Br Mw Mt Gn 32 Oz	11.9	11.5	17.0	–1.3	17.0
5	Ctl Br Mw Pm Bl Oa 32 Oz	17.2	16.5	0.0	20.7	0.0
5	Ctl Br Mw Gn Oa 32 Oz	13.0	9.1	13.1	5.1	0.0
5	Ctl Br Gn Oa 32 Oz	8.3	11.3	0.9	4.1	1.4

There are a large number of sizes, flavors, and package variations for mouthwash. The reports detail only some of the key items in the market. There are five brand groupings: 1 Listerine/Listermint, 2 Scope, 3 Plax, 4 All Other Branded, and 5 Controlled Store Brands. The market is strongly competitive, but there are significant differences among the brand groups in their usage of retail promotions.

For product volume, all brand sales have been equivalized to a standard equivalent unit. Incremental volume is reported, though it can be derived as base sales subtracted from total volume sales. Two additional derived facts are: Percent Incremental (the percentage of the total volume which is incremental) derived by dividing incremental volume by total volume, then multiplying by 100, and Average Weeks of Incremental volume, which is 52 times incremental volume divided by base volume. For item and each promotion type, the average percent price reduction is reported, as well as the average percent price reduction across all promotional types. For each item and promotion type, the Promotion Efficiency Index (PEI) is reported. This index was found by dividing the total volume sold for an item-promotional type by the base volume which occurred under the promotional conditions, and multiplying by 100.

A generally accepted analysis principle is that if the sum of the weighted weeks for a promotional type times the average percentage increase for that type totals Y across all promo types, and X is the Average weeks of Incremental volume for the period, then a change in the weighted weeks of activity that makes the new weighted sum equal to NEWY could be expected to generate on average a NEWX equal to X*NEWY/Y (Proportionate change). For example, if incremental weeks is 4.5, and the sum of weighted weeks times percentage increase is 3.7, then a change in weighted weeks of promotion that generates a weighted sum of 4.1 will lead to an 11 percent increase (100*(4.1 ÷ 3.7 - 1.)) in incremental weeks of volume, and to a new incremental volume of 5.0 times the average weekly base sales (4.5 × (4.1 ÷ 3.7)).

Question 1. Calculate average weeks of incremental volume for each item, and sort on that variable. Comment on the results—which brands sort high vs low, and are the patterns in the other variables such as weighted weeks of activity or PEI's.

Question 2. Calculate for each item the average weeks of incremental volume per total weighted week of promotion, and sort on this variable. Comment on the results.

Note: Add the two variables calculated in questions 1 and 2 to the data set for use in the following questions.

Question 3. What patterns do you find in the discount relations among the promotion types?

Question 4. For each promotion type, regress the percentage volume increase for that promotion type versus the average percentage discount on that promotion type. Graph the resulting equations over 0 percent to 40 percent discount ranges. Interpret the results. Question 5. Suppose that Plax Lg S-M Gr Or 24 Oz received the same number of weeks of support as Lmnt Mw&G/F Gn Oa 24 oz. Estimate its probable total volume under that scenario.

Question 6. Suppose that Plax Lg S-M Gr Or 24 oz received an additional two weeks of feature support in the form of 1.5 weighted weeks of feature only at its average feature only price discount and 0.5 weighted weeks of feature and display combination at its average feature and display price discount. Estimate its probable total volume under that scenario.

Question 7. Suppose that Listerine/Listermint could get the same total levels of weighted weeks of support, but could convert one week of price reduction only into an extra week of feature only at the average feature only price. Estimate the impact on total sales across all five items.

Question 8. Suppose that Listerine/Listermint lost one week of price reduction only on each item, but kept the same levels of feature and/or display activity. Estimate the impact on total sales across all five items.

Question 9. Calculate the total weighted weeks of promotion support per 100,000 base volume. Sort the brand-size items on this calculation, and comment on the results.

Question 10. Calculate the weighted weeks of quality promotion—that is, feature only + display only + feature and display. Sort the brand-items based on this calculation, and comment on the results.

CASE 12: Mouthwash II

Table 8.3 gives the results of tabulating promotional activity (observed) on a mouthwash product for one year across the total U.S. market. Also presented, as shown in Table 8.2 are the results of fitting a price promotion response model to the data (expected).

Table 8.2

MOUTHWASH PRODUCT PROMOTION RESPONSE ANALYSIS

Expected Promotion Efficiency Indices (100*actual/base)

	Pr Red	A Ad	B Ad	C Ad	Disp	A&Disp	B&Disp	C&Disp
0-4.9	.	121	111	107	169	219	202	195
5-9.9	116	139	128	123	194	251	232	224
10-14.9	123	161	148	142	225	291	269	260
15-19.9	131	188	173	166	262	340	314	303
20-24.9	141	222	205	196	310	402	371	358
25-29.9	151	264	244	234	370	479	442	427
30-34.9	164	319	295	283	447	579	535	516

Table 8.3

MOUTHWASH PRODUCT PROMOTION RESPONSE ANALYSIS

Observed Promotion Efficiency Indices (100*actual/base)

	Pr Red	A Ad	B Ad	C Ad	Disp	A&Disp	B&Disp	C&Disp
0-4.9	.	168	158	139	163	237	187	159
5-9.9	141	172	141	147	275	250	153	190
10-14.9	161	260	149	171	316	311	242	256
15-19.9	154	264	143	187	282	377	199	308
20-24.9	133	202	241	208	282	292	343	332
25-29.9	155	275	238	.	.	.	441	.

Background. Selecting a model for analyzing price promotion responses can become a difficult problem. A simple model may be dismissed as unrealistic because it does not capture many factors deemed to be important, such as competitive prices, holiday effects, special price points, and interaction of coupons with promotion. Managers with little modeling experience may distrust models in general. Considering the many pitfalls in the types of aggregate data analyses that have been conducted, this distrust may be well founded. An often-proposed alternative is to simply cross-tabulate a large sample of data and let the law of large numbers show us the form of the response.

The data on this case were developed to examine the differential effect of ad size and display quality on the response to promotion. Historically, A-Ads are considered to be the best ad type, with B-Ad second best, and C-Ads the least effective of ad types. While there are several types of displays, they are all combined into one average display effort. Conventional wisdom is that across most product categories an A-Ad will generate six times the incremental volume as a C-Ad, and a B-Ad will generate three times the incremental volume of a C-Ad. The national sales manager is questioning these values and wishes to use scanner data to revise performance requirements for trade promotion. Like many cross-tabulations, the observation count is not included for each cell. The data were developed by taking the percentage increase versus baseline increase for each observations and averaging across all observations in a cell. The response analysis was not weighted by store or market size. The reported response number is for the low end of the cell range.

Question 1. Using the cross-tabulation (observed), compare A-ad response to B-ad response.

Question 2. Using the cross-tabulation, compare C-ad response to A-ad response.

Question 3. Using the cross-tabulation, compare major display response to minor display response.

Question 4. Using the cross-tabulation, assess the impact of adding a display to an A-ad.

Questions 5 to 8. Repeat questions 1-4 using the merchandising response analysis (expected).

Question 9. Assume that the variable cost of production, handling, and distribution through all parts of the system (manufacturer, retailer, and any intermediate distributors) is 30 percent of the average retail nonpromoted selling price. Using the no-price-reduction case as the base, calculate the percentage change in system volume sales and gross profit for each cell. Comment on the relative profitabilities of the various strategies.

Questions 10 and 11. Repeat question 9 for two more cases: a variable cost of 15 percent of the nonpromotion price and a variable cost of 45 percent of the nonpromotion price.

Case 13: Ready-to-Eat Cereal

The two reports compare a six week period of sales for one year with a corresponding 6 week sales period in the previous year (Table 8.4). The reports cover changes in product distribution, regular and promoted price, and several promotional variables. The category of ready-to-eat cereals is highly fragmented, and a 2 percent share brand is considered significant. An 0.5 percent share in a single size qualifies it as a major line item. Due to the high penetration among households, and high purchase frequency among buyers, even small brands or brand sizes represent significant dollar volume.

Table 8.4

SCAN*PRO MONITOR—DEAL RATIO REPORT

For: * TTL Post Toasties 18 oz

Current Period: Week Ending 11/11/89 Thru Week Ending 12/16/89

Base Period: Week Ending 11/12/88 Thru Week Ending 12/17/88

	Eq Unit Sales	Promoted Sales	Incrmntl % Sales	Volume on Deal	Change (Point)
TOTAL US OVER $2 MILLION	1174201	754605	422100	64.3	5.5
ALBANY	40	0	0	0.0	–51.9
ATLANTA	25766	6648	3155	25.8	–28.0
BIRMINGHAM	6488	326	165	5.0	–27.8
BOSTON	5001	2993	1895	59.8	20.3
BUFFALO/ROCHESTER	0	0	0	*	*

	Eq Unit Sales	Promoted Sales	Incrmntl % Sales	Volume on Deal	Change (Point)
CHARLOTTE	5138	0	0	0.0	−18.4
CHICAGO	9038	6063	3506	67.1	32.8
CINCINNATI	15013	11033	7073	73.5	6.3
CLEVELAND	12716	8234	6914	64.8	26.9
COLUMBUS	20498	17523	11577	85.5	20.9
DALLAS	38838	31539	16818	81.2	22.4
DENVER	15830	11947	4359	75.5	−8.6
DETROIT	14070	3385	1905	24.1	13.0
HARTFORD/NEW HAVEN	16	0	0	0.0	−62.3
HOUSTON	28735	20848	4914	72.6	11.7
INDIANAPOLIS	28810	21704	14783	75.3	45.6
JACKSONVILLE	2281	323	36	14.2	−67.9
KANSAS CITY	12535	9645	2727	76.9	17.1
LOS ANGELES	7978	5564	3046	69.7	12.8
MEMPHIS	16149	13868	10003	85.9	−0.5
MIAMI	1040	0	0	0.0	−52.4
MILWAUKEE	13293	8724	7349	65.6	−6.2
MINNEAPOLIS	20030	14392	8324	71.9	12.4
NASHVILLE	12702	4651	1886	36.6	−19.8
NEW ORLEANS/MOBILE	3935	1165	160	29.6	−13.5
NEW YORK	855	82	20	9.6	9.6
OKLAHOMA CITY/TULSA	33297	21357	9534	64.1	4.8
ORLANDO	3378	573	113	17.0	−14.1
PHILADELPHIA	1643	743	442	45.2	−3.8
PHOENIX	5147	2420	875	47.0	−10.8
PITTSBURGH	6347	5330	2392	84.0	23.6
PORTLAND	15563	10771	4747	69.2	3.2
RALEIGH/DURHAM	7063	2474	909	35.0	28.7
ST. LOUIS	17692	9842	5924	55.6	0.8
SALT LAKE CITY/BOISE	12539	6135	1773	48.9	−25.1
SAN DIEGO	288	0	0	0.0	−45.4
SAN FRANCISCO	8439	4184	1601	49.6	16.8
SEATTLE	12790	9952	4723	77.8	10.2
SYRACUSE	264	0	0	0.0	−80.0
TAMPA	3757	2668	1081	71.0	44.2
WASHINGTON D.C.	4135	852	413	20.6	12.3

Table 8.4 (continued)
SCAN*PRO MONITOR—DEAL RATIO REPORT
For: * TTL Post Toasties 18 oz
Current Period: Week Ending 11/11/89 Thru Week Ending 12/16/89
Base Period: Week Ending 11/12/88 Thru Week Ending l2/l7/88

	Incrmntl Sales as % of Total	Change, (Point)	Efficiency	Change (Point)
TOTAL US OVER $2 MILLION	35.9	5.5	55.9	4.2
ALBANY	0.0	−45.0	*	*
ATLANTA	12.2	3.9	47.2	31.7
BIRMINGHAM	2.5	−10.9	50.6	9.8
BOSTON	37.9	28.1	63.3	38.5
BUFFALO/ROCHESTER	*	*	*	*
CHARLOTTE	0.0	−2.8	*	*
CHICAGO	38.8	23.3	57.8	12.6
CINCINNATI	47.1	−4.2	64.1	−12.3
CLEVELAND	54.4	34.5	84.0	31.3
COLUMBUS	56.5	9.3	66.1	−7.1
DALLAS	43.3	16.9	53.3	8.5
DENVER	27.5	−14.9	36.5	−14.0
DETROIT	13.5	6.3	56.3	−8.9
HARTFORD/NEW HAVEN	0.0	−50.3	*	*
HOUSTON	17.1	−26.3	23.6	−47.8
INDIANAPOLIS	51.3	34.5	68.1	11.4
JACKSONVILLE	1.6	−8.7	11.1	−1.4
KANSAS CITY	21.8	−14.7	28.3	−32.7
LOS ANGELES	38.2	26.9	54.7	34.9
MEMPHIS	61.9	11.6	72.1	13.9
MIAMI	0.0	−21.1	*	*
MILWAUKEE	55.3	20.6	84.2	36.0
MINNEAPOLIS	41.6	−5.7	57.8	−21.6
NASHVILLE	14.8	10.6	40.6	33.1
NEW ORLEANS/MOBILE	4.1	−9.7	13.7	−18.1
NEW YORK	2.3	2.3	24.4	*
OKLAHOMA CITY/TULSA	28.6	−0.9	44.6	−5.1
ORLANDO	3.3	−1.6	19.7	3.9
PHILADELPHIA	26.9	−14.3	59.5	−24.6
PHOENIX	17.0	−18.9	36.2	−26.0
PITTSBURGH	37.7	0.0	44.9	−17.5

	Incrmntl Sales as % of Total	Change, (Point)	Efficiency	Change (Point)
PORTLAND	30.5	−16.6	44.1	−27.4
RALEIGH/DURHAM	12.9	13.8	36.7	51.6
ST. LOUIS	33.5	6.2	60.2	10.5
SALT LAKE CITY/BOISE	14.1	−31.3	28.9	−32.4
SAN DIEGO	0.0	−19.2	*	*
SAN FRANCISCO	19.0	1.4	38.3	−15.2
SEATTLE	36.9	4.1	47.5	−1.2
SYRACUSE	0.0	−67.8	*	*
TAMPA	28.8	18.3	40.5	1.5
WASHINGTON D.C.	10.0	11.3	48.5	64.2

Table 8.4 (continued)

SCAN*PRO MONITOR—TOPLINE REPORT

For: TTL Post Toasties 18 oz

Current Period: Week Ending 11/11/89 Thru Week Ending 12/16/89

Base Period: Week Ending 11/12/88 Thru Week Ending 12/17/88

	Eq Unit Share	Change in Share (Point)	Change in Sales (Percent)	Change in Dist (Point)
TOTAL US OVER $2 MILLION	0.5	0.00	2.4	−3.1
ALBANY	0.0	−0.02	−87.5	−4.7
ATLANTA	0.9	−0.50	−31.8	0.8
BIRMINGHAM	0.3	−0.11	−25.3	−6.5
BOSTON	0.1	−0.02	−16.2	−16.0
BUFFALO/ROCHESTER	0.0	−0.01	−100.0	−1.5
CHARLOTTE	0.3	−0.09	−13.9	−8.0
CHICAGO	0.1	0.04	49.5	2.8
CINCINNATI	0.5	−0.12	−16.6	−2.6
CLEVELAND	0.3	0.06	33.5	−14.2
COLUMBUS	0.8	0.43	106.8	6.9
DALLAS	0.9	0.14	19.6	0.2
DENVER	0.4	−0.18	−27.4	8.2
DETROIT	0.2	−0.11	−31.5	8.4
HARTFORD/NEW HAVEN	0.0	−0.08	−99.3	−15.8
HOUSTON	0.7	0.00	−0.2	20.9
INDIANAPOLIS	0.9	0.42	93.2	1.3
JACKSONVILLE	0.2	−0.26	−52.1	−14.8
KANSAS CITY	0.6	−0.09	−12.8	1.0

	Eq Unit Share	Change in Share (Point)	Change in Sales (Percent)	Change in Dist (Point)
LOS ANGELES	0.1	–0.15	–72.6	–15.0
MEMPHIS	1.1	0.31	45.6	–39.0
MIAMI	0.0	–0.03	–54.6	–7.3
MILWAUKEE	0.5	0.13	30.2	6.3
MINNEAPOLIS	0.5	0.04	15.7	1.5
NASHVILLE	0.8	0.13	36.8	1.2
NEW ORLEANS/MOBILE	0.1	–0.04	–27.6	0.9
NEW YORK	0.0	0.00	–17.8	1.6
OKLAHOMA CITY/TULSA	1.4	–0.15	–5.9	6.0
ORLANDO	0.2	–0.11	–34.6	–15.9
PHILADELPHIA	0.0	–0.01	–18.5	0.8
PHOENIX	0.1	0.03	32.9	–5.6
PITTSBURGH	0.1	0.07	99.1	–1.1
PORTLAND	0.5	–0.64	–55.2	–0.6
RALEIGH/DURHAM	0.2	0.02	33.5	2.8
ST. LOUIS	0.6	–0.04	–9.5	–0.7
SALT LAKE CITY/BOISE	0.4	–0.20	–36.9	2.5
SAN DIEGO	0.0	0.09	–87.7	–21.0
SAN FRANCISCO	0.1	0.02	30.2	11.3
SEATTLE	0.3	0.11	61.7	2.3
SYRACUSE	0.0	–0.12	–91.6	–14.3
TAMPA	0.1	–0.33	–76.2	–45.2
WASHINGTON D.C.	0.1	0.00	11.6	–1.6

Table 8.4 (continued)
SCAN*PRO MONITOR—DEAL RATIO REPORT
For: TTL Post Toasties 18 oz
Current Period: Week Ending 11/11/89 Thru Week Ending 12/16/89
Base Period: Week Ending 11/12/88 Thru Week Ending 12/17/88

	Change in				
	% ACV on Deal (Point)	% Volume on Deal (Point)	Regular Price (Percent)	Promoted Price (Percent)	% Price Reduction (Point)
TOTAL US OVER $2 MILLION	4.1	5.5	9.6	9.4	–3.3
ALBANY	–13.8	–51.9	36.8	*	*
ATLANTA	–34.1	–28.0	7.7	6.4	–2.3
BIRMINGHAM	–19.5	–27.8	14.7	36.4	5.7

	Change in				
	% ACV on Deal (Point)	% Volume on Deal (Point)	Regular Price (Percent)	Promoted Price (Percent)	% Price Reduction (Point)
BOSTON	7.0	20.3	13.3	−19.9	−25.1
BUFFALO/ROCHESTER	*	*	*	*	*
CHARLOTTE	−15.3	−18.4	11.2	*	*
CHICAGO	30.3	32.8	7.8	5.5	5.2
CINCINNATI	21.0	6.3	6.8	4.3	−1.7
CLEVELAND	−1.0	26.9	10.5	−10.5	−20.8
COLUMBUS	41.0	20.9	0.4	18.7	14.5
DALLAS	22.1	22.4	10.6	6.4	−4.4
DENVER	−5.5	−8.6	2.2	9.9	4.3
DETROIT	8.5	13.0	15.2	12.5	−0.4
HARTFORD/NEW HAVEN	−25.0	−62.3	−19.6	*	*
HOUSTON	22.7	11.7	14.7	21.1	−0.6
INDIANAPOLIS	36.3	45.6	13.1	−11.3	−14.8
JACKSONVILLE	−62.4	−67.9	5.4	26.3	−5.6
KANSAS CITY	37.1	17.1	7.5	23.5	9.7
LOS ANGELES	−0.8	12.8	35.0	12.0	−15.9
MEMPHIS	−8.1	−0.5	0.7	−0.4	3.3
MIAMI	−38.2	−52.4	13.1	*	*
MILWAUKEE	−27.4	−6.2	9.7	11.1	−3.3
MINNEAPOLIS	31.8	12.4	7.9	24.6	7.6
NASHVILLE	−28.8	−19.8	9.5	22.4	−1.0
NEW ORLEANS/MOBILE	−8.4	−13.5	5.4	5.4	−1.5
NEW YORK	6.4	9.6	18.4	*	*
OKLAHOMA CITY/TULSA	9.6	4.8	16.1	12.6	−7.4
ORLANDO	−13.2	−14.1	2.2	10.0	−3.6
PHILADELPHIA	16.6	−3.8	8.4	46.1	20.6
PHOENIX	4.9	−10.8	−10.2	9.3	12.3
PITTSBURGH	42.9	23.6	9.6	2.7	−4.0
PORTLAND	17.3	3.2	17.7	25.2	5.9
RALEIGH/DURHAM	19.1	28.7	12.0	−6.3	−19.4
ST. LOUIS	−1.6	0.8	11.3	8.5	4.4
SALT LAKE CITY/BOISE	−12.7	−25.1	6.7	26.1	11.3
SAN DIEGO	−34.4	−45.4	2.6	*	*
SAN FRANCISCO	21.1	16.8	15.0	−0.2	−5.1
SEATTLE	19.3	10.2	8.1	19.8	5.1
SYRACUSE	−36.6	−80.0	0.5	*	*
TAMPA	35.1	44.2	42.9	13.2	−1.6
WASHINGTON D.C.	2.4	12.3	6.3	−1.9	−2.8

Many of the variables such as share, distribution, percent ACV on deal are naturally expressed as percentages. When comparing such variables to a previous period, the
comparison may be expressed as a point change (difference) or a percentage change
(ratio). If, for example, percent ACV was 10 percent in the base period, and 15 percent in
the current period, the change in ACV distribution from base to current period is 5
points (15 from 10) but a 50 percent change (15/10). Efficiency is defined as incremental
sales divided by promoted sales.

As an analyst for a competing similar breakfast cereal brand, you have been
asked to review these reports and make suggestions. During the time between base and
current period, there was a 10 percent increase in wholesale price, and your management believes that this increase was completely passed through to retail price by the
start of the current period. Noting that Post Toasties suffered no volume or share
decrease associated with the price increase, they are planning a similar increase in the
near future. You decide to focus your analysis on percent changes in sales.

Question 1. You decide to run a series of single variable regressions to determine
the importance of the various activities to percent change in sales. Include:

a. change in distribution;
b. change in percent ACV on deal;
c. change in percent volume on deal;
d. change in regular price;
e. change in promoted price;
f. change in percent price reduction;
g. change in incremental sales as a percent of total sales; and
h. change in efficiency.

Which variables are significantly related to percent change in sales?

Question 2. Based on the regressions performed in Question 1, what would you
tell management about the expected impact of a 10 percent increase in product regular
price. If your brand reacts similarly to price hikes as does Post Toasties 18 ounce size.

Question 3. You decide to try models which have three variables: percent change
in regular price, percent change in distribution, and one change variable associated with
promotion. Try each of the six promotion variables in turn. Which promotional variable
would you choose for a final model? Are all three variables necessary?

Question 4. If you have a stepwise regression package available, run stepwise
regression:

a. with all variables; and
b. without percent change in promoted price, percent change in price, and
    change in efficiency.

Comment on the results. What would you expect to be the impact on sales of your brand if it is similar to your brand and you take a 10 percent price increase?

Question 5. Create a new variable, Promotion Efficiency Index (PEI) = 100 * (Efficiency/(100-Efficiency)) for both the current period and the same period a year ago, and calculate point change in the Promotion Efficiency Index. Add this variable to your dataset, and repeat Question 4 with the new variable. Comment on the results.

Question 6 (Advanced). Recalculate change variables as ratio variables. If point change = current period value - base period value, then ratio change = current period value / base period value. Estimare a ratio change model using the log of the ratio change in sales as the dependent variable and the log of the ration changes of the variables mentioned in Question 1 as independents. What difficulties did you encounter in coding the variables? Did the results of this model change your conclusions about the impact of the price increase? About any other factors?

Suggested Readings

Blattberg, Robert C. and Scott A. Neslin.
Sales Promotion: Concepts, Methods, and Strategies.
Englewood Cliffs, New Jersey, Prentice Hall, 1990.

Mosteller, Frederick and John W. Tukey.
Data Analysis and Regression: A Second Course in Statistics.
New York: Addison-Wesley Publishing, 1977.

Ortega, J. M. and W. C. Rheinbolt.
Iterative Solution of Nonlinear Equations in Several Variables.
London: Academic Press, 1970.

Tukey, John W.
Exploratory Data Analysis.
Reading, Massachusetts: Addison-Wesley Publishing Company, 1977.

CHAPTER 9

PRINCIPLES OF
PROMOTION ANALYSIS

B ased upon the discussion and cases provided in preceding chapters a number of sales promotion principles and issues can be summarized. These principles and issues should serve well as guidelines for those who are managing sales promotion programs. The summary is divided into three sections: fundamental principles, the role of sales promotion analysis, and the future of promotion and trade relations.

FUNDAMENTAL PRINCIPLES. Ten fundamental principles of sales promotion have resulted from the ongoing analysis of scanner-based data. These fundamental principles are as follows:

Store-Level Data Are Critically Important. Aggregate market-level data simply are not sufficiently sensitive to detect the true sales impacts of promotional programs. Data must be measured at the individual store level and analyzed on at least a weekly basis to understand the dynamics of sales promotion. Even when the analysis is for a single chain in a single market, analysis should be at the individual store level. Promotions, particularly in-store display or shelf-price reduction, may not be equally effective across stores, offering opportunity for profit optimization. Detail results may be aggregated and summarized after the analysis is complete. Where analysis must be conducted on aggregate data, the method of analysis should have been cross-validated with store level detail data.

Sales Volume Is the Key Measure. While market share as a measure of sales performance has a strong tradition, competitive activity and other factors make it insufficiently sensitive to measure the short-term impact of sales promotion. The promoted brand's sales volume is by far the best measure of the performance of a sales promotion program.

Trade Promotions Should Generate Incremental Profit. One of the most important findings from the analysis of scanner-based data is the consistent return to the base level of business of brand after a promotional period for established products. In other words, future sales do not seem to increase as a result of the promotion. The promotion generally stimulates sales only during the promotional period. This clearly means that to be justified the promotion itself should generate incremental profit. Use of trade promotion for objectives other than profit, such as volume or share maintenance, or obtaining retailer goodwill, should be clearly identified, and should have the trade-promotion costs identified and tied back to the activity.

Package Size Is Important.   Not all consumers favor the same package size, despite their interest in the product. It is critically important to promote the package size that matches the appropriate market for the promotion to be a success.

The Demand Curve Is Kinked.   For the first time, marketing managers can begin with a realistic, empirically estimated demand curve. Both pricing and promotion decisions can be made on the basis of the fundamental understanding of the relationship of price and sales volume for the product category and brand. In many product categories, that demand curve is clearly kinked, meaning that lowering the price in certain ranges will not necessarily result in increasing the sales volume, or that raising the price would not necessarily result in decreased sales volume. Obviously, knowledge of any existing kinks greatly improves the efficiency of the revenue potential for the brand.

Competitive Effects Are Minimal Except Among Switchers.   Despite common-sense expectation, promoting one brand in a product category has very little impact on loyal purchasers of other brands. In other words, a sales promotion program does not necessarily cut into the competing brand's business. Promotion clearly has the greatest impact on brand switchers. It is the switchers that promotion is most likely to influence, with additional volume potential available from infrequent category buyers.

Price Sensitivity and Promotion Responsiveness Are Different.   Not all brands will respond in the same way to price. Some products may behave entirely on the basis of price, while impulse-driven items may respond primarily to promotion elements, such as an in-store display. Responses depend upon the loyalty characteristics of the brand.

Retail Trade Performance Is Essential.   Even the most successful consumer promotions can be substantially enhanced by the trade. The cooperation of the trade with in-store displays, ad features, and its own promotional programs create a special synergy that can result in sales that far exceed what either the manufacturer or retailer could do alone.

Reduction of Promotion Results in Loss of Volume.   Generally, every time a promotion program ends, the sales volume substantially declines. Clearly, there is a strong relationship between the promotion and the sales volume for the brand. However, the loss of sales volume does not necessarily mean that profit is lost. The revenue lost due to lower prices and the cost of the promotion itself may mean lower profit during the promotion.

Analysis of Real Data Maximizes Profit.   The most important point of this discussion is that promotional programs should be analyzed in terms of the incremental sales generated and the additional costs incurred. Local competitive conditions and volume response differences can lead to dramatically different profitability from region to region, or even from store to store in a market for apparently similar promotional activity. The profitability of the promotional program should be the ultimate criterion for the management of promotional programs.

ROLE OF SALES PROMOTION ANALYSIS. Beyond the fundamental principles of sales promotion is the evolving role of analysis in managing an integrated marketing communications program. The special role of sales promotion analysis can be summarized in the following seven ideas:

Competitive Promotion. Not only should a brand's own sales promotion programs be analyzed, but competitive promotions should be analyzed as well. This additional analysis not only aids in understanding the competition, but also provides insight into the product category.

Head-to-Head Promotion with Competition. In those instances when two promotions are in direct competition, the sales results of the brand, the direct competitor, and the product category need to be understood. Analyzing scanner-based sales data is the only way to understand the impact of the head-to-head competition.

Display Wearout. While displays generally are the most effective way to build short-term sales volume, the effectiveness diminishes over time. Assessing the effectiveness of displays requires a special store-level analysis over time.

Holiday Promotion Effects. Understanding any special synergy that may exist from holiday—or other event—related promotions is very important in stretching a limited promotional budget. Analyzing holidays requires special attention to temporal detail.

Coupon Drops and Other Direct Promotion. Understanding the sales results from coupons drop and other direct promotions in the context of the marketplace and category is very important. Expanding the analysis beyond the in-store displays and feature advertising to include other consumer promotions is vital to managing an integrated marketing communications program.

Short-Term TV Advertising. Advertising analyses are also critical to managing integrated marketing communications programs. Special attention needs to be given to the role of competitive advertising and its long-term effects.

Temporal Response for Price Reduction. How long should a special price reduction be maintained? Such questions can be answered directly through analysis. The impact of a price reduction is related to both its magnitude and its duration.

FUTURE OF PROMOTION AND TRADE RELATIONS. Sales promotion will undoubtedly continue to grow in importance as a marketing tool for both manufacturers and retailers, based on its ability to stimulate sales. However, as time passes, sales promotion will be increasingly managed as part of an integrated marketing communications program and will be considered along with other marketing communications such as advertising, personal selling, and public relations.

The future of trade relations is a major complicating factor in understanding the future of sales promotion. The issue of trade relations seems to be tied directly to the analysis of scanner data. The future of trade analysis can be summarized as follows:

Struggle for Channel Profits. The current climate in which the manufacturer and retailer operate is becoming increasingly competitive. Much of the promotion controversy, such as slotting allowances and diverting, can be seen as little more than competition for channel profits. As retailers are increasingly realizing the value of the data that they are collecting, access to the data becomes an increasingly important issue. Certainly the expectation would be for the struggle to both continue and intensify.

Retailer Demands. As retailers grow in their own analytical sophistication, they are becoming ever better users of their own data. This makes them much more skeptical of manufacturer's proposals and more demanding in negotiation with manufacturers. Retailers are also increasingly able to take advantage of the competitive environment faced by most manufacturers. Demands from retailers will no doubt continue to escalate.

New Era of Cooperation. While retailers seem to be increasingly gaining the upper hand in negotiations with manufacturers, the retailer still needs strong and competitive manufacturers to provide the high-quality merchandise to sell. It is the manufacturer that has traditionally been the innovator of new and better products, that has traditionally best understood the consumer, and that has developed the analytical tools.

Given the mutual dependence between the manufacturer and retailer, the future should hold a new era of cooperation between them. A key will no doubt be in the analysis of scanner data to the benefit of both. This era of cooperation may have public policy implications, as the nature of the business relationships between manufacturers evolves.

Performance Guarantees. Manufacturers should increasingly insist on performance guarantees in administering their trade promotion programs. Some of the current problems in trade relations are to be blamed on some manufacturers' reluctance to institute and enforce promotion performance requirements. Increasing the levels of performance requirements that are tied to real store-level sales data would be a step in the right direction.

Fact-Based Marketing Is the Key. The solution for both the manufacturer and the retailer is fact-based marketing. Marketing and selling strategies for both retailers and manufacturers should be based on a thorough understanding of both base and incremental sales volume and the impact of marketing communication programs. This will put the success of any marketing program in the hands of the consumer, where it belongs.

SALES PROMOTION HANDBOOK, 8TH EDITION BY TAMARA BREZEN BLOCK AND WILLIAM A. ROBINSON

The management of sales promotion has become increasingly sophisticated and complicated. The need for a handbook on the topic is perhaps greater than ever before for anyone involved in the planning, implementation, and analysis of sales promotion programs. Every chapter is written by an expert working in the field of sales promotion. Hundreds of real examples and case histories are included throughout, often accompanied by pictures and exhibits to bring each promotion to life. Since the introduction of the first edition more than 40 years ago, the **Sales Promotion Handbook** has been regarded as a "must-have" reference book for every marketer's shelf.

900 pages; fully illustrated and indexed; $69.95;
Book Code: 1212

MARKETING MANAGER'S HANDBOOK, 3RD EDITION BY SIDNEY LEVY, HOWARD GORDON, AND GEORGE FRERICHS

Newly revised and updated, this exhaustive compendium places the wisdom of marketing experts from all over the world at your fingertips. Each chapter is written by an authority in a particular field of marketing, working hand in hand with a marketing executive team to offer insights and ideas on such topics as organizing the marketing function; establishing your objectives; developing plans for consumer products and services and industrial products; industrial marketing; and more.

1,200 pages; fully illustrated and indexed; $69.95;
Book Code: 1203

WINNING WITH PROMOTION POWER: 100 BEST OF THE BEST PROMOTIONS BY FRAN CACI AND DONNA HOWARD

Featuring the 100 top award-winning sales promotions of the past decade, this guide to powerful promoting is all you need to push your sales to the top of the chart! The Reggies (as in "cash register") are bestowed by the Promotion Marketing Association of America to companies of all sizes in all types of fields. This compendium gives you a chance to study and learn from the winners of business-to-business promotions, consumer-oriented companies, and both product and service providers. In each "winning" case, you'll learn the company's marketing background (including problems encountered and overcome); the strategies and tactics each employed; a step-by-step description of how the winning program was executed; and what the company did with the results of the winning promotion to help you create your own winning campaign.

250 pages; hardcover; $59.95; **Book code: 1204**

ANALYZING SALES PROMOTION, 2ND EDITION BY JOHN TOTTEN AND MARTIN BLOCK

This is the expanded second edition of the landmark work on sales promotion strategy and management. Using sales data generated by in-store electronic scanners that track product movement and promotional programs, the book explains sales promotion strategy and how it should fit with the overall integrated marketing program; fundamentals of promotion analysis, including sources and uses of data; the nature of consumer response to sales promotion, including such key factors as brand loyalty vs. price sensitivity; strategy development from both the manufacturer and retailer perspectives; uses of analysis techniques for disaggregate and aggregate data; and the basic principles of promotion analysis that can be applied to all sales promotion and brand management. New sections include: integrated marketing communication; characteristics of trade and sales force "audiences"; an all-new chapter on sales promotion strategy, including marketing communication strategy and "fact-based marketing"; strategic responses; distribution channel conflicts; and principles of promotional strategy and analysis.

258 pages; paperback; $34.95; **Book Code: 1229**

QUESTIONS THAT MAKE THE SALE BY WILLIAM BETHEL

Propel your sales to ever-higher levels by asking the right questions. Eleven information-packed chapters show you how to: Rivet attention on your presentations; identify and clarify your customers and their needs; and motivate, qualify, prospect, probe, and close with greater success. The final chapter contains 365 questions ("a question a day") to achieve greater sales success.

198 pages; paperback; $19.95; **Book Code: 1196**

THE IDEA-A-DAY GUIDE TO SUPER SELLING AND CUSTOMER SERVICE BY TONY ALESSANDRA, PH.D., GREGG BARON, AND GARY COUTURE

Set your goals even higher—and reach them! Start each workday with a 15-minute session with this personal sales "trainer," and you'll find yourself overcoming your selling weaknesses, shoring up your strengths, and learning new techniques. You choose how to use this skill-building tool: build good sales habits day by day; read the carefully organized sections as you need to reinforce specific areas; or do both at once. Fifteen sections include 250 hard-hitting ideas, as well as handy checklists, information sources, worksheets, and a self-diagnostic test, all designed to keep you on the road to success.

320 pages; $19.95; **Book Code: 1185**

PERFORMANCE DRIVEN SALES MANAGEMENT BY GEORGE ODIORNE

Manage your sales force more profitably with this step-by-step management guide. You'll learn how to set realist profit and performance goals; develop team-driven sales goals and strategies; measure progress fairly and accurately; and train for maximum effectiveness. An 80-page "Sales Management Workshop" shows these ideas in action in real-life situations. 260-page text; 80-page "Sales Management Workshop"; 3-ring binder; 60 exhibits; $91.50, **Book Code: 1189**

YES! SEND ME THE BOOK(S) I HAVE CHECKED. I UNDERSTAND THAT IF I AM NOT COMPLETELY SATISFIED, I MAY RETURN THE BOOK(S) WITHIN 30 DAYS FOR A FULL REFUND.

___ *SALES PROMOTION HANDBOOK*; $69.95; **Book Code: 1212**

___ *MARKETING MANAGER'S HANDBOOK*; $69.95; **Book Code: 1203**

___ *WINNING WITH PROMOTION POWER*; $59.95; **Book Code: 1204**

___ *ANALYZING SALES PROMOTION*; $34.95; **Book Code: 1229**

___ *QUESTIONS THAT MAKE THE SALE*; $19.95; **Book Code: 1196**

___ *THE IDEA-A-DAY GUIDE TO SUPER SELLING AND CUSTOMER SERVICE*; $19.95; **Book Code: 1185**

___ *PERFORMANCE DRIVEN SALES MANAGEMENT*; $91.50; **Book Code: 1189**

Bill my: ___VISA ___ American Express ___MasterCard ___Company

Card # _____ Exp date _____

Name/Title_____

Company _____

Address_____

City/State/Zip_____

Signature _____ Phone (___) _____

(Signature and phone necessary to process order.)

Copies may be ordered from your bookseller or from Dartnell.
To order from Dartnell, call toll free (800) 621-5463 or fax us your order (312) 561-3801.

D A R T N E L L
CHICAGO • LONDON • BOSTON

___ Please send me your latest catalog.   94-5500